REMARKABLE JOURNEY:
ROSE NOTEHELFER AND THE
MISSIONARY EXPERIENCE IN
JAPAN

Remarkable Journey:

Rose Notehelfer and the Missionary Experience in Japan

F. G. Notehelfer

Library of Congress Cataloging-in-Publication Data

Notehelfer, F. G.
Remarkable Journey: Rose Notehelfer and the
Missionary Experience in Japan
ISBN-13:978-1974643981

This book was originally published   in 2006 by
EastBridge books of Norwalk, CN, in its "Missionary
Enterprise in Asia" series. All rights were returned to
the author by EastBridge in 2017 and it is now being
republished by the author to meet reader demand.

F.G. Notehelfer
Salt Spring Island
2017

To my wife Ann

Who loved Mama and Papa,
and without whom
this book would not have been written.

Contents

Preface
Mama

Rose Henner Notehelfer

In 1993 my mother, Mama as we all called her, celebrated her 90th birthday. For the occasion she had only one wish, and that was that her whole family could be with her. The result was a wonderful birthday party that included hundreds of guests. Only Papa could not be there. He had died ten years earlier. But we felt his presence, especially as we talked about the past.

The book that follows began that day in 1993. Curiously it started with a verse I composed for her on that occasion, which is included in the epilogue. Mama's life was full of surprises, constant challenges, and a degree of adventure that suited her well. Her experiences and career incorporated a vast territory, physically, spiritually, and at the level of personal growth and self awareness. In many ways she was ahead of her time. As a woman who emerged from a small German village she sought the broader world. Thinking to go to China as a missionary, she ended up in the South Pacific and Japan. Rejecting the idea of marriage in her early years, she subsequently became the mother of six children. In the wake of her World War II experiences in Japan she added another cultural environment by coming to the United States. In all these spheres she was remarkably independent and self reliant. In essence she was a woman seeking a meaningful role to play in life that went beyond traditional boundaries. Sitting down with her to put together her life story was itself fascinating. At times it was difficult, especially as I wanted to create a picture of the whole person. Mama was a woman of great faith, but she was also a very down to earth being. I hope to show all her faces. One side of her was very social, loved people, and reveled in the public sphere, but she could also be introspective and self-critical. Her spiritual life was never passive. She not only followed the "inner voice," which she trusted implicitly, but she was prepared to wrestle with God when occasion warranted. All through her life she maintained a strong voice of her own. I have tried to retain this voice in her story. Writing this book has been quite different from other books I have written. It is essentially Mama's book. I hope that it conveys something of the complex and caring individual she was. She always thought her life was rather ordinary and to me she demonstrates that it is often precisely in the ordinary that we find the extraordinary.

What this book presents is essentially an oral history. For nearly five years after 1993, I sat with Mama and transcribed her narratives on my computer during visits to her apartment in Turlock. The process was never one of pure narration, however, as I interposed questions and opened further areas for exploration. Later I assembled the narratives and filled in the historical details. She reviewed the final product and agreed to its publication. In many ways, then, this is an autobiography as well as a biography. It is both her book and my book.

I want to gratefully acknowledge the help of my brothers and sisters, and their spouses, who generously reviewed the manuscript and provided me with useful corrections and additions. I also want to thank Karin Henner, my mother's grand niece, for advice and corrections that dealt with German language materials. The late Hans Rogger kindly read the manuscript and helped me with other German matters, including the name of the funny automobile, the Hanomag, that my father owned in prewar Japan. Hans recalled a childhood jingle, *"Ein bischen Farbe ein bischen Lack da hat Man einen Hanomag,"* which suggested the car was glued together with paint and lacquer, and not much more.

I would also like to thank Erika Greber, the daughter of Adelheid Zilly, for providing me with several interesting and useful photographs that were in her mother's possession from the time she lived in our home in Karuizawa during World War II. Erika was able to read the manuscript while serving as a visiting scholar at the University of California, Irvine, on leave from the University of Munich. My father was an avid photographer and left us an extensive photo record of life in Japan, and elsewhere, that I have liberally used in this book. The majority of the images in this volume are therefore from the Notehelfer family collection. A few came from other sources, and I wish to thank the U.S. Army, the California Zephyr Museum, and the Buss Family, for allowing me to use images from their collections.

I am greatly indebted to Douglas Merwin and Kathleen Lodwick of EastBridge for the help they have given me in getting the manuscript ready for publication. It was interesting to observe that Doug and I were born to missionary parents in 1939 just a few months apart--he in Peking and I in Tokyo. I also recall that it was one of my teachers at Harvard, John K. Fairbank, the historian of China, who first alerted me to the importance of missionary writings and memoirs for the history of modern East Asia. It is my hope that this book will take its place among other missioanry accounts of what it was like to live through such a fascinating period in the development of the modern world.

Finally I want to thank my wife Ann for her warm support. Without her encouragement this book would not have been written.

F.G. Notehelfer
Los Angeles, 2005

Chapter One
Bernstadt

Mama as a child.

I was born in Bernstadt on December 11, 1903. Bernstadt means the "city of bears," but our town was not a city. It was really a small village about twelve kilometers from Ulm. Bernstadt and Ulm are both in Swabia, and the people of this part of Germany speak *"Schwäbish,"* a funny dialect that is associated with country people. I can still talk up a storm in *Schwäbish* when I get a chance. It always makes me think of home.

My father was Julius Henner. My mother's maiden name was Margarete Roeger. My father was a cartwright. He had his own shop. My mother's family, the Roegers, were brewers. Unfortunately her parents died young. They had three girls and one boy. The boy died as a teenager. With their parents' death, the girls were all placed in foster homes. My mother was taken in by Mrs. Steck, who had a country store. Mrs. Steck was an unusual woman. Every week she bought eggs from the local farmers, and every Saturday she could be seen carrying a big basket on her head with six to eight hundred eggs in it. She could walk and balance those eggs without using her hands! She was also very strong. One night she carried a buck on her shoulder the whole way from Bernstadt to Ulm because an officer had shot it and wanted it delivered to his house. He had poached it, so she had to bring it at night. Mrs. Steck was also rather large. She was so large, in fact, that when the King of Würtemberg saw her at an exhibition for the Zeppelin in Friedrichshaven, he said to his assistant, "Have you ever seen such a corpulent woman!" Unfortunately she died not long thereafter. My mother, her only heir, inherited the store and house. But for years it was always called the Steck House. And even after our new house was built it was still called the Steck House.

I don't know much about my father's family before they came to Bernstadt. My great grandfather lived in Ballendorf. My grandfather, Kasper, moved to Bernstadt and built a nice house with a big workshop for his cartwright business. He was an interesting man. He had a big beard and a long pipe, and the pipe was always in his mouth. He was not only the wagon master, but also the postmaster, telephone master, and dentist. For his dental work he had three instruments—a pair of big pliers, a pair of small pliers, and a pair of tweezers. These were wrapped in a piece of soft cloth. He also had a big leather chair in his room, which was unusual. When people came with a toothache it usually meant that the tooth had to be pulled. There was little more that could be done. Then, if the man was big, Grandma had to stand behind the chair and hold his chin, while Grandfather extracted the tooth. Sometimes the patient let out a big scream. A glass of water was placed beside him so that he could rinse out his mouth. Then Grandfather would finish by putting a big piece of cotton in his mouth, and the man could go home. Needless to say, we children were always dead scared if we had a toothache and were sent to Grandpa! But our teeth, that is our baby teeth, came out like nothing, and he just lifted them out with his instruments. I should add that he was also the mailman, and every day delivered the mail from a big leather bag filled with letters and newspapers. Nearly everyone took a newspaper. He had a telephone, the only one in the whole village. I remember the phone being there even before 1910. But electricity did not come to our village till after that year.

Bernstadt had about 900 to 1000 residents. Most were farmers. The nearest railroad station was an hour-and-ten-minutes walk in Beimerstetten. It was six kilometers from Beimerstetten to Ulm. When the railroad was built, the farmers of Bernstadt were not willing to give up their land, so the railroad never came to town, much to their later regret.

Our village was square. From East to West there was the Römer Strasse, or the Roman Road, because the Romans had once built a road there. But in the middle of the town there was the Schmied Gasse, named for two blacksmiths. At the end of the Schmied Gasse stood an old castle that was used as a school when my father and mother

The Castle and later the City Hall of Bernstadt.

2

Fields and Meadows near Bernstadt Today.

were students. In my youth the castle also served as the town hall, or "Rathouse," where the Bürgermeister had his office. All important business was conducted there. In the basement was a prison, and when we heard that a prisoner was there, we were always excited. On the Eastern edge of the village was the Frauen Strasse. The other major street was called the Platz Gasse. On it there was an open square where the carnival came once a year with its carousel.

The Gypsies also came every year with their wagons. They tethered their horses at the front of the Beer House. Their wagons were placed at the corner of the Schmied Gasse and the Platz Gasse where they carried on their business. They made baskets and repaired old pots and pans, and whatever the farmers couldn't repair they brought to the Gypsies. I was very interested in the Gypsies as a child. One day my father came running into our house and said "Is Rosel here? The Gypsies have come!" I left everything and went down to the Beer House. My father and mother went upstairs to watch what I would do. I walked several times around their wagons and slowly tried to go up the steps of one of them. They had a three or four tier home-made step, and I stood on the first step and looked into the wagon. Then I climbed into the wagon and looked all around. My mother and father were surprised, because no one dared to go into a Gypsy wagon. But the Gypsies smiled and didn't do me any harm, and let me go again. One evening, not long thereafter, my Grandmother made a point of telling me a story about a boy who had been kidnapped by the Gypsies. They painted his skin with coffee and made him dark brown so that he looked like a Gypsy, and he never saw his parents again. It scared me, but it never took away my interest and love of the Gypsies, and I was always glad when they came to our village and our houses. Once a young Gypsy boy brought a little white Spits dog and asked my mother to give his dog some milk. I was so happy when my mother filled a dish with milk and put it outside. The Gypsy boy and I watched the dog drink the milk.

Beside the castle there was a path that led through some meadows to a beautiful forest called the Bergwald. We loved this place. Early in spring we would always find the first flowers there, anemones, violets, or snowdrops. By May and June the forest was covered with lilies of the valley. And in July and August we picked wild strawberries and raspberries from which mother made the best jam. One of my pleasures was to walk in this forest on Sunday afternoons. There was also a great Linden tree that stood at the East end of the Schmied Gasse. We liked to climb in this tree as children. When it bloomed we picked its flowers for a medicinal tea that mother made. This tree was important in other ways. On Sunday evenings the young people of the village regularly gathered there to sing folk songs.

At the right side of the Beer House was a big farm house which belonged to a family named Erne. The Ernes had seven children and the youngest were twins, Andreas and Mary, who were exactly my age. They became my best friends. From the age of three I spent almost every day with them. That was really because my mother had so little time for me. They had a big house with a large attic, and we had a wonderful time playing hide and seek. Upstairs there lived a retired school teacher from Ulm. We always called her "Fräulein." Sometimes she would invite us into her lovely living room, which seemed rather fancy to us, and sit us on the floor and tell us a story. We loved her stories. Occasionally these were accompanied with a candy for each of us. We also liked to play in the barn. There was a wonderful place where we could play in the hay. We would climb a ladder to the loft and then jump down into the dry hay and straw below. None of us were ever hurt. Some of the older boys made us a carousel-like swing. This consisted of two round poles that moved horizontally over a square vertical pole at the center. The horizontal poles moved over some greased metal held up by the square center beam. We would be suspended from these poles by rope seats and would fly outward as the poles rotated. We loved "flying" on this contraption.

School! That was something. My father died on the 21st of April, 1910. On the 26th my youngest brother was born. I was to start school for the first time on the 28th. It was customary, in our village, for every mother to bring her child to school on the first day with half a pound of butter or half a dozen eggs for the teacher. But my mother could not accompany me because of my

brother's birth. So my grandmother took me to school and introduced me to the teacher. The teacher talked to all of us and explained that starting tomorrow we would have to come to school by ourselves. He also showed us the

The Bernstadt School House where Mama went to school, originally built in 1902, and recently remodeled.

4

schoolroom and told us where to sit. We were the biggest class that year because it was the first time that they put two years together, those born in 1903 and 1904. We had about twenty-eight students in our class. The other classes had about fourteen.

The teacher was Herr Schmidt, he taught me from the first to the fourth grades. We started school at 7:00 A.M. in the summer and at 8:00 A.M. in the winter. At 10:00 we had a morning break, which meant we could run home and get a piece of bread and jam. My job was to go to the Beer House to get Herr Schmidt his morning snack. That was usually a fresh-baked-hard-crusted roll which was filled with ham or sausage. When I brought this to him and he bit into it, there was always the mouth-watering sound of the fresh crust crackling. For my part, all I had was a piece of black bread with a little jam. Then and there I decided to become a teacher, so that I could have a roll like that every day. But I never did, till I came to America.

I loved school. School was the dearest place for me. I liked to read and write, and I was always number one. In those days we were seated according to our rank, I always kept the first seat from the first through the seventh grade. Only, one day I came home to tease my mother and said, "Mother, I lost the first place seat, and I'm now seated second." She got very angry and was about to give me a spanking, saying "I will show you what it means to lose your first place!" But I cried out, "No, No, I kept it, I just wanted to tease you." But she didn't appreciate such teasing! For her there could be no levity in loosing one's first position. Education was a serious matter. So was the performance of her children.

When I was ten years old war came and the male teachers were all drafted. Then we had two women teachers, Fräulein Müller, she was such a beautiful woman, and Fräulein Nuding, she was heavy and plump and the boys made lots of jokes about her, but she was a wonderful teacher. Fräulein Nuding taught us poetry for the first time. The men teachers never taught us literature. But she taught us to express things in a beautiful way. She made us memorize a lot of poetry, such as *"Meine Mutter"* (*"My Mother"*) by Dettlef von Lilienkron. I can still remember these poems, and later taught them to my children. She was very concerned about how poetry should be read. And she instructed us to place the proper emphasis on each word. I remember reciting the lines from *"My Mother,"*

Wie oft sah ich die blassen hände	How frequently I saw those pale hands
nähen, ein Stück für mich,	Sewing, a piece for me,
Wie liebevol du sorgtest	How lovingly you cared

and how she taught me to emphasize *"liebevol!"*

But I forgot to say something about the village police. The policeman had a black uniform with gold buttons, and a hat that went with it. When the Bürgermeister wanted make a special announcement, the policeman took his bell and walking up and down the streets would ring it quite loudly every hundred feet or so. All the people would come out to hear what the had to say. Then he would announce that the Bürgermeister would like to meet with the men of the village that evening, and that all the men should come to the Beer House. And if someone had a cow that needed to be slaughtered, the policeman went around and said Farmer Hans Jork has to slaughter his cow and everyone interested in buying meat should go to the farmer's house where the cow was butchered. He also announced the butchering of pigs. Every important thing that happened in the village was announced by the policeman with his big bell. And when there was a wedding in the village, that wasn't announced with the big bell, but the policeman went from house to house with a folder and asked everyone if they would attend the wedding. If they said yes, they had to pay five marks for the dinner, which he collected. Even when I came home in 1954, after being away twenty-four years, the policeman went through the village with his big bell and announced: "Mrs. Rose Notehelfer, born Rose Henner, came home from Japan after twenty-four years and will speak at the Church tonight; everyone is welcome." And the whole church was full that evening.

Our village was a rural place. That meant we lived with the animals. The slaughtering of pigs was particularly a spectacle. We always got quite excited as children when the Policeman announced such an event. Pigs were usually butchered early in the morning before school, and we would all watch. The butcher usually brought the pig out with a rope tied to one of its hind legs. Then he tied it to a pole, took a big wooden hammer and hit it over the head. When it fell unconscious, he took out a big knife and cut the pig's throat. The farmer's wife stood nearby with a big pail and a wooden spoon to catch the blood and then stirred it with the spoon to keep it from curdling. Later the blood was used to make a kind of sausage that everyone liked. After the blood was removed the pig was put into a large wooden container and the farmer and his wife brought boiling water from the kitchen and poured it over the pig. Then they scrubbed the pig clean with a big metal scrubber until it was perfectly clean. Finally it was taken out of the water and the butcher cut it open and cleaned out the inside, separating the usable from the unusable parts. The intestines were carefully washed because they would serve as the wrappers for many of the sausages the butcher prepared. That afternoon everyone in the village would receive a piece of broiled meat and a liver or blood sausage as a present.

At home we made our own game out of this spectacle. Once in a while

The Village of Bernstadt and the fields surrounding it where Mama "gleaned" and worked as a child.

father would come home before we were put to bed and would play with us. On these occasions we always wanted him to play "pig," and he was a good sport. He became the pig and we would tie a rope to one of his legs. Then he had to crouch on hands and knees and we would pretend to hit him on the head with a small wooden hammer. He would fall over "unconscious," and we would start scrubbing him from head to toe. But just as we started to "butcher him," he would always wake up with a loud scream. That was lots of fun!

My early years were quite carefree. I remember we particularly enjoyed winter. Father made each of us a sled and we always had lots of snow. When the snow was frozen hard we could slide down the Schmied Gasse all the way to the castle. Sometimes we put two sleds together and then a third on top. We would all get on the top sled and go as fast as we could. We used to call this the "Ride of the Three Kings." Christmas was always the best time. Father had made us a beautiful store with a real set of scales and little weights for a pound, half a pound, 100 grams, 50 grams, and 10 grams. The cupboards of the store were filled with sugar, flour, chocolate coffee beans, and raisins. There were also apples, pears, plums, and other fruit, all made of marzipan. During the holidays the store was open every evening and we were able to shop there with play money. My sister, Walburg, was the store keeper and we came from our own little places which we built with a chair and a blanket in one of the corners of the living room and bought everything we could and started to cook our own meals. Only, we were not allowed to eat what we cooked, for when mother came in from the real store and said, "Children, it's bedtime," we had to bring all the things we had bought back to the store and

The Steck House in which Mama was born which also served as the village store. Mama's sister, Walburg, stands before the house in 1969.

Walburg put them away. The next evening the store was opened again. We played this way for two weeks. January 6th was the last day of Christmas. On that day the store was closed. Then Mother took all the good things from the store and divided them equally among us, and we were allowed to eat and enjoy them.

Father also made a wonderful little kitchen for us. This had a real stove that burned alcohol and we could cook our own soup and hot chocolate. Once a week we were allowed to invite our friends for a party. Mother baked lots of cookies, tiny little Bundcakes, which were specially delicious and we made the hot chocolate on our little stove. None of the other children in the village had as much fun at Christmas time.

I was the third child. The oldest was my sister, Walburg. She was born in April 1901. Then came my brother Karl; he was born in September 1902. After me came my sister Gretel (or Margaret). She was born in September 1906. Last was my younger brother Julius, born in 1910, just five days after my father's death. Karl was killed in May of 1945 as he was fleeing the Russians—he was killed just as he was about to board a bus that would have led to his freedom. Julius died in a train accident in 1943 during the war. Some said he threw himself before the train. Gretel died of cancer in 1979.

My father was a hard worker. From early morning till late in the evening he was in his workshop. In the spring of 1910 he was working on a new wagon for a farmer. He had nearly finished the wagon, but when he tried to put on the last wheel he badly injured himself. He was in terrible pain and could hardly walk home. My mother put him right to bed. She also asked his father, who had the telephone, to call the doctor who lived an-hour-and-a-half away. The doctor finally came in his horse-drawn wagon, examined him, and announced, "This man is perfectly healthy, give him castor oil and he will be well again tomorrow." Tragically the doctor was not aware that my father incurred a serious hernia that damaged his intestines. Giving him castor oil was the worst thing one could do. My mother didn't know this either, and on the doctor's advice she gave him a big dose of castor oil. Father's pain became unbearable and after midnight he said, "Now the pain is coming to my heart, I have to go, 'Father, into your hands I commit my spirit.'" These were his last words. Mother and we children stood by his bed crying. Our neighbor, Gottlieb Stängle, who was the leader of the Pietistic Community, was with us that night, and prayed with us. He also called Mrs. Meyer, who took care of the dead. She came early in the morning to wash father's body with a special water and clothed him in a beautiful white gown. Then the cabinet maker brought a casket he had made. Father was put into it and placed in a little room near our bedroom, where he lay for three days. Every day I would look in. I couldn't understand why he didn't wake up. He had always done so when we played pig. I was six and had no understanding of death. I never associated the animals I had seen butchered with people.

On the third day the casket was closed and some men carried it downstairs and out in the garden. Many people in black clothes were waiting there. Even some soldiers and the policeman had come in their uniforms with their guns, and I was quite scared. After several men spoke kindly about my father, the soldiers lifted up their rifles and fired three times into the air. This scared me even more. "Why should they shoot my father?" I didn't realize that this was a final tribute to him as a soldier. Now four men picked up the casket and carried it to the graveyard. Grandfather, grandmother, mother and we children all followed. Then came friends and relatives. Finally the whole village joined the procession to the cemetery. There the Pastor waited to give father the final rites. I was horrified to see men lower the casket in a big hole in the ground and cover it with dirt. "Will he never come back again?," I wondered. We all took father's death very hard. But mother was truly heartbroken. All of our lives suddenly changed, and much of the carefreeness of my early years ended.

Because I was so young when he died, I remember very little about my father. But I know he just loved to sing. In Ulm they once put on a play about William Tell, and my father was asked to play the main role and had to shoot the apple from the boy's head. On that occasion, the Bürgermeister of Ulm said to my Grandfather, "Henner did you really produce this boy?" My father was very honest and direct. Once, when I was five years old, my mother said something in criticism of my Grandfather, who had drunk a little too much, and it embarrassed her. I remember, he stood before my mother and said, "Woman, don't you ever say anything about this man—he is my father!" I also remember that my father and grandfather were the barbers of the village. Every Saturday evening our living room was full of men who came for a haircut and shave. They sat around and talked, and one after the other got his shave and haircut for Sunday. My father was paid ten pfenig for each shave and haircut.

My mother was very intelligent. She was also very good at knitting and crocheting. She had a knitting machine and knitted socks for the whole village. And she had the little store. After my father's death, she had to work very hard to keep the family solvent. There were lots of debts, because just before father died, they had built the new house, store, and workshop. These were newly finished and needed to be paid for. At the start she didn't think she could manage. She later told us that one night she was really discouraged and wanted to give up. Then she heard a clear voice saying, "I will never leave you nor forsake you." Knowing that God was with her gave her renewed strength. On another occasion a businessman who had come to show her some wares realized that she needed encouragement. He told her, "Frau Henner you must not give up, your children need both a mother and a father, and you must be both to them." And so she really worked day and night. My sister had to help her with the socks she knitted and also with the store. In summer, when the store was open only in the evening, my mother took all of us children into the fields to glean during the day. Like Mrs. Steck, she carried all the sheaves we gathered home on her head. Then we would thresh out the grain at home, and often had a whole sack-full of wheat that we had milled for the winter. All of us worked, and from the age of four we were already gleaning in the fields.

I sometimes think about lessons we learned then. We had so little money, and my mother worked so hard to hang on to the little store and house. The money to build both had been borrowed from a wealthy farmer. Payments had to be made on a regular basis. I recall that one year my mother put three beautiful gold coins in a white paper and asked me to take them to Mr. Bühler, the "New Farmer." This was the interest on our loan. I asked two of my girlfriends to go with me. It was a dreary day and the streets were full of mud because it had been raining. I don't know how it happened, but when we arrived at the farmer's house, I had only two gold coins. I had no idea where I lost the third coin, but I knew how important it was, and I was really scared. I prayed in my heart, "Please dear God, help me to find the coin!" My two

friends and I retraced our steps carefully looking everywhere. But how could we to find such a small coin in all that mud? And believe it or not, Hilde, one of my two friends, found it! Oh! How glad and thankful I was! My mother rewarded Hilde with a bar of chocolate and I was truly happy for her. Thereafter I was always very careful with money.

Chocolate was really my

Bernstadt village.

downfall. I loved it so much, but I never got a bar of chocolate from my mother as a child. So one day I stole one from our little store and buried it in the garden. In the evening, when everyone was in the house, I went out to get a piece of my chocolate bar. But I couldn't find it any more. It was gone. All that was left was the heavy sense of guilt that I carried with me for many years.

In the summer of 1913 one of my relatives came and picked me up to baby sit for her daughter's little girl. But an old woman was soon found for this job, and I was put to work in the fields and in cleaning the kitchen and doing the dishes. I was not used to regular field work. Soon my hands were so swollen that I couldn't hold the sickle anymore. I was also terribly homesick and cried day and night. One day out in the fields I went behind a wild rose bush and cried out to God that he might have mercy on me and send me home. The following Sunday my aunt said to me, "You have no hands for farm work; you have the hands of a teacher. You can go home to your mother, but I have no time to take you. On Sunday morning I will show you the way. And you can go." Nobody was happier than I. I couldn't carry anything, not even my little basket, because my hands were so sore. My aunt went with me until we reached the edge of the village where there was a small hill. From there I saw our church steeple in the distance and I said to my aunt, "You can go home now, I can find my way from here." So I started to walk over the recently harvested fields till I came to the next road, and I focused only on the steeple and constantly made my way towards it. I arrived home in about two-and-a-half hours. But when I came close to our house, I got scared. I was afraid that my mother would be mad at me for leaving the people she had promised I would help. I had a hard time going in. We had a bell on our house door, but I opened it so quietly that the bell didn't ring. Then I stood before the living room door and opened it very slowly. What I saw was my mother, sister, and brothers sitting at their "vesper," which is a kind of second breakfast. I ran towards my mother, fell on my knees before her, and laid my hands in her lap and said "Mother look at my hands!" She was shocked, and tears started to run down her face. She laid her hands on mine and said, "poor child." Next she ordered my sister upstairs to bring a pillow and blanket, took off my shoes, laid me on the sofa and covered me, giving me something to drink. Lying on the sofa, I felt so good, so wonderfully good, as if I were in heaven. And then my sister asked, "Has Rosel to go again to these people?" And my mother said, "No!" Now I really relaxed and my heart was full of joy and peace. Oh! How happy I was to be home again!

Three weeks later my sister, her friend, and I went to the village where I had been to pick up my things. At the entrance to the village we met a very fine and elegant man who greeted us and asked us where we were from and where we were going. Then he put his hand in his pocket and took out three little bars of chocolate which he gave to each of us. So that was the first kindness shown me in this village, and later I found out that he was the pastor of the village. I will never forget him for his chocolate; I will even remember him in heaven for his chocolate! What a little kindness can do!

The following year war broke out, and most of the farmers had to join the army. One of my mother's acquaintances, was a farmer whose wife was pregnant in August of 1914. Soon a little girl was born. But the farmer's wife had no one to help her with the farm and her children, as her husband had been called up. So she asked my mother if I could be sent to take care of the children. There was one girl two years old and the new infant which was just three weeks old when I took over. I was ten years of age at the time, and I gave the little girl a bath every day, fed her, and took care of her and her sister. The farmer's wife, Mrs. Hausler, spent almost all of her time in the fields with the servants. She had to take over for her husband. Meanwhile, I took care of the children and the chickens. I did this for two years.

By the age of twelve I graduated from taking care of children and had to do much harder work. There was a farm run by an elderly couple called the Hausers. They had only a son and daughter, and the son was called up by the army. He was later killed in the war. They needed help, so they approached my mother and asked her to lend them Karl and me. She agreed. Thereafter Karl and I went every day at 5 A.M. to their house to help. Karl worked at the Hausers two years; I only one. We had to feed the cows, carry the feed in from the cutting machine, and bring the milk in every day. At the same time we still had to go to school for four hours. After school we went to work again. We also worked in the fields and did everything the grownups did. We worked so long, that I never had time to read, and I wanted so badly to read. The only free time we had was from one to five o'clock on Sunday afternoons. That was the only time we got off. But the old couple really loved us and were very kind to us. Only the food was terrible! Oh! What miserable food! Mrs. Hauser just couldn't cook. She made such dumplings that when you shut your mouth you couldn't open it again. But it didn't matter, we ate everything. How different from children today. We didn't even dare to complain about that awful food. Still, she was a cheery person and treated me just like her child. When we had to work in a distant field she took only bread, which was always good, and a little coffee—that was our lunch. After lunch she had a song she would sing:

Kaffeele du bist zuckeret	My coffee you are sugared
Kaffeele du bist süss	My coffee you are sweet
Und wenn I d'Schuh vertanzed han	And when I've danced these shoes away
Dann han I doch noch d'Füss	I'll move on to bare feet

Then she would stand up, take me by the hand, and we would dance around the meadow together.

In February 1916 I started to work on the farm of Frau Angela Fuos. She also needed help because her husband was in the war, and only the old grandfather was left to assist her with the farm. She went to my mother and my mother agreed that I should work for her. Of course my mother got paid for my work, but I never saw a penny of the money. At the Fuos farm I had to work so hard from early morning to late at night, at home and in the fields, that I had little time to read or study, which I wanted so much to do. Sometimes, I remember, I went to the toilet and stayed there long enough to read a few pages. On one of these occasions the cow got out of the stable, while I was reading a story, and everybody was howling outside, and the cow was running wild. This was all my fault, because I got lost in my reading.

That was a terrible period in my life. A hard, no, more than hard, time. In the winter of 1917-18 I wanted to die. I longed to get pneumonia and die. I even gathered up all the snow that came in the window and ate it. And I lay on the floor only in my nightgown waiting to get sick. And yet, when I got so cold that I was shaking, I wanted to get back into my bed, and did. I didn't get sick and I didn't die. But a woman who saw me working so hard at the Fuos's, went to my mother and told her that if she wanted to turn me into a cripple she would soon accomplish that end by leaving me with Angela. This scared my mother who arranged to transfer me to another woman's farm.

The new farm belonged to Agnes Müller and her husband. He, too, was away in the war, and the Müller's had three children. I stayed a year with the Müllers. Mrs. Müller was kind to me and she was an excellent cook. Then the war ended; that was in 1918. We all rejoiced. Soon Agnes's husband came back from the army. Now I was no longer needed at the Müllers. It was also at this time that my older sister Walburg said to my mother, "You know how much Rosel likes to study, can't we help her to go to school." My mother thought this over. Not long thereafter a new world opened before me. In 1918 I turned fifteen. We were still poor. But as a family we had survived the war and the difficult years after my father's death. For me the worst was over.

Location of Bernstadt (*) between Stuttgart and Munich.

Chapter Two
Breaking Out

Christuskirche Mannheim.

My mother and sister wanted to help me with my education. They thought I should leave Bernstadt to learn something of the broader world. For them a woman's education consisted of learning how to manage a household. This meant knowing how to cook and clean house. Till then my experiences were limited entirely to country life and farm work. They found me a family with six children in Ulm. And there I learned how to cook and to take care of the house. The family's name was Schmidt and they were kind and treated me well. Even today I still correspond with their children. The Schmidts paid me 15 marks, or about three dollars, a month. This was the first money I was allowed to keep for myself.

I was at the Schmidts about nine months when my aunt in Mannheim, my father's sister, made an agreement with my mother that if she supplied her with food, my aunt would take me in and make it possible for me to attend a Kindergarten Training School in that city. So in September of 1919 I took the train from Ulm to Mannheim and started a new life.

In Mannheim I attended the Kindergarten Seminar and learned how to educate and care for young children. At first I felt a stranger in the city. I was very lonely. Then I came to like it, and before long I was part of it, and I felt proud of being part of the city and able to go to school. I was still scared, but I liked it. I felt secure in the city. I was happy when I walked through the streets. Till then there had been only work, now I could enjoy life, walk about and gaze into the stores. Before I felt more a part of the animal world, now I felt more a part of the world of people. With my hard-earned money I bought some clothes. I was so poor, I had almost nothing in the way of clothes. So I had a dress made, and that cost ten marks just for making the dress. It cost me five marks for the material. I still sent money home on a regular basis, and I bought my own ticket home once a year. I also bought a few books which remained my treasures.

It was at this time that I met a very nice group of young people. They were called the Christian Endeavor, and through them I found peace with God and peace with man. I came to know God in a personal way, and this meant a great deal to me. My real desire became to please God.

Growing up in Bernstadt I had, of course, gone to church. In keeping with the tradition of the Lutheran Church, children under six were not allowed to attend service, but thereafter we went every Sunday. And yet, the God to which I was introduced in our village church was only a God to fear. For years I was afraid of God. And yet, I was also longing to know him. When my mother started attending the meetings of a Pietistic Christian Community, which was quite different from the Lutheran Church, she sometimes

The Bernstadt Village Church.

took me with her. But here, too, I heard how strict God was. The emphasis was on punishment, particularly of those who disobeyed him and failed to do right. One of my mother's friends, a Christian woman, taught us how to pray. So lying in bed at night I often prayed that God might forgive me for my many wrongs. But I had to wait until I came to Mannheim and the Christian Endeavor group to realize that there was a different God, one who was kind and loved me, and with whom I could have a personal relationship. We loved each other dearly and tried to help others whenever we could.

There were about thirty young women in the Kindergarten Seminar that I attended for a year and a half. When we finished our training we were given the choice of working in a Kindergarten or being employed by a private family. I chose the latter. There was a very nice Jewish family in Mannheim by the name of Sostheim. Paul Sostheim was a highly successful oriental carpet merchant. He had a booming business and two lovely children. Rolf, the oldest was four, and Hans, the younger was two. Frau Sostheim was a very elegant lady, and she and her husband asked me to live in their home and serve as governess for their children.

For the next four years I lived with the Sostheims. I really had little to do but to attend to the children. For the first time in my life I had it really good. We had a cook and a housekeeper and good food, and everything seemed to go well. Frau Sostheim was chic and cultured. Every New Year the Sostheims gave a party, for which I had to dress as a Bavarian boy with lederhosen, and the cook had to dress-up in a dirndl. We served about twenty guests on these occasions. At one of these parties, I recall, a businessman wearing the costume of a medieval musician and entertainer, sang a song about all the guests who came. I still remember the lines about the lady of the house, Mrs. Sostheim:

Ella ist 'ne schicke Dame	Ella is an urbane lady
Das weiss jeder der die Mode kennt	So say those who style invent
Ist für Wirths 'ne blendende Reklame	Shining ad for her designer
In der Kleidung zeigt sie viel Talent.	In her dress she shows us great talent
Einmal ging in Baden Baden	Once she strolled in Baden Baden
Auf dem Ludwigs Platz sie stolz umher	Proudly round the Ludwig's Place
Plötzlich fühlt sie was an ihrer Waden	Then her legs felt a new omen
Und schon nahte sich ein gross' Malheur	Of misfortune soon to face
Leise und ohne viel Beschwerden	Without sound and without warning
Loest sich ein intimes Kleidungsstück	Loose came a most private dress
Und fiel ploetzlich runter auf die Erde,	Suddenly to earth it bounded,
Es war Sommer, das war noch ein Glück!	It was summer, Oh, what luckiness!

That was Ella. She liked to travel. Every summer she went to another spa, or visited her family in Hamburg; she knew her children were in good hands.

The Sostheim's had a lovely home full of beautiful carpets, fine silver, and crystal. But what I liked best was their library. They had a wonderful collection of books. There were many volumes on literature, and many novels. Mr. Sostheim encouraged me to read, and told me I could read anything I wanted. For the first time in my life I had ready access to books, and I took full advantage of it. Mr. Sostheim also had a car and chauffeur, and sometimes even the children and I were allowed to be driven around. It was very unusual to have a car in those days, and Mr. Sostheim was clearly a man of means. One summer we spent our vacation in Freudenstadt in the Black Forest. The parents lived in a splendid hotel, and the children and I stayed in a Pensione. Everyday we went into the woods and picked berries and flowers. And when we came home we had a good meal that had been prepared for us. In the afternoon we met the parents at a cafe and had a delicious piece of torte. Then we would go hiking again.

One day we came home from our hike in the woods, and I discovered that I had lost my watch. It was the first watch I had ever owned. I had bought it with my own money. And it was really precious to me. To lose it was really terrible. So I prayed, "Oh, Dear God, let me find my watch again." But how does one find a watch in the woods? Early the next morning, when the sun was coming up, I said to the houseboy, "I am going to the woods, please watch over the children, and if they wake up, and I'm not back, tell them I will be back soon, so they will not worry." I took the same path we had taken the day before. I remembered that we had been singing and had clapped our hands. It must have been then, while we were clapping our hands, that my watch had come loose. But where exactly that might have been remained a mystery. I was constantly praying that the Lord should let me find my watch. Then I came to a spot where there was a slope on the left side, and at the bottom of the slope a fallen tree. I stood still. In my heart a voice said, "Go down to the tree and look for your watch." I said, "But we never went down there!" Still the voice inside me compelled me to go down and look. I stirred the leaves and examined the ground for a while, and lo! and behold! there was my watch! I fell on my knees and praised the Lord with all my heart, and walked back with joy. The children were still asleep when I arrived at the Pensione.

The following summer I returned on a visit to Bernstadt. My mother was going blind. She had glaucoma. None of the doctors seemed to be able to help her. Then she heard of a man in the Black Forest who had a special gift for healing and she wanted to visit him. My sister helped her to get there and to stay at Möttlingen near him for a few weeks. She didn't get back her sight, but inwardly she was restored and returned home with great joy and peace in her heart. She was now able to accept the fact that she would soon be completely blind. In the Black Forest, not far from this man, there was a beautiful town named Bad Liebenzell. This town was known for its hot springs and for its mission and a mission school. My mother visited there with several guests from the home where she stayed. While in Liebenzell she heard three missionaries from China who spoke about God's work there and the need for more missionaries. My mother thought, if only my Rose were willing to go to China. She remembered that some years earlier a missionary from India had come to Bernstadt and spoken at our church. On that occasion the missionary had asked if there was anyone in the audience who was prepared to go to a foreign country to present God's word. I had stood up and said, "I will go!" Maybe now, she thought, I would be willing to go to China. So when she returned to Bernstadt from Möttlingen and Liebenzell she was really excited about mission work and her heart was full of what she had experienced in the Black Forest. When I met her on my visit she said to me, "Rose, you are young and strong, you could go!"

But I didn't want to go. For the first time in my life I had it good. I couldn't think of leaving Mannheim and going somewhere else—especially not to China! But strange as it may seem, when I got back to Mannheim, the very first Sunday, I was invited by a young girl I had met on my way to the railway station, to attend a meeting at her church that evening. "Please come," she said. So I promised that I would. At that meeting the speaker was a Sister from the Liebenzell Mission who spoke about China. When she finished her talk, she said, "The Lord needs workers for China. If there is a girl here who the Lord has called to go, let her be willing to go." I was really surprised because I had never met her, and she didn't know me. I didn't go up to see her afterwards. In fact, I left by the back door, and went home. But I couldn't sleep. Finally, I fell on my knees and said, "Oh! God. If you really want me to go to China give me love for the Chinese people and make me willing to go."

Through the Liebenzell Sister I received various publications that dealt with the Mission's work in China and the South Pacific. I learned that the Liebenzell Mission had been founded in 1899 as the German branch of the China Inland Mission. The more I read, the more my heart was warmed towards mission work in China. When I turned twenty-one in 1924, I wrote to Liebenzell asking for an application to the mission school. At the time only twenty-one-year-olds were accepted by the mission. They sent me a set of forms, which I filled out, and sent back. That was in April or May. But I received no reply. I had already told the Sostheims that I would leave them and go to the Mission School. They couldn't understand my decision. They tried to do everything they could to keep me, but I had made up my mind. I went home, leaving Mannheim, to spend a few days with my mother. I knew that school started in September, and it was now July and August, and I still

The main street of Stuttgart in 1954 when Mama returned to Germany.

had no word from Liebenzell. So I thought, well, I tried my best, and if they don't want me, that's all right with me. I will go and find another position in Stuttgart. I went to my uncle's home in Stuttgart and began to look for another job as a governess.

While walking down one of the main streets of Stuttgart I saw a book store. And in the window of this store there was a large open Bible. I looked at it and read: "I will also give you as a light to the Gentiles, that you should be my salvation to the ends of the earth." This was a verse from Isaiah, Chapter 49. Then a voice inside me said, "Don't look for another position. Go to Liebenzell!" I went home to my mother and wrote a letter to Liebenzell saying that I had sent in my papers in April and still had no word from the school. What should I do? I received a hurried reply that I should come, that my name was already on all the shelves, and that they were waiting for me to arrive. "Your class is already here," the Mission wrote, "the Class of 1924." So my sister helped me to get ready as quickly as possible. We had to bring our own bedding, sheets, blankets, and even our own featherbed. All these were hard to get in 1924. Fortunately the Sostheims generously provided me with all the materials, and my sister helped me with the sewing.

This was the period of the terrible inflation in Germany. We, too, lost all our money. The price of a bun rose to four million marks. There was also a lot of social unrest. Already when I was at the Sostheims in 1923 people painted a swastika on the house. One day when Mrs. Sostheim was away, and only the cook and I were at home, I heard Mr. Sostheim come in late in the evening. He paced through the house from room to room. I went out to ask why he was doing so. I saw that his eyes were bloodshot, and he said, "Fräulein Henner have you ever hated a person so much that you wanted to kill him on the spot?" I said, "No, but have you?" He said, "Yes, tonight! One of my own brothers!" He meant a fellow Jew. "He was speaking, and he said you are not Germans, you are Jews; you must leave this country and go to Palestine!" "What a fool!" "What a fool!" "Am I not German, just like you?" And then he lifted his sleeve to show me a big scar on his upper arm and said, "See! I was wounded in the last war. I gave my blood for Germany, and I am still willing to give my blood for Germany!" Mr. Sostheim saw himself as a loyal German. It was hard for him to accept the fact that some Germans now sought scapegoats for their own economic problems and identified them with the Jews. I kept in touch with the Sostheims until 1933, hearing from them once in a while during my years in the South Pacific. Then suddenly all letters stopped. I do not know what happened to them. When I returned to Germany for the first time in 1954 and came to Mannheim, I immediately inquired about the Sostheims. But, as in so many other cases, nobody knew anything.

In my heart I fear that the worst happened.

Before going to Liebenzell I had to take care of one piece of unfinished business. This was very hard for me. Years earlier, while at Angela Fuos's, I had been sent to buy sausages at the local butcher shop. The butcher had just finished making the sausages. They smelled wonderful. I had brought a ten mark note to pay for the sausages and the butcher had to go upstairs to get change. While he was gone I took a sausage off his tray and put it in my pocket. My purchase was all wrapped up. On the way back I ate the sausage. It was still warm. And tasted so good! But I knew I couldn't go to the Mission School and to China with this stolen sausage on my conscience. So I walked to the butcher's house. It was Sunday. I remember how hard it was to knock on his door. His son answered. I asked, "Where is your father?" He said, "In the kitchen." I said, "I have to speak to him." He showed me the way. The butcher was sitting at a large table cutting up lard. I told him the story of the sausage I had taken, and I put a one mark piece on the table. He said he didn't want my money. I said I had to do this because otherwise I could not go to Liebenzell. Suddenly there were tears in his eyes. He told me that my taking a sausage was nothing in comparison to his working on the Lord's day. I assured him that God could forgive both of us. How strong a force guilt is.

After my hasty preparations and my visit to the butcher, I took the train to Liebenzell. Arriving at the station I looked around trying to get my bearings when a man in a great apron came towards me and said, "Fräulein, are you going to the Mission?" I said, "Yes." He said, "I will carry your suitcase. You follow me. I am the gardener of the Mission." So I gladly followed him. After a while we came to big black iron gate. He opened it with a key and let me through. A few steps beyond the gate was a large white stone with "God is present" carved on it. I was moved by this. From here our path zig-zagged upward to the "Villa," the headquarters of the Mission. The gardener took me to the Director, Heinrich Coerper and his wife Ruth. Both welcomed me most graciously. Then they asked their daughter, Elizabeth, to show me the whole Mission compound and my new quarters. In the garden I saw some men working. They were all students of the school. We were called "Sisters" and they were the "Brothers." I knew one of the men working from our Christian Endeavor group in Mannheim. So with great joy I waved my hand and called out, "Hello Brother Gibeler." But he didn't answer. Fräulein Elizabeth took me by the hand and said, "Sister Rose from now on you can't greet a 'Brother' on the Mission compound." And I never did!

When I went to Liebenzell I knew we had to wear special clothes, dark colors, long skirts, and a black hat. Because our class was still on probation none of us received the usual Sister's uniform with its distinctive cap. Still the

Mission had a strict rule about hats, and whenever we went out into the community we had to wear one. If we did not have an acceptable one of our own, the Mission had a closet full of hats from which we could choose. I had my own hat. But it was a funny hat. It was rather old fashioned. Once I was going to Geislingen to visit the

Mama as a "Sister" in the Black Forest, after she convinced the Mission to allow her to wear a habit.

daughter of a teacher who lived there. I had my long dress, my hat, and carried my suitcase. While walking, I ran into a group of children. I said, "Children can you tell me where I can find your school house?" They said, "Yes, we are going there." Then they looked at me from head to toe and got very excited. One of them said, "Fräulein, do you have anything to show." I said, "What do you mean to show?" He said, "You know, like snakes or butterflies in your suitcase." They thought I was a traveling school performer who brought around strange and unusual things to show to school children. At least that is what my appearance suggested to them. I marked the occasion with a poem to the Mission's governing committee, suggesting that we be allowed to wear a uniform that clearly indicated we were Sisters, not traveling entertainers. Not long thereafter we were allowed to wear our Sisters' uniforms and caps and that ended the confusion.

Conditions at Liebenzell were also affected by the hard times. For breakfast we got a thin oatmeal soup, more water than oatmeal, and for lunch potatoes and vegetables. Once a week, usually on Sunday, we got a small piece of meat. And for supper we had a kind of soup and bread, or potatoes and milk. That was our diet. We lived poor, but we were all healthy. I loved the school. We were twenty-four women in one room. And we had one senior who watched that we kept order in everything. I still remember one occasion when I was ordering some of my classmates around saying, "You do this," and "You do that." One of the girls stood up and said, "Sister Rose, you think you've come to the Mission to command people. You came here to learn obedience!" After that I learned to keep my mouth shut. But we really loved each other and helped each other whenever we could. All the Sisters had to buy a uniform, but I had no money to pay for mine. Again I prayed. I said, "Dear Lord where can I get some money to pay for my uniform?" One day I came into our big bedroom, and there lying on my bed was a complete new uniform. Till today I do not know who paid for it, but I know that some of my classmates did. I really felt at home and was happy in Liebenzell.

We didn't pay tuition to the school, but we had to work in the afternoons for the Mission. All the office work and all the housework was done by the students. On Sundays we all went to the nearby villages and towns and taught Sunday School and Ladies' Classes, or participated in other Sunday services. In my last semester I went back to Mannheim for six months to work in a hospital so that I could get some experience in dealing with the sick to prepare me for patients on the mission field. Thereafter I was sent as an intern to the Black Forest. There I had eight little villages where I held Sunday School and Ladies Classes, and where I visited the sick, helped the poor, and performed other social services. All of us had to prove that we were capable of such work before being sent to the mission field. That was interesting work, and in the year I spent in the Black Forest, 1929-1930, I came to know many poor, and some wealthy, families. I usually made the circuit either on foot or by bicycle. On one occasion there was an older missionary lady from the South Sea Islands who wanted to go with me. It was the middle of winter and the streets were so icy that we couldn't walk, except by pulling ourselves along by holding on to the trees. But somehow we managed to reach the next village.

We tried to help the people as best we could. Working with the poor was always a challenge. All of us hoped that our work was pleasing to God and a help to our fellow man. We knew that only God could transform people's lives. And we tried to give Him the glory. But the people we met were also

very human. I had always been interested in the Gypsies. In my group of villages there were no Gypsies, but one of my fellow Sisters worked with an old Gypsy woman. The woman was greatly helped by her in both a physical and spiritual sense. She did everything she could to make the old lady comfortable. At the same time she tried to teach her to do right. When it came time for our Sister to go on to a new work, the old lady broke into tears. She sobbed and sobbed. When asked, why she was crying, she said, "You have done everything for me, and there is nothing, nothing, that I can do for you. I just feel terrible." After crying some more,

Heinrich Coerper (1863-1936).

Mama at her Ordination in Bad Liebenzell in June 1, 1930. At the center are Pharrer Coerper and Mrs. Coerper (with her arm around Mama). To Mrs Coerpers right stand Käthe Wenzel (later Mrs. Buss), Magdelene Röste (later a China Missionary), Thea Barth (later Mrs. Lang) and Lydia Mueller (who accompanied Mama to the South Pacific). The men are not identified.

she suddenly stopped. An idea flashed across her face, and a smile replaced her tears. She took Sister by the hand and said, "You wait here a moment." "I know what I can do for you. I'll go out and steal you a chicken."

In the spring of 1930 the Director of the Mission, Pharrer Coerper, who had become my spiritual father, called me in and said, "Sister Rose, are you ready to go to the South Sea Islands?" I said, "To the South Sea Islands? Shouldn't I be going to China?" "Yes," he said, "but we need a young woman for those islands, a woman who is cheerful, because life there is very lonely, and we have been watching you and you are always cheerful. Therefore we would like to send you." I said, "Herr Pfarrer, if the Lord wants me on the Islands send me." So I was ordained on the first of June, 1930, and then on the 26th of August I left Bad Liebenzell and went to Berlin. There I met two young women who were engaged to missionaries in Japan, and another woman who had been chosen to go with me to the South Pacific. The two going as brides to Japan were Thea Barth and Käthe Wenzel. Thea married Ernst Lang and Käthe married Bernhardt Buss, two of the pioneer Liebenzell missionaries in Japan. My fellow missionary for the South Pacific was Lydia Meuller, "Tante Lydia," as she came to be affectionately known in our family. We were all full of youthful energy, adventuresome, and heading for a new life. I was twenty-seven in 1930. Twenty-seven is a good age. One is young enough to remain idealistic, and old enough to temper that idealism with a dose of reality.

Chapter Three
East to the Islands

Truk.

We left Berlin on August 26, 1930. The train took us to Warsaw, and from there to Moscow. In Moscow we had to change to the Trans-Siberian Railroad. Porters came and took our luggage, our passports, and everything to the new train. We spent a day in Moscow and wanted to buy bread and butter for the journey east. Going down to Red Square we found a store that sold excellent dark bread, but we wanted butter, and none of the stores had any. Finally we found a store that had a little butter, but it was so covered with flies that we could not bring ourselves to buy it. In the end, we resigned ourselves to eating our bread dry.

We had a small spirit stove in our compartment on the train. But we soon discovered that at all the stations there was good soup for sale. So we bought soup. At one station, while we were getting our soup, thieves stole the coats of several of the passengers. You had to be very careful in Russia. We had third-class tickets, which meant we had only wooden benches, and at night we got a sponge rubber cushion, a pillow, and a little blanket. It was August, so the weather wasn't cold, and we didn't freeze. Lake Baikal was particularly beautiful. One morning we woke up as someone cried "fire!", but it was no fire, only the sun rising. The whole forest seemed on fire. I wrote a long poem about our trip across Siberia. At one point the axles of the train caught fire, and while they were being repaired we picked berries on the slopes near the tracks. Finally we arrived in Harbin and had to change trains. We were at a loss where to go, but there were three Japanese doctors on the train who spoke German, and they helped us to transfer our luggage and showed us where to take the train for Korea. From Harbin we went to Pusan, and from there we caught a ship to Shimonoseki. We all got terribly seasick. The sea was so wild. The water was all yellow. Having hoped for a wonderful sea voyage, we were quite disappointed. Finally, we arrived in Japan on the 6th of September.

We took the train from Shimonoseki to Tokyo. Herr Buss and Herr Lang were waiting for their brides in Shimonoseki dressed in pure white suits. They looked very smart! The train ride up to Tokyo took about a day-and-a-half. In Tokyo we lived near Omori, and learned our first words of Japanese—*konnichiwa, ohio gozaimasu,* and *konbanwa* (hello, good morning, and good evening). Later we added *ikura desu ka* (How much is it?) and learned to count. What struck me about Japan were all the shops open to the streets, with their goods practically spilling out on them, and no one took anything. It was also strange to see so many tiny houses. In 1930 almost no Japanese women wore foreign dress and most went out in their kimonos. All the children wore school uniforms. I was impressed with the big department stores in Tokyo and Yokohama. What surprised me the most was the way that Japanese women would bow right to the floor when we visited a Japanese home.

In getting ready for the Lang and Buss double wedding, which was held on September 18th, I helped with the decorations. It was then that I met Herr Notehelfer. He was a tall, thin man with a shy smile and a love of flowers. We made floral arrangements, hung up garlands, and prepared the tables. I had little inkling at the time that we would later marry. The wedding, I remember, was very festive and full of fun, a part of which included a long poem I wrote on behalf of both couples.

In order to go the South Sea Islands in 1930, one had to get permission from the Japanese Church as well as from the Japanese Government. Although German missionaries had been active in Micronesia for many years, when the islands had been under German control, after World War I they were mandated to the Japanese by the League of Nations. To get Church clearances we went to see Kozaki Hiromichi. He was a well known Japanese Minister who became a Christian in Kumamoto under the influence of an American

Mama arriving in Japan from Korea with her traveling companions. From the left, Lydia Mueller, who went with her to the South Pacific, Thea Barth who married Ernest Lang, Mama, and Käthe Wenzel who married Bernhard Buss.

Civil War Officer, Captain Janes, in the Meiji period. We visited him at his house. He was now an old man, but I recall he had a broad face, a big smile, and a mustache. There was a sense of samurai dignity about him. We also met his wife who wore a beautiful dark kimono. He spoke excellent English and wished us well in the *Nanyō*, as the Japanese called the islands. How curious life is. I could hardly have imagined, as I sat in Kozaki's parlor that day, that my son Fred, as a university professor, would later write a biography of the American who converted Kozaki to Christianity and taught him the beautiful English in which we now conversed. Kozaki was far more enthusiastic about our going to the *Nanyō* than was the Foreign Ministry. The Japanese government was already very strict about where they would allow foreign missionaries to go in the South Pacific. Some islands were clearly off limits. Later when I was on Mortlock, and wanted so badly to visit Ponape, which was known to be very beautiful, the Japanese never gave any of the German missionaries permission to go there.

We finally got our visas and on the 16th of October Tante Lydia and I went on board a little black steamer that was bound for Truk. I can still see the people at the pier and the many ribbons. All the missionaries came to see us off, and then the ship began to move away till the last streamer was broken. The ship had only three or four cabins, besides that of the captain. We were the only foreigners aboard. The rest were all Japanese traders and businessmen going out to the islands. When we disembarked on Truk, the first thing I learned was that the Japanese were in charge and that everyone had to bow before them.

Lydia Mueller and Mama departing for Truk.

We were greeted at the ship by one of the Japanese missionaries from Kozaki's group. He was quite different from the Japanese officials, and took us to his house which was surrounded by papayas and palm trees. We stayed there till the Liebenzell missionaries, who were coming from the island of Moen could reach Truk. From Truk we went to Elise Zuber's. She was known as the "Queen of the Islands," and had been there since 1906. Everyone knew her and respected her. She was a powerful figure. Her home base was Udoet, where she ran a girls school. So we went with her and stayed at the girls

26

school. Tante Lydia had been chosen by the mission to become her assistant. My own assignment was to help Sister Anna Schneider on the island of Tol. This was an island on which Herr Maeder ran a Bible school for preachers. Anna Schneider's mission station was just six miles from this school, and it was here that I joined her for half-a-year to learn the language. It wasn't hard to learn. After six months I could already get along. The children were a happy lot and we learned from them as we taught them. At that time, the only schools available were the mission schools. Later the Japanese required all the islanders to go to Japanese schools. The children were my best teachers, they always corrected me and laughed about my mistakes.

After being on Tol for six months, a request arrived from Mortlock, a group of eight islands, that I should be sent there. On Mortlock there was only one missionary and his wife who needed help. So the mission decided to send me to Mortlock. I remember I took a very small, dirty steamer full of copra, pigs, and chickens to Mortlock. I had a tiny cabin that was airless, and I preferred sleeping on the deck with the chickens and pigs. When I reached Mortlock, the whole island was there to greet me in white dresses, white shirts and white trousers. They welcomed me with a German song they had learned especially for the occasion. About a hundred to a hundred-and-fifty people were there.

Protestant Church on Lukunor.

Half the population of Mortlock was Catholic. The other half was Protestant. The Island to which I was assigned was Lukunor. It took about three hours to walk around the whole island. Everything was flat, nothing but coral sand. It was hard to keep a garden, because after a heavy rain all the good soil was washed away. Food production was very meager. It consisted of breadfruit, coconuts, and taro. Even bananas were scarce. Taro was the main meal when there was no breadfruit. This was for about three months of the year. In preparation for this period, the islanders made a special preserve of breadfruit which they mashed and wrapped in banana leaves and buried in the ground. It fermented, and if they ate too much of it, they often broke out in serious rashes. Most of the people went fishing every day.

At the mission station we had about six boys who helped us with the work. They got some special training, and took care of the boat and buildings. Their only pay was food and clothing from the mission. In most cases the boys stayed with us for a year and then went back to their home islands, or to the mission seminary.

I had a sweet little house. A wooden house, with a big veranda. Inside was a living room, bedroom, and kitchen all in one. It was right at the edge of the water. During storms the ocean would go under the house, which was built on cement pilings. What I liked best was the big porch that went completely around the house. There was also a large water tank, because rain was our only source of water. It was scarce so we were very careful about using it for bathing, cooking and drinking. The Church also had a large water tank for the whole island, and every house had a small barrel of water. The natives bathed in the ocean and swam every day. The women usually went fishing, not out beyond the reef, but in the shallow part of the lagoon. With their babies on their backs, they caught small fish about the size of sardines in little nets.

Mortlockese family with Breadfruit, the staple of the local diet.

Our day started every morning at six when a man blew a great conch shell. The people got up and gathered at our church for early prayers. Then we went to eat breakfast. I taught school in the mornings from eight to eleven. From eleven to twelve I had the sick people come for medicine. I

Mission Schooner.

cleaned their wounds. Many had such terrible sores! I would do what I could. Often all they wanted was an aspirin which they believed could cure anything. For them Aspirin was a wonder drug! Still, many of the children died of tuberculosis. I always thought the Japanese might have done more to deal with this disease. But later, in Japan, I realized that even there the problem remained unsolved. I remember two twins who came to school every day, and each day they became a little weaker; both were only fourteen or fifteen when they died.

From twelve to two was my rest period. Then all the ladies came to learn how to sew and to make dresses for themselves and shirts for their husbands. From two to five we sewed. At six we met again at church for Bible study and singing. And then the day was done. Because we were close to the equator, the sun rose at six in the morning and set at six in the evening. It got dark very quickly after the sun set because there was little twilight in the islands. Everyone had a lantern, but there was no electricity. None of the islanders burned candles in their homes for fear of fires. Their houses were all made of palm fronds, so they had good reason to be concerned. At night, most people kept a small fire burning before the entrance to their homes. This was to keep the evil spirits away. The hardest thing was that they had no doctor and no hospital. When they became seriously ill they had to be taken to an island like Truk.

Because we had the responsibility for eight islands, I often had to go from one island to another. Getting around the islands was very difficult for me. I

The Mortlock Islands. Mama's home base was Lukunor.

Canoe with Max at the prow.

had real trouble going beyond the lagoon. The mission had a thirty-six foot sailboat that it used for inter-island travel. This boat was twelve feet wide. But whenever I took this boat I got terribly seasick. I usually lay on the deck, and with every shift of angle I would roll around. There was very little protection from the sun, and I got terribly sun-burned and often peeled like a potato. I hated to travel, but it had to be done.

It was easier for me to go by outrigger canoe. The canoe did not swing as much as the boat. But going by canoe could be dangerous. Once I was on the island of Oneop. I had been there two weeks when the boys said, "It is such a beautiful day today Miss Henner, shall we bring you home to Lukunor?" I said, "Yes, make the canoe ready." They got the canoe ready, and they even rigged a new sail for it. But that morning it was Lua, that meant "wind-still" in Mortlock-ese, so Max, one of my boys, stood up in the front of the canoe and said "Lord send us wind now, and do it quickly, we must bring Miss Henner home!" I scolded Max, saying, "Max, we cannot speak to the Lord like that. He is King of Kings, and Lord of Lords, and if you want something from him you have to ask him and not command him!" But half an hour later the wind came. And the clouds too. And we were in a storm. The boys couldn't manage the canoe anymore. The sail was torn, and then the canoe capsized.

Mama's outrigger canoe with its crew of young men.

We were all thrown into the ocean. And I couldn't swim! When the rain started I had put on my heavy oil slicker. It had lots of air under it, and it managed to keep me afloat until one of the men swam after me. I was more worried about my boxes. All my supplies were contained in water-tight boxes that had been specially made for the tropics. My stove was also in one of these special boxes, and now everything was drifting away in the storm. After they grabbed me, the boys went after my boxes, dragged them back, and succeeded in righting the damaged canoe. This was hard work for an outrigger with a sail. Finally they managed to put me and the boxes back in the canoe and we made it home safely. The boys were exhausted, so I said, "Come to my house. I will cook a good soup!" But they all insisted on going to church first. They wanted to apologize to the Lord for having ordered him around. Then they came to my house to eat.

Incidents like this did not keep me from visiting the other islands. The people were so interested in having us come, and they were so generous in bringing and sharing with me whatever they had. I thoroughly enjoyed my work, even if travel was difficult.

The other missionaries on Mortlock were Frau and Herr Joswig. They had a little girl, Lotte, who was one and a half years old. Mrs. Joswig was pregnant and Mr. Joswig took her to Truk for the delivery of their child. Because traveling was so hard, they asked me to take care of little Lotte while they were gone for six weeks.

With Mr. and Mrs. Joswig, Lotte and Michael on Lukunor.

Two weeks after they left Lotte came down with dysentery. No matter what I tried, she wouldn't get better. On the fourth or fifth day she was so weak that she couldn't lift her head anymore in her bed. I knew she was dying, there was no life left in her little body, and she was growing cold. So I threw myself headlong on the floor and cried out to the Lord with all my heart to save this child. I pictured the scene of the parents coming back, and my standing on the shore to welcome them, and they asking me "Where is Lotte?" Then I would have to answer, "She is in the graveyard." "Dear Lord," I prayed, "Save me from this! But Your will be done!" I don't know how long I prayed. I finally stood up, took my little Kerosene lamp, and lifting the mosquito net that covered Lotte's bed looked at her. Just as I did, she opened her eyes and

31

The boys who took Mama on her circuit preparing the outrigger canoe.

recognized me, and I was certain that she would live. How I praised the Lord! From that day forward, she became better and stronger, and when her parents returned from Truk with their new son Michael, I stood there with Lotte in my arms full of joy and thanks for what the Lord had done. Next to Papa's death many years later, that was one of my hardest experiences. How I wrestled with God for little Lotte's life!

In February of 1932 I wanted to visit Truk, so the boys took me to Truk and to Tol. Because I wanted to spend a few days with Sister Anna Schneider, I left the boys with the boat, and wished them a good trip home. As I was walking towards Sister Schneider's house, two natives came running up behind me to tell me that Richard, the captain of our boat, had died. I said, "How could this be, I just left him and he was well?" They said that they couldn't bring up the anchor because the chain had wound around a great rock. Richard dove down to loosen it, but could not do so. He came up again and asked the boys to tie a rope around his waist. He told them that when he shook the rope they should haul him up. But he never gave the signal. When one of the boys dove down to see what had happened he found that Richard's rope had also been caught in the rock and trapped him. He had to go up to get a knife and cut him free, but by this time Richard was dead. Richard was such a nice man, and he had a wife who was six months pregnant. I felt badly that he had to lose his life because I wanted to visit Truk.

By 1933 I had been on the islands for three years and my health was beginning to fail. The other missionaries also thought that constant travel was too hard for me. They agreed that I should go to Truk and teach at the girls school there. I was looking forward to the possibility of this new assignment, because I always wanted to be a teacher.

Then one day a letter came from Herr Notehelfer in Japan. He asked me if I would be willing to come to Japan, marry him, and help with the missionary work there. I didn't like the idea. I had been called as a Sister, and I felt that I had committed myself to my work as a Sister, and not in Japan, but on the islands. So I thanked him for his letter and told him it might be different if he were to come to the islands because we needed another missionary, but I would not go to Japan because my work was in the South Pacific. He wrote back and said that Japan was also an island, and if I came there, I would still be working on an island. I knew this, but I still thought I should stay where I was. I wrote him to this effect with the next mail.

Our location was so isolated on Mortlock that only every six weeks or two months a ship would come to our island. The next ship that came brought a letter from Thea Lang in Kikuna near Yokohama. She was the only person who knew that Mr. Notehelfer had asked me to marry him. Thea wrote, "Dear Rosle, I don't think you will need to come to Japan. Mr. Notehelfer is very ill. All the doctors have given up hope for him. His lungs have hemorrhaged and they cannot stop the bleeding. By the time this letter reaches you, he may already be in heaven." She explained further that Mr. Notehelfer had been operated on for appendicitis in a Japanese hospital and that complications has set in due to a switch in anesthesia. I was surprised by this letter. But I said quietly, Dear Lord, if you want to take Mr. Notehelfer to heaven, please do so, I will stay here on the islands.

With the next mail a letter came from Bad Liebenzell. It was from the Mission Director. He wrote: "Dear Sister Rose, Mr. Notehelfer has asked the Mission Committee to give you freedom to go to Japan to be his wife. We prayed about this, and we know he needs you. So we give you complete freedom to leave the islands and go to Japan to marry him. But do not go at this time because he is very ill. If the Lord should make him well again, take it as a sign and go to be his wife." I was very moved by this letter, and I asked the Lord what to do. I wrote a brief letter to Mr. Notehelfer in which I told him that if the Lord should make him well again, I would come and be his wife. But I felt certain that this would be unnecessary. Weeks passed and I heard nothing further from Japan. So I concluded that Mr. Notehelfer had died.

Then one day a telegram arrived. The telegram said: "Go on with your work in the islands. I am going home to Germany." It was signed, Notehelfer. I couldn't understand this telegram. But at least I knew that he was still alive. Yet, I wondered why he refused me, now that I had

Mama on Lukunor shortly before her departure for Japan with Michael Joswig.

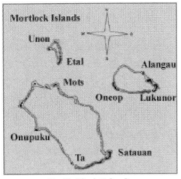

The Mortlock Islands.

written that I was willing to come. I was so mad at myself. I said, "Why did I say yes, I will come. I should have said no from the beginning!" I thought, "All right, I will stay on the Islands!" Then I asked the boys to prepare the boat, and got them to take me to the furthest island on my circuit, the island of Etal, which I had never previously visited. From morning to night I worked on Etal with the people there, and I got sick, very sick. I had fever and such a terrible ear infection, that I was in pain day and night. After two weeks the boys brought me home again. And there was the mail, and on top was another telegram. The telegram said: "Forgive me, come as soon as possible to Japan, love Karl."

I couldn't understand the first telegram and I couldn't understand the second one either. Then a letter came from Mr. Notehelfer which explained things. After he was released from the hospital and came home to his little Japanese house he went every day to the mailbox, hoping to find a letter from me, but there was none. I was not aware that my letter, in which I had written that I would be willing to go to Japan, took three and a half months to reach Tokyo. Without that letter he thought, well, if she is not willing to come, I will have to let her go. Since I am due my furlough, I will return to Germany and see what the Lord has for me there. Then my letter arrived and he quickly sent the second telegram to let me know that he was still waiting for me.

But I was still not willing to go. I was afraid. I knew Mr. Notehelfer, what he looked like, because we had gone to the same seminary, but we never spoke, and we only briefly came to know each other in Tokyo before the Lang and Buss wedding. I had no clear idea of his character. Furthermore, I was annoyed with the mis-communication that had taken place. I thought if he is going to toy with me like this, one day in, and one day out, I would not like to be his wife. I went on with my work, but I had no peace. So one day, I prayed all night long, and I said, "God, I have to know what to do." Early in the morning it was as if the Lord stood by my side and said, "Go! My disciples always went where I sent them. Go to Japan." Later that day, at our prayer meeting, I said to Mr. Joswig, "Mr. Joswig, I have to go to Japan." He looked at me and said, "You have to? No! We need you here on the islands and you will stay here!" I said to him, "This is what I also thought, but this morning the Lord spoke to me and told me that I have to go , and I will go! Poor Mr. Joswig. He couldn't accept my going. He couldn't understand the Lord's command to me. Still mad at me, he said, "You are like all other girls. You just want to be married!" How little he understood my inner qualms.

Chapter Four
Japan -- The Early Years

Once again my life was to be greatly changed. I left the islands with fear and hope. I regretted leaving the people to whom I had grown so close. I knew I would miss the children with their smiling faces. And the simple island people, so straight forward and direct. I knew I would also miss the sounds of the islands. The sea, the wind, the way the people could sing. Oh, how the people of the islands could sing in beautiful harmony! My life in Japan, I thought, will be very different, with its big cities, factories, and urban noise. I wondered how I would fit into a society in which women bowed to the floor. Everything, I told myself, will be new and strange. And in one way I was scared.

The people of Lukunor sent me off the way they had received me. They all came out in their white dresses, white shirts, and white trousers. They sang, as the mission boat taking me to Truk pulled away. I can still see them waving. Even the Joswigs were there, though Mr. Joswig never accepted the idea that I should go to Japan. And there stood little Lotte waving her arms and Michael who loved me dearly. That was special. Over there were the boys who had rowed me in that canoe to so many islands. I knew I would miss them too. But I took a little bit of the islands with me. One of the boys gave me a set of sharks teeth. Another a stuffed sea turtle. I was also given a story board from Palau that later made its way to the UCLA museum. Some Mortlock masks with their curious white and black trimmed faces. And a simple set of wood and stone tools that had been used by islanders for generations. In later years my children's were often amused by these curios. Young Bill, I recall, developed a special fascination for those shark's teeth.

From Truk I caught a steamer for Japan. As we made our way toward Yokohama, I had plenty of time to think about my future life. I was still anxious. The night before we arrived in Yokohama, I prayed really hard and asked God to fill my heart with love and confidence towards Mr. Notehelfer.

Mama and Karl at the reception of their wedding in Kikuna with Thea and Ernest Lang (right) and Käthe and Bernhard Buss (left). The children are Siegfried Buss (left) and Ernest Lang Jr. (right).

When we reached the pier, I was ready. I wanted to see no one but Mr. Notehelfer. But he was not there. All the other missionaries arrived to greet me. Each asked, "Where is Karl?" No one knew. I couldn't prevent the fleeting thought, "Has he again regretted asking me?" But I was now in Japan, and there was no turning back. Then a tall Japanese fellow came toward me. He was from the shipping line. He asked if I was Miss Henner. I said, "Yes." "Are you waiting for a Mr. Notehelfer," he continued. Again I said, "Yes!" "Oh, he just phoned," he said, "It seems the company gave him permission to go out to your ship with the health and immigration officials, but they made a mistake and sent him to the wrong place. He will be here in half an hour." So in half an hour, there he came, running down the pier with a beautiful bouquet of red roses and red carnations. He wore a brown suit, and I never liked brown suits on men! And he was sweating profusely. We went quietly into my cabin, knelt down, and prayed together. Then we kissed each other for the first time. That was a funny feeling! Fear, joy, and everything was mingled together. Three weeks later, on November 13, 1933, we were married. The wedding was in Kikuna. Mr. and Mrs. Lang did everything to make it beautiful.

For our honeymoon we went to Karuizawa. One of Papa's Japanese friends, Professor Yamazaki, offered us the use of his cabin at this resort in Nagano Prefecture. This cabin was located at the upper end of what was called the *machi*, or main street of Karuizawa, toward the road that led to Sunset Point, one of our favorite hiking spots of later years. From there you could look out upon the whole plateau, of which Karuizawa was a part, and at the surrounding

Karuizawa Station at night with Taxis in the early 1930s.

hills, with Mt. Hanari close up, and Mt. Asama, a still active volcano, some twenty miles in the distance. Karuizawa was a favorite vacation spot for missionaries and diplomats who wanted to escape Tokyo's summer heat. But few foreigners lived there in the winter.

Mama and Karl on their Honeymoon in Karuizawa.

We arrived at Karuizawa at four in the morning. Papa hired a taxi to take us to the Yamazaki's place. It was already cold in Karuizawa and the leaves were off the trees. Because of the narrow streets, the taxi could not make it all the way to the Yamazaki's. So we had to walk the final stretch. I had a suitcase and some food and Papa had a suitcase and a kerosene stove. When we reached the cabin it was still dark and we groped around to find the lights. There was a cold, dank smell of mildew in the cabin, and I thought, "What a place for a honeymoon!" We brought our own sheets, but the *futon*, the Japanese comforters, also reeked of mildew. It was so cold that it was hard to feel romantic.

The next day Papa heated up the Japanese bath, and after we had taken an *ofuro* together we were more in the mood. He had also brought some German sausages from Lohmeyer's, the German butcher in Tokyo, and I had not had a German sausage during all those years on the islands. How good they tasted! The second day in Karuizawa it snowed, and it all looked very beautiful.

We stayed in Karuizawa for two weeks and took many hikes together.

Hiking near Karuizawa with Karl.

Once we walked all the way down the mountain pass to Yokogawa. This was the town from which the engines of the cog-railroad pulled trains up the mountain to Karuizawa through twenty-eight tunnels. As we came down the mountain we occasionally heard the sound of the train and its engines as they echoed through the hills between tunnels. Each

37

engine had its own horn, and when six of them—four in front and two in back—sounded their horns in sequence the effect could be both charming and haunting. We stopped at a Japanese inn along the way to eat. So by hiking and spending time together we came to know each other better. In our wedding bands was engraved the phrase "to bear each other's burdens." This we soon learned to do. Karuizawa remained dear to both of us, but soon it was back to Tokyo. I had to learn about life in Japan. And that meant learning Japanese. How hard this was for me. How many tears I shed over that language!

Japan in 1933 was still the "old fashioned" Japan, nothing by comparison to what it is today. The ladies all wore their kimonos. Everyone walked in the streets. There was hardly a car. We still saw rickshaws. Taxis could be found at the stations, but they were not widely used. One either walked, or went by train. Many of the men already had bicycles, but I almost never saw a woman on a bicycle. If you wanted to find a place you asked the rickshaw man to take you there. I still recall my first rickshaw ride. I wanted to visit Mr. Yamaguchi, the Japanese missionary from Truk, who had returned to Japan. I had his address, but didn't know where he lived. So Papa and I took rickshaws. I was surprised how fast the rickshaw went through those narrow streets. Sometimes I thought we would run into people. But we got there safely. Everywhere we went there seemed to be large crowds, and I was overwhelmed by the sheer numbers of the Japanese. Not only were there

A rickshaw parked before a traditional Japanese house.

many people, but there were also many rats. And I was so afraid of rats! The people I came to know were very kind, however, and they treated me well. Whenever I visited a Japanese house, everyone would bow. I didn't like the idea of having people bow to me, but I slowly got used to it. The food was extremely simple, and I sometimes wondered how the Japanese got the nutrition they needed. There was rice and vegetables and cabbage and a little fish. Sometimes radishes and carrots. Occasionally a little fruit. I watched the typical housewife shop. She

Mama's first home in Japan located in Horinouchi, Tokyo, with Karl in Japanese Yukata.

would buy a carrot, two leek-like onions, and a radish. I thought, "How can she make a meal out of that?" And yet, these women knew exactly what they wanted. Shopping was a daily routine. Every woman went to the market once a day. After the war there were many vendors who came to the house to sell vegetables, fruits, or meats. But in the 1930s there were few such hucksters.

We didn't have much money, but living in Japan was very reasonable. Papa and I occasionally went to Shinjuku, to the Fujiya Restaurant, for dinner. At this restaurant we used to get a whole meal—soup, salad, entree, dessert and coffee—for fifty sen, or half a yen. At that time the yen traded at about three yen to the dollar. So our meal cost about seventeen or eighteen cents!

We lived in an interesting house in Horinouchi. It was quite large with three stories and a Mansard roof. The roofline made it look European, but it was really a mixture of East and West. On the inside it was half Western and half Japanese. I still have a nice photograph of Papa standing before the house in his Japanese *yukata* beneath the wisteria arbor. Upstairs we had three rooms on the second floor, and on the third floor there was a beautiful straw mat, or *tatami*, room that opened at one end through a set of doors on an elevated veranda where we often hung our laundry. No Japanese house had a veranda like this. Downstairs there was a fourteen-and-one-half mat *tatami* room which we used for a Christian kindergarten during the day, and for meetings in the evenings. There was also a little Western room at the corner by the

39

entrance in which we had two chairs and a table. It served as a miniature parlor. The kitchen was small and dark. I enjoyed cooking. And I liked to have a nice, bright kitchen. I could never under-stand why almost all Japanese houses had such dark and unin-viting kitchens. Next to the kitchen was a

In Japanese attire with Tante Lydia and friend in the garden of the Horinouchi house.

dining area where we had a few chairs and a table. It was a curious house, but it had a beautiful garden with lots of bamboo trees. Horinouchi was near Shinjuku. Most of the houses of the neighborhood were small and densely packed together. Few had space for a nice garden.

Our landlord was Mr. Hasegawa. He and his wife were Christians. He owned a rubber factory and made all kinds of things out of rubber. He even made a bed for John of rubber, so that he did not need diapers. It was a rubber box covered with a soft rubber mattress with holes in it so that the urine could pass through. It made the baby sore, however, so I did not use it long. Mr. Hasegawa thought he would try it out, and if it worked, he might be able to market it commercially. He was always trying out new ideas.

Near our house was a famous temple called the Myōhōji which was one

Myōhōji Temple grounds in Horinouchi where John used to play.

of the most popular centers of Nichiren Buddhism in Eastern Japan. Every year there was a big festival there in October to which visitors came from all over Japan. We often took John, our first son, to play on the temple grounds. Near us lived a priest who awakened us every

40

The Hōnan Church and its Sunday School.

morning with his drum.

We lived in Horinouchi from 1933 to 1938. In 1934 we built the Hōnan Church which was our main center of activity during these years. Behind this church was an interesting story. It involved another family with the name of Yamazaki. These Yamazakis were also prestigious but they were not related to Professor and Mrs. Yamazaki, in whose cabin we had honeymooned in Karuizawa. Mr. Yamazaki worked for the Imperial Household Ministry. This meant that the family maintained close ties to the Emperor. The Yamazakis had six children. One of the sons, Yūzo, was constantly in trouble. He was only a high school student at the time, but his behavior was a concern for the whole family. On one occasion his brother warned, "One day I will kill Yūzo because he brings so much shame on the family." The mother loved him and went from shrine to shrine, and temple to temple, to pray that he should change his ways. In the autumn of 1934 we had tent meetings near a hospital on a piece of land the hospital provided. We had an excellent preacher named Matsuda Sensei who

worked with us in these meetings. One night Yūzo came to our tent and was converted. The next morning his mother heard him speaking to someone in his empty room, and she thought he had lost his mind. When he returned from school she asked him if he was sick. He assured her that he was now "quite well," and explained how he had become a Christian. Mother, he said, I was speaking to God, asking him to help me lead a new life. His mother and sister, Ritsuko, were so impressed with the new Yūzo that they decided to attend the meetings themselves. They too were converted. And later much of the family became Christians. Yūzo, who was an excellent

Mrs. Yamazaki, Yūzo's mother.

guitarist, used his musical talents to reach other young people. The Yamazaki's opened their family home to meetings and they became central figures in the Hōnan Church. When we left Horinouchi in the late 1930s the Hōnan Church was still flourishing. But then the war came. The area around Horinouchi was heavily bombed and the Hōnan church was burnt to the ground. Everything in the neighborhood was destroyed. Most of the people had to move away. The Yamazaki's also lost their home and had to leave Tokyo. They moved to Osaka. Meanwhile, we had gone to America, and I heard nothing further from them.

One day, after our return to Tokyo from the United States in 1953-1954, someone knocked on our door in Todoroki. I opened it, and saw a tall man. I looked at him, and he said Mrs. Notehelfer, don't you recognize me anymore. I shook my head and said, no, excuse me, I don't know you. He said, "I am Yūzo Yamazaki." Then I threw my arms around him, which I never do to a Japanese, and I said, "Yūzo are you still alive!" And he said, "Yes, I am still alive, and I am still a Christian." I asked him to come in. He told me he had come on a special mission. His father had died. And the family wanted to bring his ashes back to Tokyo to be buried in the family plot. The family asked to have Papa speak at the graveside. So we went, and found thirty members of the Yamazaki family gathered for the funeral. Each had become a Christian. What a joy it was to see them.

After the funeral the family wanted to give us a special gift. They presented us with one of the family's treasures. This was a pair of silk *tabi* that had once belonged to the Emperor Meiji, and had been given to the family for its loyal service to the Imperial House at the time of the Meiji Emperor's death in 1912. They remain an interesting memento of the Yamazaki's and of our days in Japan. One of these white socks had obviously been worn and was slightly soiled. The other was like new. I was aware that under the Meiji Emperor the signboards proscribing Christianity as an "Evil Religion" had been removed. It was also under his reign that Christianity made important inroads in Japan. It seemed appropriate to have these socks. But more important was the Yamazakis' faith in God. For them, as for other Japanese Christians, the Emperor was human, like his soiled socks. They did not believe, as so many in the war believed, that he was a god whose every command must be obeyed.

Speaking of the Emperor, one of the things I remember about living in Hori-nouchi, was a day when early in the morning I heard shooting and yelling. I rushed out to see what terrible thing had happened. Everyone was out in the streets shouting to one another, and when I asked *"nan desu ka"* ("what is it") they told me that the Crown Prince had been born. This was a great event. The day was

December 23, 1933, the day before Christmas Eve. After four daughters the Empress, Nagako, had finally born the Emperor a son.

My own first son, John, was born on September 19th of the following year, 1934. I remember I made *Apfelkuchen* in the afternoon, then I started labor. So Papa called the Japanese midwife. She lived about two hours away from us. Professor Yamazaki's wife was associated with the Red Cross and she had introduced us to the midwife. Labor lasted more than twenty-four hours and we were really glad to hear him cry at last. He weighed in at ten pounds and was a happy baby. We were very pleased to

Mama and baby John, her first son.

have a healthy boy. The Japanese all came to congratulate us on having a son. As on other formal occasions they were polite and restrained. But we joked among ourselves that no one was willing to make as much noise for John as they had been prepared to make for the Crown Prince.

When John was two-and-a-half years old he disappeared one day. We couldn't find him anywhere. We were terribly worried because he did not reappear for several hours. Then a Japanese woman came carrying him on her back. She said she found him wandering around the temple grounds, and the people of the temple told her that he belonged to those "foreigners who lived in the neighborhood." There were so few of us foreigners that everyone knew where we lived. She had no trouble in finding us. And we were only too

John in Carriage in Karuizawa.

happy to see John back. But this was not the first time he disappeared. Two summers earlier we had been in Karuizawa. We rented a room in a Japanese house with kitchen privileges. It was Sunday and after coming home from church I was in the kitchen preparing dinner. Papa was reading in our room upstairs. John was just ten months old and I had him in a carriage outside the kitchen door. Two nice looking Japanese women came in and asked me something about the baby. My Japanese was still so poor that I

43

didn't quite understand what they said, but I answered *hai, hai*, which means yes, yes. The women smiled and left. When I came out to get John for dinner, there was no John, only an empty carriage. I called Papa and we started to look all over for John. We even went to town looking for him, but there was no John near or far. My heart was beating fast, and I was in a real panic that someone had abducted him. We decided to go to the Police Station. Then suddenly I saw two Japanese women coming out of a photo shop. One of them had John in her arms. It was the same two women. What a relief! Praise the Lord! The women had asked me if they could take John to have a photo made, and I had said *hai, hai*, without understanding what they requested. How dumb I was! And how hard I had to struggle with Japanese! Poor Mama!

On November 2, 1935, Anne-Marie, our first daughter, was born. It was also a Saturday, and I had once again baked a cake. Her birth was not as hard a John's and she was a beautiful girl—every baby is beautiful—but she had the loveliest hands I ever saw. I placed those hands in God's and asked him to take care of her. Every Sunday I put the children in our baby carriage and pushed them to church. Japanese were fascinated by Western children, and invariably I would be stopped along the way by people who wanted to see John and Anne. This often gave me a chance to give them some Christian literature and invite them to our church.

In the summers we usually went to Karuizawa. In the 1930s no one had air conditioning in Japan, and Tokyo was very hot during the summer months. Most foreigners, and many Japanese, would try to get away during the "dog days." Some went to Hakone, or to Lake Chuzenji, near Nikko. Others to the seaside towns by Kamakura. We liked to go to Karuizawa for the cool fresh air. Karuizawa had also become a center for summer missionary conferences, and missionaries from many denominations gathered there. We enjoyed these meetings, and Karuizawa allowed us to interact informally with other missionaries. Two American missionary families, the C. E. Carlsons, and Joel Anderson and his wife became good friends. We often visited each others houses. Both had come to Japan with the Scandinavian Alliance

Mama, Papa, John and Anne-Marie in the Karuizawa House in 1937.

Birthday party in Karuizawa with the children and their friends.

Mission. Joel was particularly fluent in Japanese. I recall, he gave the main address at the dedication ceremony of our Hōnan Church. Those present commented on his unusual command of the Japanese language. I always wished I had just a little of his talent. Because so many people wanted to be in Karuizawa each summer, finding a place to live there was not easy. But in 1935 Papa's sister, Emmi, sent us five hundred dollars from Germany. She instructed us that the money was to be used to build a summer home.

In Karuizawa there was a small hospital. We often passed this hospital on our walks. It was just off the main road leading up to the Mampei Hotel. This was the best hotel in Karuizawa. There was a small creek that crossed the Mampei road and a path ran along it. About two hundred yards down this path stood the hospital. The area beyond was largely woods and meadows scattered with pretty wild flowers. My favorites were the blue and yellow forget me nots. There were also lovely white acacia trees that bordered the narrow path. In the spring the whole area was filled with azaleas which grew splendidly in the volcanic soil. Many larch and birch trees nearby reminded me of home. There was even a cuckoo, which always sat on the very top of one of the large fir trees to sing. It made me think of the Black Forest, and Papa thought of his home in Bavaria

Walking by this favorite spot in 1935 we noticed that just east of the hospital a lot had been marked and prepared for building. The ground had been leveled and gravel, rocks, and foundation materials assembled. But for two years no further work was done to put up a house. Papa asked the mayor of Karuizawa to whom the land belonged. The mayor told him that the owner was Dr. Monroe, who was the chief doctor at

Visiting the Carlsons and Andersons in Karuizawa.

45

Road leading to the Karuizawa hospital.

the hospital. So we went to Dr. Monroe and asked him why he did not build on this lot. He told us, that his wife, who was Japanese and a nurse by profession, did not like living so close to the hospital, and that they had decided to build elsewhere. We asked him if he were willing to sell the property. He said, "Yes, When the right people come." I said, "Are we not the right people? We are missionaries from Germany and we need a place for our family." He told us he would talk it over with his wife and would give us an answer the following day. So we went again the next day, and with a big smile he said that he would sell the land to us. The price was only $200, which was very cheap.

We went immediately to the Japanese carpenter who lived at the northern end of the *machi* and asked him to come to the site and take a look at it to see what kind of house he could build there. We wanted only a simple summer house that could be built as cheaply as possible. The carpenter came. He

Karuizawa no.1391, the Notehelfer house built in 1937.

46

The family in Karuizawa in 1939. John and Anne-Marie in center. Bill is next to Papa. Fred is in Mama's lap.

looked at what was there. And, I remember, he started to count. He counted and counted, and then he counted some more, and finally he said, "If I make it very cheap it will be ¥900." We were really happy with this price, and asked him if he could build it by the following year because we were expecting another child. He promised to do so and really did a wonderful job—we were delighted with the house. And by the following July we could move in. He even made a crib for the new baby that was about to be born. When the house was finished it seemed to us the most beautiful house in Karuizawa. Even strangers came to look at it because it was so beautiful—and the whole house was built for ¥900, or about $300. It was amazing how we managed to buy the land and build the house exactly for $500.

We moved into our new house in July 1937, and on the 27th of that month our son Bill was born. He was the ugliest looking little fellow. I had a special crib made for him with curtains, and I said, "Shut the curtains so that nobody sees him!" To my surprise, by the age of three he had become the cutest little fellow! When he was about six weeks old I took him down to the living room and there was a terrible thunder storm. Lightning hit the corner of the house and ran down the rain gutters. The whole house shook. Bill started to scream, and no matter what we did we could not stop him from screaming. I will never forget how he screamed. I thought that maybe the lightning had harmed him. But afterwards he was all right

The year Bill was born was a restless year. Just three weeks before his birth the "China Incident" had broken out, and Japan was soon at war in China.

47

The Army's First Division parading in Tokyo after the February 26 "incident" of 1936.

It was also that summer in Karuizawa that several of our American missionary friends came to see us with tears in their eyes. They were so worried about Japan's future. They also thought they would soon be leaving for home. We were not worried about being sent home, but we were concerned about the ominous signs of change taking place in Japan. I was not in Japan in 1932 when Prime Minister Inukai was assassinated by group of radical officers who wanted to carry out a coup d'etat. But by 1936 I knew that the Japanese Army was increasingly involved in politics. I was not a political person myself, so I didn't always know what was going on, but I remember that already in February of 1936 a major "incident" had taken place in Tokyo. We didn't know exactly what happened on February twenty-sixth, but the radio went off the air, and I know all the neighbors were scared. Everyone was talking. I was so ashamed that I couldn't make out enough of what they said to understand what was going on, but I knew they were worried. And for several days we could not go into Tokyo. I also remember that 1936 was the year in which many of the young people left for Manchuria. Even some from our church. They were paid to go, and they always said they would have a better life in Manchuria than in Japan. I was not so sure. But when Bill was born, I know we were worried because when it came time to select a name for him we decided on Rudolph, Wilhelm, Traugott. "Traugott" means to "Trust in God," and we must have realized that the years ahead would not be easy.

In the autumn of 1937 we returned to Horinouchi and continued our work at the Hōnan Church. The only change was that the police now watched the church and we were ordered to have the congregation sing the national anthem at the start of all church services. Whenever we had meetings in our house we also had to report them to the police. Despite such police interference, there was no decrease in the number of adults and children who attended our church and home services. Then in 1938 we were asked to leave the Horinouchi House because the Hasegawa's needed it for their family. By this time, our Church at Hōnan had become largely independent, with its own Japanese pastor, and we were ready for a new work. Our children were entering school age and needed to be closer to the German School which was located in Ōmori. So we decided to move.

Chapter Five
Todoroki

Mama at the Great Buddha in Kamakura.

Todoroki, I quickly learned, was written with a complicated Chinese character. It came from the word thunder. Perhaps it was appropriate that we moved there in 1938. The China War was already thundering along by that year, and soon war broke out in Europe. Little did we know that when we left Horinouchi we were moving at least partly out of harm's way. During the years that followed I often felt God near us in difficult times, and sensed a wisdom that went beyond my own. I firmly believed in God's help, but at the same time felt that he expected us to do our part. There was nothing passive about our response to the changing environment and challenges that lay ahead.

In searching for a new place to live and work we had a few priorities. The first was that our new location should lend itself to the kind of missionary work we did. We had already built our first church and were anxious to lay the foundations for a second. This required an area where we could utilize our tent, and where people would be willing to attend our meetings. With the growing nationalism of the late thirties and the war mentality that gripped the Japanese leaders after the outbreak of the China War, Christian work became increasingly difficult. It was this realization that had brought tears to the eyes of our American missionary friends in Karuizawa. We also sensed this in Horinouchi. Papa was convinced that the more urbanized Japanese, the type of Tokyoites we had worked with in Horinouchi, were increasingly reluctant to expose themselves to foreign ideas. By the late thirties western ways had become suspect. Japanese who maintained contacts with foreigners drew unwanted attention to themselves. In a world in which even modern dress, and hair-

Papa and Pastor Hertel reading the Japan Times "extra" with news of war in Europe, 1939.

49

styles, could draw criticism, such associations marked an individual for censure, and in some cases, police harassment. Certainly by the time that war broke out with America, that was the case.

After 1936 the Japanese authorities became very strict about what could be said about the Emperor. We never saw the Emperor in person, though once we saw his motorcade. Neither Papa nor I ever heard him speak. Sometimes, in the newspapers, there was a picture of him in military uniform on a white horse. He was spoken of as a god, and people were not supposed to look at him. We knew that many supporters of the Emperor regarded Christianity of the type we preached, which stressed a personal relationship to God that transcended all other relationships, as potentially subversive. There were some among them who openly declared that it was impossible to be a Christian and a true Japanese. For the Japanese citizen of the imperial state there could be no higher authority than the Emperor. Martin Luther's idea of following one's conscience, and not the orders of the king, was anathema to the Japanese and their state religion, Shinto. Forcing all Christians to sing the national anthem at the opening of every church service, was one way of enforcing the Emperor's power. The police, who came to all our meetings after 1938, were there to make certain that we toed the line. While they were usually courteous and did not give us trouble, their presence could not help but intimidate us and those who came to hear God's word.

In some cases police interference was much more direct. In 1938 the head of the Osaka police department circulated a questionnaire to all Christian pastors of that city demanding categorical answers to questions regarding their faith. The questions put to these pastors were: "What is the Christian concept of Deity?" "What view of the Emperor do Christians hold?" "What

Women showing proper obeisance before an Imperial Shrine.

The Emperor's motorcade at Meiji Shrine in the late 1930s.

are the views of Christians regarding Imperial Rescripts and Pronouncements?" "What is Christianity's attitude towards worship of the Japanese national gods?" The implications were quite clear. Christians were potentially subversive. By maintaining loyalty to God, and not the Emperor, they challenged the authority of the imperial state. So they had to be brought under control. By 1941 the government pressured much of the Church to form a single organization, the *Nippon Kirisuto Kyōdan*, or Church of Christ in Japan, which the authorities felt was more amenable to state supervision. This was part of a broader effort to bring all religions under government sponsorship. Christians and their churches were relentlessly pressured to conform to the orthodox values of the secular state. With time this meant not only proper obeisance to the Emperor, but an endorsement of state Shinto and a recognition of Japan's sacred mission in Asia. Missionaries and mission work were naturally suspect under these circumstances. Both were seen as potentially seditious. Japanese Christians were encouraged to be independent. The new united church was advised to rid itself of outside influences. There were even those who called for a distinct Japanese Christianity. We were never strong supporters of the *Kyōdan*, but with time even our churches felt compelled to join the new structure. We were not interested in politics; we just wanted to preach the Gospel. But this was no longer easy. Particularly when the presence of a foreign missionary could become troubling for a native pastor. By 1941 there was also a clear shift in the public's attitude towards the few missionaries who remained in Japan. In former days people riding on a bus or train would

One of our Todoroki neighbors planting rice.

look at you and whisper *"yaso,"* (Jesus) to their seat-mates, now it was not uncommon for them to mumble *"spai"* (spy).

Papa thought we could work better in the rural areas, than in the city. In one way he was right. The country people were often more direct and less concerned about appearances. I may be wrong, but the police also seemed less interested in them. Papa got on well with farmers. We could therefore work more freely in Todoroki, than we could have worked in the heart of the city. At the same time, we thought more fresh air would be good for the children. So we moved to Todoroki.

Todoroki was really in the countryside in those days. There were still lots of fields to be seen, both rice fields, and vegetable fields. There were also many farmers. When they manured their fields with nightsoil, you knew you were in the countryside. Todoroki was in Setagaya Ward, which made it a part of Tokyo, but it was really halfway between Tokyo and Yokohama near the Tama River. A railroad from the Toyoko Company, which owned the big department store in Shibuya, ran through it from Mizonoguchi to Ōimachi. This was very convenient for the children, for it was only one stop from Ōimachi to Ōmori where the German school was located. Three stops away was Jiyūgaoka. There our little train crossed the main Toyoko line that ran from Shibuya to Yokohama. This train also went through Kikuna where the Lang family lived. So while Todoroki was in the *inaka*, or countryside, it was

Typical farmhouse of the type found around Todoroki.

also conveniently located for us. The Tama River ran just below where we lived and there were lots of places for the children to play and explore. Nearby ran a stream that flowed out to the Tama River and was crossed by a big black steel bridge. Along this stream there was a well known grotto and a temple that was a favorite playground for the children. It was also a nice place to take walks. In later years Todoroki became quite a fancy residential part of Tokyo. Then we had a neighbor who was a Kabuki actor, and one with a miniature golf course. But before the war most of the houses in the area were traditional farm houses with heavy thatch roofs. There were only three new houses close-by. The first belonged to the Nakamura sisters, one of whom taught music. The second housed a Yugoslav businessman, Mr. Korbe, who was married to a Japanese. And the third was owned by another Japanese family.

Before the war it was very difficult to buy property in Japan. Few landlords were willing to sell their land. But some were prepared to rent on a long term basis. Japanese houses were often built on leased land. And in our case, too, we entered into a twenty-five year lease with our farmer land-lord. Our experience in building the Karuizawa house had been so good, that we decided to ask the

Papa with the Karuizawa carpenter at the Todoroki house.

same carpenter to build our new house in Tokyo. We wanted a similar house, only a little larger. But this time our experience was quite different. In fact, the Carpenter cheated us. When the house was nearly completed with its roof and flooring in place, the rainy season set in. To our surprise the whole house soon filled with water that came through a roof that leaked like a sieve. Our new wooden floors were all warped. And there was extensive damage throughout. We had paid for most of the house in advance and were very troubled. The carpenter did little to help us. Finally we had to go to a lawyer and bring charges against him. He later admitted that he put most of the money we had paid him into another house in Karuizawa, the Mason house, which was not far from our own. It seems Mrs. Mason was very demanding and insisted on things for which he had not budgeted. Unable to deal with her he had tried to make up his shortfall by putting a used tile roof on our Tokyo house which was the cause of the flooding. We finally forced him to redo much of the construction, including a new roof, and by the fall of 1938, after

The Todoroki house completed in 1938.

returning from Karuizawa, were able to move in. Despite the grief it had caused us, the house itself was full of light and sunshine, it had lots of space, nine rooms in all, and it was very nice. I always liked that house. The only thing I didn't like was the toilet and bathroom. I don't know why they built such poor bathrooms and toilets in Japan. We had to dig a well for water, and I remember we had to go down over a hundred meters before we hit it. Our water was so hard, and it was so full of iron that everything got brown. I had to use great quantities of blueing to make things white again. After the war we were the first people in the neighborhood to get running water, that was really something! What a relief it was to stop pumping all our water by hand.

Our life in Todoroki was pleasantly simple. Still, there were also elements of modernity. Papa always liked gadgets and machines. He had originally wanted to fly to Japan on the Zeppelin, and had actually put in an application to do so on its original trans-Pacific crossing. But his application was turned down. He always liked cars, and even in Horinouchi we had a funny three-wheeled vehicle made by DKW, that was more like a motorcycle than a car. The Japanese later imitated these, but theirs had handle bars rather than a steering

Papa in his DKW three-wheeler, with tent on the back.

wheel. In Todo-
roki Papa traded
up and bought a
Hanomag from
Mr. Lang. This
was also a funny
car, and riding in
it was often an
adventure! When
we got to the pass
that led to
Karuizawa we
would have to put
the Hanomag on
a truck to haul it

Inside the Todoroki house. Mama with Bill, Fred, John and Anne-Marie in 1939.

up the mountain. Papa also enjoyed his cameras. I always though he was a better
driver than photographer, but none of us could tell him that. He just loved taking
pictures, and I never understood why most of them were out of focus. I still
have boxes of his photographs. But there was one thing he didn't care for,
that was the telephone. In all the years we lived in Japan we never had a
phone. It was far more common to get and send a telegram. This could be
done at the Post Office. Telegrams were delivered by a man on a red bicycle.
In those days, people would often just appear at the door for a visit. They
would bring with them some small cakes, or fruit, and one would invite them
in and have a visit. Nearly everything was done by mail, and the mail came
twice a day. Special Delivery would connect us to most of our friends by the
next day. For news we depended on the radio and the newspaper which was
delivered in the morning and evening.

We did our local shopping in Jiyūgaoka or Mizonoguchi. Todoroki had
almost no stores in 1938. There was only one small grocery and vegetable
store near the Todoroki station. For bread the nearest bakery was in
Jiyugaoka. There was also a milkman who came every day, although drinking
milk was not yet common in Japan. Butter and cheese we usually ordered
from Hokkaido where there was a famous Trappist Monastery that produced
both and shipped them in tins. If we wanted German meats or sausages we had
to go to Lohmeyer's butcher shop not far from the Ginza. Nearby was also
Kettles, one of the few German restaurants in Tokyo before the war. In those
days the train was cheap and convenient. Shibuya was about half-an-hour
away, and for clothing and other things we would shop there. But we often
went to Yokohama. As an international port, with many foreign residents,

John and Yuki-San, one of our maids.

Yokohama provided a variety of stores with western goods not seen in Tokyo. There was an excellent German Bakery and several good restaurants in Yokohama that we liked. The Lang's home was nearby, so we could often combine a shopping expedition with a visit to them. With time, Todoroki expanded, and more and more people moved in and built their houses there. I recall that one of the distinct sounds of those days was the clatter of the wooden *geta*, or clogs, that most Japanese still wore as they walked past the house toward the little railroad station. Our house was located at the end of a stretch of road that was bordered by cherry trees. These usually burst into wonderful blossoms in the first week of April. And then our neighborhood was filled with sightseers.

Fred was the first child born in the Todoroki house on April 13, 1939. I remember the cherries had just bloomed. His birth was very difficult. He had his hands over his ears and the umbilical cord was wrapped over them around his head. When he came out he was all blue. He nearly died. The midwife told me that he would always dislike loud noises. And she was right. He was a quiet child. He was also very shy, just the opposite of Bill who was social and gregarious. Fred always liked to draw and loved to take things apart, particularly clocks.

Our life was now getting harder and harder. We were being watched very carefully. Whenever we had a meeting in our house, even for the children, we had to report it to the police, and a policeman would come. I always provided him with tea and crackers. He would listen to everything that was said. In 1938 Japan mobilized for the China war, and the young people were all encouraged to work in industry. We had a maid. The police came to see her and said that she should not work in the home of a foreigner, but should go to work in a factory. We lost another of our maids when her brother, who was with the military, objected to her working for foreigners. She was from Noborito. Then we got another maid who came to us through the Lang family in Kikuna and she stayed with us.

We always treated our maids as if they were members of the family. The Japanese told us not to do that, because a maid was regarded a servant in a

Japanese house, and servants could never be treated as family members. Most of them were very good workers, except for one we had at the time of Bill's birth. She was really lazy and always wanted to lie down. When I was still confined upstairs and Papa asked her to bathe the children, she left them alone in the bathtub. She was generally careless, and we finally asked her to leave. She did the dirtiest cleaning I ever saw, nothing was clean after she cleaned. But she was clearly the exception. Occasionally we would encounter different attitudes towards child rearing. I remember one maid who was very upset if I spanked the children. "No, No, you can't do this *okusan!*" she would say, and sometimes she would stand between me and the child to keep me from doing so. Japanese socialized their children quite differently. Young children were allowed to do almost anything they wanted. Parents rarely, if ever, subjected their children to physical punishment. This was radically different from my German tradition. And yet, I marveled at the way that Japanese children, became so well behaved as soon as they went to school. Most of our maids were country girls. They worked for very little pay. Their families were glad to have them get their food, a few clothes, and a small allowance. I thought of my own early days in Bernstadt when we were so poor that I had been put out for similar work.

Not far from our house in Todoroki there was a Buddhist temple with extensive grounds. We often went there for walks. Nearby there was a secret path that led to a bamboo grove with a grotto and a small waterfall. Sometimes we saw the priest standing half-naked in the ice cold water from the fall meditating. It was his cleansing ritual. The children liked to play on the temple grounds. Both John and Anne had gone to Japanese kindergartens and spoke Japanese fluently. But they too felt changes in attitudes towards foreigners. One day John came running into the house screaming, "They will get me! I must hide!"

Then he crawled as far as he could under Papa's big writing table. I asked, "Why are you so scared?" "Who is coming to get you?" He said, "The Priest and his wife are coming to get me because I hurt their son." It seems that

Todoroki Temple.

Anne-Marie and friend in Temple Grotto near our Todoroki home.

John and the Priest's son had gotten into a fight over something that was said, the fight ended by both sides throwing stones at one another and one of John's stones hit the boy on the head causing a cut with considerable bleeding. I tried to calm John down, but it was impossible. A little while later the Priest and his wife came with their son who had a small wound on his forehead. The bleeding had already stopped. We apologized and asked them for forgiveness. John had to come out of his hiding place and tell them that he was really sorry this happened. Then we asked the Priest and his wife to go to the doctor and agreed to pay the bill. This they did, and we were in peace. But the children didn't go to the temple anymore.

With the outbreak of the war in Europe the German community also became more nationalistic and polarized. When I arrived in Japan we didn't hear that much about the Nazis and Hitler. But by the time the war started in 1939 the Nazis were on the rise in the German community in Japan. We used to always attend the annual reception thrown by the German Embassy in May. At first I remember it was not so political, there was always lots of good food, and all the Germans went to be together. But now when we went, we didn't have such a good time. There were many party members among the Germans. And the Nazis didn't like missionaries. Still, I realized that if we did not attend we would be in trouble, and would be labeled disloyal Germans. The Japanese also started watching us carefully. Our mail from Germany was always opened, and I don't know who read it, the Japanese or the Germans, and it was regularly censored. Any references to food shortages, or an increasingly powerful military, would be blocked out in black ink. Later I learned that the Nazis actually used the Japanese police to watch us.

John and Anne-Marie, and later Bill, all went to the German School in Ōmori. This was a good school. It was a typical German school abroad. For many years the principal of this school was Mr. Redecker. He was a fine man who served the school for more than twenty years. Mrs. Redecker also taught there. But she was forced to give up her position after Hitler came to power. Even at the school the spirit now changed. There was a growing emphasis on the Hitler Youth, and there was great pressure to have the children go to the Hitler Youth summer camps. Because all his classmates were going, we sent John to camp one summer at the Fuji Lakes, but it was not a good experience for him, and we never sent any of our children thereafter. There was also some pressure to join the various auxiliary organizations that were associated with the party and the embassy. I did not like joining such groups, but others, even among our missionary circle, did.

Many of the tasks undertaken by the German Embassy were important for the community and helped people in distress. Onkel Lang, as we always called him, served on the Embassy's Relief Committee. Strangely enough, one of the other Germans working with him was Richard Sorge. We met Sorge once or twice at Embassy parties, but I had no idea that he was one of the greatest spies of World War II. In fact, Onkel Lang later told us that the day before he was arrested by the Japanese Sorge came into the Relief Committee Office, slapped him on the back, and said with a big laugh, "Herr Lang. Now they say I'm a spy. Isn't this the funniest thing you ever heard!" The next day he disappeared. I remember riding the train up to Karuizawa not long thereafter, and a Japanese man, sitting beside me on the train, said to me in German, "Herr Sorge macht viel Sorge," punning on Sorge's name which meant grief in German and hinting that he now made grief for Japan and Germany. Sorge had, in fact, gotten word to Stalin that the Germans would attack Russia. He had also informed him of the Japanese decision to attack the United States in 1941. He was later tried and executed by the Japanese. Of course we knew little of this at the time, but we felt the consequences. The German Ambassador, Eugen Ott, who was a man of liberal inclinations, had been taken in by Sorge. He was now blamed for the breach of security at the Embassy and in May of 1943 he was replaced by Dr. Georg Stahmer. Stahmer was the man who negotiated the Axis Alliance between Germany and Japan in 1940. He was a hard liner, and wanted to be sure that there were no other disloyal Germans in Japan. The Gestapo attaché, Col. Josef Meisinger, helped him to keep an eye on all potentially disloyal Germans.

Fortunately in Todoroki we managed

May 1st German Embassy Party with Elephant in late 1930s.

The three German missionary families of the Liebenzell Mission in Japan gathered at the "White Thread Waterfall" near Karuizawa in 1939. In the rear from left to right are Mama, Lydia Becker (Tante Lydia), Mr. Buss, Mrs. Buss, Mrs. Lang and Mr. Lang. Twelve of their children are pictured in the foreground.

to stay out of the limelight. We had few contacts with other members of the German community except at the School. We socialized almost exclusively with our fellow Liebenzell missionaries, the Lang and Buss families. At least once a month we would get together at each other's houses for Bible study and fellowship. Each of our families now had four children who were close in age, so our get-togethers were not only spiritually rewarding, but lively and full of fun. The Buss family loved music and when we went to their house we usually enjoyed a miniature concert. Everyone loved to come to our house to eat. Both the Lang and Buss families had returned to Germany for furlough in the 1930s. They each traveled by way of the United States. When the Langs returned shortly before the Pacific War broke out, I remember, we had a gathering at our house, and Mr. Lang brought the first home movie projector any of us had seen. He showed us movies of America, particularly of city life there, and the children were really excited. Little did we know at the time that we would all move to America after the war.

Once in a while we had visitors from abroad. In 1939 Tante Lydia came back to Japan on her way to Germany on furlough. I had not seen her since I said goodbye to her on Truk in 1933. She arrived just a few days after Fred was born, and spent some time with us before going home by way of the

Trans-Siberian Railroad. We took her to see a few Japanese sights like Kamakura and Nikko and spent the summer together in Karuizawa. In 1940 she visited us again on her way back to the islands. Before leaving Germany she had acquired the proper Japanese visa to return to her station on Truk, but when she arrived in Japan the Japanese Foreign Ministry would not allow her to continue to the South Pacific. Papa tried very hard to get her a visa to go to the United States where the Liebenzell Mission had a farm in New Jersey for recuperating China missionaries, but the American authorities would not give her a visa. She was still living with us in January of 1941 when Rosalie was born on the fifth. Finally I said to her, "You have to go back to Germany!" And she said, "Please don't send me back to Germany. You don't know the Germans any more. You don't know the spirit of Germany! When I went back to Germany, I promised myself I would never shout 'Heil Hitler.' But when Hitler came to Mannheim and I was in the crowd I could not keep myself from crying 'Heil Hitler' with the others. Later I wept bitterly in my room over my failure." But there was nothing we could do. In the spring of 1941, Papa took her to Manchuria and put her on the train for Germany. She managed to get the second to last train that crossed Russia. On June 22nd the Germans invaded Russia from the West. Now we were largely cut off from our homeland. News and letters from our families became sporadic. By the end of the year, only German blockade runners linked us to Europe.

Tante Lydia's departure was followed in the summer of 1941 by the arrival of many German women and children, literally hundreds, from Borneo, Java, and Sumatra. All the Germans were forced to leave by the Dutch. The men were arrested and imprisoned, the women and children were sent to Japan to catch the Trans-Siberian Railroad home. But with the railroad closed there was no way for them to return to Germany. They were stuck in Japan. These women were billeted with various Germans in the community. We took in Mrs. Schweitzer and her three children who came from Borneo, and her cousin Adelheid Zilly. The Schweitzers stayed with us for a year. Unfortunately they brought with them a virulent form of amoebic dysentery which all the children got, and of which Fred nearly died. Fresh apple juice was one of the few things

Tante Lydia with Joel Anderson in Karuizawa.

61

Gudrun Koch, Adelheid Zilly and Mrs. Schweitzer at the birthday party for Bill in Karuizawa on July 27, 1942. Fred is in the foreground.

that the sick children could eat that provided some therapeutic value. But it was summer and apples were very scarce. So papa went to the Embassy and they managed to get us a basket of apples that helped cure the children. I had always been a firm believer in homeopathic medicine, and a spoonful of fresh apple juice every two hours combined with cornstarch enemas is what Doctor Hoppeler advised. As on many other occasions he was right! The Japanese health authorities took communicable diseases like amoebic dysentery very seriously in those days, and I remember they came and fumigated the whole house after the children became ill.

The Schweitzers eventually went to Hakone, but Adelheid Zilly remained with us and went with us up to Karuizawa. A part of the program initiated by Hitler and the National Socialist Party was that all girls should gain experience by living with a family with many children. Consequently we had several German girls living with us during these years. One of them was Ingrid Funke, who was with us until the end of the war and then went to Shanghai for nurses' training. When I had to have surgery in Hakone, right after the war, she was the nurse of Doctor Schröder who operated on me and took care of me. The other was Gudrun Koch, she was the daughter of a German-American missionary family with the Seventh Day Adventist Church. She decided to stay in Japan and be "German" when her parents returned to America on the eve of the Pacific War. After the war she was only too glad to go back to America and rejoin her parents. She wrote us after getting to America that she could now enjoy her favorite meal every day, which was spaghetti with cheese on it. During the war food was so scarce that spaghetti with cheese was a luxury.

The ominous sounds of war, which had been rumbling in the distance for several years in China and Europe, now drew distinctly closer. In December of 1941 our quiet world in Todoroki was suddenly shattered.

Baby Rosalie with two Japanese friends. 1941.

Japanese Soldier at Meiji Shrine.

Chapter Six
War Erupts

On December 8, 1941, I was in the grocery store in Todoroki buying my weekly supplies of, rice, sugar, and soya sauce, when a man came running into the store with both hands raised. He was screaming, "How Terrible! How Terrible!" The owner asked,"What is so terrible?" He said, "Haven't you heard! We bombed Pearl Harbor last night! How foolish! How foolish! It's just like a dwarf making war against a giant! We will never win!" I was shocked both by the man's behavior and by what he said. Normally the Japanese were highly restrained. I rarely saw them excited. I wondered what the police response would have been had they been there. I hurriedly went home and told Papa. Soon we received confirmation from the radio. We spoke with our neighbors and they were also worried. None of us could believe the news. But it was true. Thereafter all we heard about was the war.

Although the average Japanese did not fully understand the reasons for the attack on the United States, and there were some like the man I encountered at the grocery store who were doubtful about Japan's chances for victory, once the war got under way the Japanese people were ready to sacrifice everything for it. After that initial outburst, I never heard a single Japanese complain about the war. Old and young united behind the war effort. A commitment to victory could be seen everywhere. Even in church we had to pray for Japan's success. The Japanese people sacrificed a great deal for the war. Patriotic contributions of all kinds were solicited from them. I remember that we were now organized into neighborhood groups called *tonarigumi*. About ten to fifteen household were in each *tonarigumi*, and everyone had to be a member. This organization was designed to handle civil defense and fire-fighting. But it did many other things; it distributed government orders, sold government bonds, passed out rationed food, and generally watched the neighborhood. All members of a *tonarigumi* were mutually responsible. I remember that our group used to come around and ask whether there were any extra pots or pans in my kitchen that could be

Papa standing behind the Hanomag.

contributed to the war effort. Every scrap of metal counted. There were also members of the *tonarigumi* who went from house to house telling people to black out their windows.

We had the little car, the Hanomag. It was a really funny looking car. It had four wheels, but it looked just like a caterpillar.

Still on level ground it could go quite fast. When I was pregnant with Rosalie, the car was still running, but gasoline was already difficult to acquire. One morning I looked through the window of our bedroom and saw fire coming out of the car. I jumped out of the window with a bucket of water and poured it over the car to put the fire out. Papa wasn't home. The fire went out, but the car wouldn't run any more. It sat there in the garden next to the house. We could no longer buy gasoline, so Papa just left the car unrepaired. Then one day, not long after war with America broke out, two policemen came to the house and said they wanted our car. I told them that it would no longer start, and I gave them the key to try. I don't know where Papa was, but he was not home. They took the key and tried to start the car, but with no success. Then they came in again and started to talk with me about the war. They said, "Do you think the Americans will come and bomb our country?" I replied, "Why not? Look at what they do to Germany." Then one of the police-men laughed rather scornfully and said, "We are not Germany! We are Japan, and America is afraid of Japan!" They suggested that we contribute the car to the war effort. When I told them that we preferred not to do that, they said they could confiscate the car if necessary. I told them that this was fine as long as they brought the proper papers. I knew how bureaucratic Japan was and how everything required papers. When Papa came home I told him that the police wanted our car. He became angry and said that he had no intention of contributing his car to the war effort. Instead, he decided on a different course of action. With all our help he took the car apart. Every piece of it. Until there was nothing left. Now there was no more car to confiscate! Later, when you could buy absolutely nothing, the car helped us to make many new things. One of these was a stove for our

Karuizawa house. Another was an ingenious cabbage cutter Papa made using the leaf springs of the car, ground down as blades, that helped us, and other people, to put up sauerkraut in the mountains. It was interesting to see how parts of our funny car came to life again and helped us to survive the war.

In the early phase of the war the Japanese were highly successful. All we heard about were Japanese victories as the Japanese army moved through the Philippines and into what is now South East Asia. It seems that Americans could be defeated more easily than anyone at first imagined. The radio and newspapers spoke constantly of "Glorious Victories," which came with few lost lives. The two policemen who visited the house reflected this early mood of confidence. Then came a big surprise. The Doolittle raid on Tokyo of April 18, 1942.

I remember how excited we all were to see the Doolittle bombers flying over our house. They flew so low. Papa and I even ran out into the street to see them better. But a Japanese man said to us, "Go in! Go in! This is real! It is dangerous!" We went in, but we didn't really know how dangerous it was until the children did not come home from school at the usual time. John and Anne were just at Ōmori station on their way home when the American planes arrived. Adelheid Zilly was with Bill at Ōimachi. Both were taken by Japanese strangers to shelters. Unfortunately Bill got lost because a Japanese woman took him by the hand and led him to another part of the shelter. Finally he was found again. Because the B-25s bombed in the Ōmori and Ōimachi areas, the trains were no longer running. So all had to walk about an hour before they reached a station where the train still ran. They got home very late. We did not know what had befallen them and were terribly worried. I asked Bill later that evening, "Were you not scared today?" He replied, "No, I said to myself, 'und ist kein einziger mensch mehr da, so ist der liebe Gott doch nah,' ('And if not a single person remains, God is still near')." This was a verse from our nightly prayers. And I thought, "How much better is the faith of a five year old child, than that of us adults."

Not long thereafter we built a bomb shelter to one side of the house in the yard where the car had once been parked. As usual Papa built it himself. It was like everything that Papa built, a solid structure. Papa also ordered large quantities of sand. Some of this he used to build the shelter, but the rest was kept in piles. The children thought these sand piles were grand places to play and to build things. But Papa had his own ideas. He had served in the German Army in World War I. After a stint with the ski troops he had been selected for pilots training. It was then, while learning to fly, that his best friend had been killed in an air accident. And the death of this friend led directly to his conversion and his decision to go to Japan as a missionary. As a result of his

Onkuru, Mr.Hayashi, with the children in Karuizawa. He died on Okinawa.

training Papa knew something about bombs. He knew that phosphorous bombs could not easily be put out with water. He also knew that sand was an effective extinguisher of the fires caused by such bombs. Later we had good reason to be thankful for his foresight.

While the Doolittle raid served as a wake-up call for the Japanese and led to a boom in bomb shelter construction, there was little American follow-up. Soon Japanese confidence was renewed and people were making fun of Doolittle's name. As far as damage was concerned, the raid had in fact done little. The Japanese radio and newspapers continued to announce victories, although the words "strategic retreats" now also appeared from time to time, and we were curious as to what these meant. We knew from German sources that the war in Europe was not going well, and that by 1943 and early 1944 the fighting, and especially bombing of German cities, had become worse. In Japan we had seen no more American bombers, but the people increasingly felt the effects of war. Everything was now being rationed, and there were hardly any civilian goods for sale in the stores. Already there was a growing black market. I remember items such as butter, which were part of our normal diet, were becoming extremely hard to find. More ominous was the number of war dead whose ashes were returned to their families and solemnly buried in local cemeteries. Schoolchildren were now regularly taken to Shinto shrines to pay homage to the war dead. This became an issue even for our children at the German School, which was now required to send its students on similar pilgrimages. The Langs, Busses, and we decided that our children should be instructed not to bow before the Shinto shrines when taken there. At least on one occasion this became a serious problem, and Mr. Buss had to go to the school to explain our position.

By the summer months of 1944 things were becoming quite tense in

Japan. The American push across the Pacific was really picking up steam. In February of 1944 the American naval forces had already smashed Japan's "impregnable" position on Truk. How thankful we were that Tante Lydia had not been allowed to return to this island in 1940. Elise Zuber, her partner in the Girl's School on Truk, and the best known of our missionaries in the South Pacific, starved to death under Japanese house arrest. In the Manus Islands near New Guinea another group of our missionaries were machine gunned after being assured that they were being taken to safety. I sometimes think that had I remained on Truk as a teacher, I would now be dead with the rest. Of course, it was not long before we ourselves would face such dangers in Japan, but we were not aware of them. At the time, we knew nothing about the tragedy that confronted my fellow missionaries on the islands. What we did know, was that the war was coming to Japan. The first of the new American B-29 bombers attacked Kyushu on June 15th flying from China. By the end of the first week of July, Saipan fell to the Americans, and this island in the Marianas was to become the major bomber base for attacks on Japan. The first B-29s from the Marianas flew over Tokyo on November 24, 1944, and bombed the Nakajima aircraft plant near Mitaka. It is always interesting how God works. After the war the land on which this plant stood was bought by a group of Japanese and American Christians and became the campus of International Christian University in Tokyo. Thereafter bombing raids became very common in Tokyo. Soon it seemed the whole city was being targeted. One of these raids destroyed our Hōnan church and the whole neighborhood of Horinouchi where we had lived. The worst air raids came in the spring of 1945. On the night of March 10th a large part of Tokyo was destroyed in a massive air attack. There were terrible fires, and more than 100,000 people were killed. Tokyo was not alone in this devastation. Nearly every major Japanese city was bombed and the destruction was terrible. The Japan we had known in the 1930s was being turned into smoke and ashes. Everywhere there was only rubble. Those who survived the fires fled

Lining up for rice rationing in our neighborhood during the war.

American B-29 Bombers with bomb bays open over Tokyo in 1945.

to the countryside.

Of course, by then we were in Karuizawa. But by the summer of 1944 the war was getting very close to us personally. I remember that earlier that year our preacher, Hayashi Heikichi, who all of us in the family called *Onkuru*, or "uncle," and who we treated as a member of the family, was suddenly drafted. At the farewell meeting we held for him, one of the boys of our church, who was crippled and loved him dearly, started to cry, knowing the fate that awaited him. A college student, seeing this, severely reprimanded him saying, "No one should cry for one who gives his life for his country!" Dear *Onkuru* died in the battle for Okinawa the following spring! How we grieved over the loss, and shed inner tears for him, when we heard of his death. Still, I never saw a Japanese mother cry for her son when she was told of his death in the war. The Japanese were very self-controlled and accepted their sacrifices with great stoicism.

By the spring and summer of 1944 the fate that awaited Japan became apparent to most of us living there. The European war, while not yet in its final stage, was rapidly moving in that direction. And Germany's defeat seemed inevitable. Some of the Nazis in the community continued to bluster, and spoke of secret weapons, but it didn't take much looking in the sky to see that those gleaming silver B-29s with their bomb bays open were in fact the very weapons the Nazis wished on their side. The Japanese had nothing like them either. Among the more sensible members of the community we now heard increasingly subdued voices. There was also a general and growing feeling that living in Japanese cities would become dangerous. Just looking around at the wood and paper construction of most Japanese houses, all closely packed together, made one conscious of the catastrophe that uncontrolled fires would produce. The Japanese authorities were themselves concerned about how the public would respond towards foreigners when their cities were under air attack from abroad. Most Japanese regarded Westerners, whether American, German, or Italian, as all the same. Few could distinguish between one caucasian and another. For the Japanese authorities, the solution was to recommend that as many foreigners as possible should leave the cities.

January fourth, 1944, was Rosalie's third birthday. I started labor that evening, and I remember the children sat in the dining room from where I could hear them having a big debate. The boys all insisted that the new baby should be a boy. Anne-Marie and her little sister were calling instead for a girl to establish gender equity in the family. The boys were, of course, much louder. When Peter was born the next morning, January fifth, Anne-Marie was greatly disappointed, but after I allowed her to hold her baby brother she brightened up and returned to her former cheerful self.

Not long thereafter we received the first notice that we should move away from Tokyo. By spring the "recommendations" became more urgent. We were told by the authorities that our house would be given to a White-Russian engineer and his wife who worked in a strategic war industry for the Japanese government. Of course many Japanese also knew what lay ahead for the cities and tried to take their families into the countryside.

Food became increasingly scarce. Rationing began, I remember, in 1942. The *tonarigumi* distributed the portion of rice and vegetables that we received every week. We got about a cup of rice per person, and a few vegetables, sometimes a head of cabbage, some carrots, or a Japanese radish. There was also a little bread, and a special annual allocation of potatoes. But by 1944 there was less and less. We now spent more time just trying to stay alive. As the Pacific War intensified there were also fewer and fewer German blockade runners that made it to Yokohama.   In the past when these naval vessels reached Japan, they usually brought in supplies of food, often from merchant ships they had seized along the way. The German Embassy was careful to distribute this food fairly among the German community. On one occasion we received quite a supply of Australian Corned Beef in blue tins from the German Relief Committee. But this source now came to an end.

Our own mission support was largely cut off. Towards the end of the war in Germany the Liebenzell Mission was no longer allowed to send money abroad. Even if it had, it would have been difficult to get to us. The lines of

Bombed out buildings near our house in Todoroki. By 1945 most of Tokyo looked like this.

69

communication were completely broken. After 1944 we heard nothing further from our families. What little income we still received came from the Embassy's relief fund for displaced persons.

We now had six children. Little or no income. And the world was collapsing around us. If there was ever a time for faith, this was it! Papa and I decided that the best course of action for us was to move to Karuizawa. There we would be safer from the bombing. Nagano Prefecture was largely agricultural and certainly our summer house would be more adaptable to the requisites of living off the land that now confronted us. Our mind was further made up by the fact that the German School decided to move to Karuizawa as of the summer of 1944. In fact, there was some disagreement about where the school should move. At first it was suggested that all children in the fifth grade and above be sent to a boarding school that was to be run by the Hitler Youth at one of the Fuji lakes near Hakone. But we didn't like this idea. And neither did many others in the German community. So the decision was made that the main part of the Omori school should move to Karuizawa. In the end some six or seven hundred Germans joined us in the move to the mountains.

We packed up what we could take from the house, put ourselves and the children on the train, and arrived in Karuizawa in May of 1944. Karuizawa was always beautiful in spring. Looking at the azaleas blooming all around us, at the forget-me-nots, and the lilies of the valley, it was hard to reconcile nature's beauty with the human killing that drove us here seeking refuge from the coming storm.

The children in 1944 in as we packed up to move to the mountains. Bomb shelter is left, behind them..

Mt. Asama from Karuizawa.

L ife in Karuizawa was a little easier than it had been in Tokyo. This was because Papa was able to make a beautiful vegetable garden. As a young man, Papa had apprenticed for a time in the Kaiser's garden. He loved plants and possessed a natural affinity with growing things. He was also good at making and inventing things. These natural talents now came to the fore. Pressed into service by the demands of the war his ingenuity blossomed.

There was some land around the house that could be used for growing food, but Papa realized that we needed additional land if we were going to meet our basic needs. He was always good in dealing with Japanese, and he persuaded the Mayor of Karuizawa to allow him the use of one of the town's older garbage dumps as the site for his garden. He knew that years of compost had been piled there. While cleaning up the site was very hard work, we were soon rewarded with a wonderful garden that produced excellent beans, tomatoes, cucumbers, cabbage, and potatoes.

We also bought a goat. A beautiful goat which gave birth to two kids. Every day she gave us more than a gallon of milk. I never saw a goat that gave so much milk. A wonderful milk that had little goat smell about it. The next year one of the little one's gave birth to her own kid and we had more milk. We even had enough milk to give to other members of the community. We called the goat *Lisel* and the little one *Gretel*. And then we bought sixteen chickens for which Papa made a beautiful chicken house. We now had milk and eggs. A little flour was still being rationed to us. So we had the basic ingredients for baking. But there was little meat or butter. I remember that

71

Lisel, our goat, with her two kids.

later, when one of our goats had to be slaughtered, I made such a delicious goat-stew, but none of the children would touch it. They just couldn't eat *Gretel*! So I had to give my good stew to others to enjoy. During the war nothing was wasted. And nothing was ever left on one's plate. I recall how surprised I was after the war when the first American soldiers visited us in Karuizawa and I cooked dinner for them. They often left food on their plates. Even today I find it hard not to eat everything on my plate.

There was a duck-farm in the woods on the other side of Karuizawa. The weasels got into the farm and killed many of the ducks and wounded others. As a result the wounded ducks were sold. We got four of them, and nursed them back to health. Every Christmas, thereafter, we had a duck for Christmas dinner. But there was one we couldn't eat. She was the "policeman" among the chickens. And before Christmas she would always start laying eggs. From the moment she arrived she was determined to live in the chicken-house with the chickens. Every morning she would be covered with chicken droppings. So Papa took pity on her and built a special house for her. A very nice, and beautiful house. But when he put her in it, she started quacking in protest. She continued quacking all night. Neither of us could sleep! So I told Papa, "Put her in with the chickens!" Which he did. And finally she was at peace.

The stream beside our house was largely dry, except for the rainy season in spring. But just as it reached our house it was fed by a

small artesian well, so there was usually a pool of water that came out of the ground. We often used this water in the winter when the weather got cold and the pipes froze. Papa

Duck Policeman.

The path leading to the hospital that ran past our house.

72

said "Let's take the duck swimming." And we all went out to
watch her swim around this pool.
She had a wonderful time swimming. But after a while she looked
to the right, looked to the left,
started quacking, and headed for the
shore. She seemed to be concerned
that none of the chickens joined her
in the water. Thereafter it became
something of a ritual for her to take
her bath while the chickens watched
from shore. She was clearly the

Farmhouse in Nagano Prefecture.

"boss" among the chickens. Once, I
remember, when two chickens were
fighting, she started to scold each in turn,
but they paid no attention. She then
grabbed the tail of one of the chickens
with her beak and dragged the chicken
away from the other. Then she put
herself between them and brought the
fight to an end. We never could eat that
duck. When we left Karuizawa in 1947

Papa bartering with farmers.

we took her to the Buss family's house
in Kutsukake which had a large pond on which she could swim to her heart's
content. I wonder how she got on with their chickens.

Even with all our efforts food was now quite scarce. Still, the Lord
provided in marvelous ways. I remember that every fall we continued to be
rationed a portion of potatoes. We had very little money, and one fall I
couldn't pay. Papa was in Tokyo, and I was informed that the potatoes would
be available the next day. But I didn't have the money. I prayed to the Lord
with all my heart that somehow he would give me the money to pay for the
potatoes. When I stopped praying and went downstairs, I saw a man coming
to our house. He was one of the Nazi leaders. Of course I was scared. He
knocked at the door and I opened it. Then he asked, "Can I come in?" I said,
"Please Dr. Miller, come in." When he entered the room he said, "Mrs.
Notehelfer, do you have money to pay for the potatoes that are coming
tomorrow?" I said, "No I don't." Then he put his hand in his pocket, pulled
out a sum of money, and laid it on the table. It was exactly the sum I needed

for the potatoes. I asked him, "Dr. Miller, How did you know that I had no money for the potatoes?" He said, "Well, my wife couldn't sleep last night, and several times she woke me up and said, you have to go to the Notehelfers and see if they have the money to pay for the potatoes." So I thanked Dr. Miller warmly, and praised the Lord for his wonderful help.

Once in a great while a German naval vessel still made it to Yokohama with seized food from allied ships. This usually consisted of canned goods, some canned milk, canned meat, and some canned salmon or tuna. The Embassy distributed this food fairly to each German family according to the number of family members. This was a great help. But by the end of 1944, few such supplies reached Japan. What kept us going, as much as our garden, were Papa's forays into the countryside. Money was now virtually meaningless. But clothing, cigarettes, and *sake* were highly prized by the farmers of Nagano Prefecture. Barter became the standard form of exchange, and Papa often traded old clothes and his rationed cigarettes and *sake* for walnuts, apples, and cabbage. How thankful we were for those walnuts! With apples and cabbage we could make sauerkraut for the winter. Walnuts provided us with a vegetable substitute for meat and butter. Papa's inegnious cabbage cutter, made from the old Hanomag springs, was now in high demand not only at our house, but with others who were grateful for his invention. When people borrowed it, it usually came back with a return gift, a box of matches, some toilet paper, a little bar of soap. Even here barter was the accepted norm. By the time we reached Karuizawa you could buy almost nothing, not even a needle or a nail. In fact, we gathered up all the old nails we could find and pounded them straight again. A nail was a treasure! Sometimes Fred would take a little of our goat's milk to an old man who lived nearby. He would reward him with a sugar crystal, the only candy still available.

Our biggest problem was getting a stove. Karuizawa was bitterly cold in winter, as I knew from my honeymoon. At that time we used a kerosene stove to keep warm. But now there was no more kerosene. Wood was the only fuel available. Which meant we needed a wood stove. But there were no stoves for sale. Once again Papa's ingenuity came to the fore and the Hanomag saved us. Papa made a wonderful stove using parts of the car. This stove even had a kind of baking oven, in which I could bake bread and cakes when Papa managed to barter for that rarest of all treasures, a sack of flour.

Even rarer than food was soap. During the war the only available laundry soap was like fine sand. It had almost no washing power. So what I did was take ashes and poured boiling water over them, and let them stand overnight. The next day I filtered the liquid through a fine cloth. Then I boiled my laundry in this lye. After cooling it, I washed it and rinsed it in clear water, and hung it on the line. The method was effective, but the lye ate up my fingernails and my fingers were sore all the time. This was really hard on me.

Like everything else, shoes were no longer available in Japan. People were consequently concerned about repairing their old shoes. Papa went and studied how to repair and resole shoes with a Catholic priest. Through the German Embassy he got some leather and he was often up till well after midnight resoling and repairing old shoes for some of the Germans in Karuizawa. He was an excellent cobbler and really did a wonderful job. Clothing was also unavailable. So what I did was take apart all the old sweaters we had, and combining the wool with some black cotton thread I had been able to get earlier from a Japanese store, I reknitted clothing that would keep the children warm in winter.

We all had to work together to stay alive during those years. Each of the children had his specific chores. Getting feed for the animals was a regular task. Helping with the housework was another. One of the children would often be sent to guard the vegetable garden which was a little distance from the house. If no one was there the vegetables simply disappeared. Bill liked this assignment. He often went to the garden with one of our German walking sticks that had a big crook on the end. One day a Japanese started to help

Papa farming the garbage dump.

himself to Papa's beans. Bill came up from behind him with the stick, put the crook around the man's neck and pulled. The man was so surprised that he dropped the beans he was picking and ran off into the nearby woods. Bill was always dramatic in relating his adventures and he just loved to show us how he had saved our beans with the walking stick. There were also hours that went into sawing and splitting firewood. We would all go to gather wood in the forest. One of the duties of every able-bodied male German in Karuizawa, who did not officially work for the Japanese, was to go out into the woods and help to fell trees. The Japanese government needed the timber, so they were not allowed to take any of this, but they were allowed to gather branches and other debris left over from the trees. Every clear day, we took the children, even after school, and

The German School in Karuizawa at the end of the war.

went out into the woods to gather firewood. Papa made a wagon which we pulled by hand, and the children had their own hatchets to cut off small branches. This wood we sawed into firewood at home. Then we stacked it into great piles under the eaves around the house where it dried so that it could be burned in winter.

We also went to pick blueberries at the foot of Mt. Asama every summer. On these occasions we had to walk nearly fifteen miles to get to the foot of the mountain. All of us marched along together. I still marvel at how we could do it. The children were often very tired, but we kept our spirits up by singing. It was always good to come home and rest. I cooked the blueberries with the little sugar we received in our ration and sealed them in beer bottles with some wax. We tried to preserve enough berries so that we had one bottle per week. Once a week I would make a treat for dinner, that was pancakes with blueberries. I can still taste them. We also went on outings with our bicycles. Papa used to have two children's seats on his, and he also made a little wagon for two of the children that he could pull behind. I never could ride my bicycle with a child on it, but we went to many places like Kutsukake, where the Buss family lived, and to the Seizan Hotel on our bikes.

The fact that the German School moved to Karuizawa was very important to us. The school was located in an old building next to the Karuizawa Tennis Courts, where many years later Crown Prince, and now Emperor, Akihito, met his wife-to-be, Michiko. The building was rather run-down, but the quality of the education remained high. There were many excellent teachers among the German women who came out of South-East Asia. These included Sister Hannah, and Fraulein Roehm. Adelheid Zilly was also an excellent teacher, and she continued to live with us in Karuizawa while taking charge of the kindergarten of the school. The children did not particularly like going to school. The tensions in the German community were quite severe and these often spilled over into the children's lives. There were children of the Nazi Party members attending, at the same time there were those who, while patriotically German, were not willing to be members of the party, and then there were a number of German Jews whose children attended as well. School arguments sometimes broke out, and John got into a rather nasty fight one day with another boy over being called *"Mission's Narr,"* or *"Missionary fool."* We felt sorry for him. What the children did like about the school was that it was only a ten minute's walk from our house. The Nazi leaders were, of course, interested in controlling the community, but this was not always easy. The Germans who lived abroad were quite diverse. We were officially instructed not to patronize Jews, for example, but such instructions were often violated. There were many able professionals among the German Jews and one of them was my dentist. Missionaries were hardly popular among the Nazis either, and by 1945 most of us realized that our survival depended on mutual cooperation. Meanwhile, the course of the war in Europe and the Pacific served to undercut the community's most strident voices.

The children did make a number of new friends. While the outbreak of war was difficult on us as adults, for the children it was even more difficult. For us it meant an end of our missionary work among the Japanese. For them there was a sense of rejection. Suddenly their Japanese friends disappeared. Neighbors could no longer afford to have their children play with ours for fear that this would invite police interrogation. "What had little Hans said to Toru?" John's fight with the Priest's son was indicative of the growing estrangement and perhaps his own sense of anger and betrayal. In Karuizawa there were many German children living in close proximity to one another.

In the house next door lived Dr. Müller, who was with I.G. Farben, and whose son Utz was about John's age. He often came to our house to do his homework. Another friend was Dieter Eckhardt. His father was also an engineer. Dieter had been struck with polio and walked with braces on his legs. The boys often went to play with him. He was a very kind and sensitive fellow. When the Eckhardts left Japan after the war, he gave his much loved electric train to the boys. I often wonder what happened to Dieter.

While formal missionary activity with the Japanese was no longer possible, we

John and Anne-Marie at the German School.

Reinhard Buss with the Buss' cow, Kushi.

continued to have some meetings in Karuizawa. Once a week we had the ladies from South-East Asia to our house. We also had regular German Church, which met in the English Church of Karuizawa. I taught Sunday School in that church for all those years. The German pastor was Pfarer Jaekel. On Sunday afternoons we usually had some friends to the house for coffee and cake. I don't remember a time when we could not bake a cake for a Sunday gathering. Papa somehow got a whole sack of raw coffee beans in the early phase of the war. These beans were unroasted, and at first we thought of throwing them out. But then Papa made a coffee bean roaster and we roasted our coffee in the roaster over the wood stove. So we always had coffee during those years when no one could buy coffee anymore. For the children we made a kind of barley coffee, *Malz Kafee*, which they drank mixed with milk from the goat. Every month we missionaries gathered at each other's houses for lunch and fellowship. This brought all the families together and continued a tradition we had established in Tokyo many years earlier. The children particularly liked to visit the Buss family in Kutsukake because they had a cow, and that meant they sometimes got *schlag sahne*, or whipped cream, which was a special treat!

In a way our life in Karuizawa was curious. On the one hand we lived off the land, growing as much food as we could, cutting our own firewood, raising our own animals, and even manufacturing some of the things we needed. On the other, we were only a step away from the urban world in which we had spent most of our adult years. Meeting the necessities of daily living was now our primary challenge and the Lord graciously provided. For the children, too, this was a very different life than they had become accustomed to in Tokyo. But children are marvelous. They seem to rise to challenges. I remember that they just loved to read stories about American Indians. Their favorite author was Karl May, whose many stories about native Americans were extremely popular in Germany. The children lapped these up. Living at the edge of the woods allowed them to develop their own American fantasies. One day the boys took the goat to graze in the woods. While the goat grazed they started to play "indians" with some of their friends. They completely forgot the goat, which had been tied to a tree. *Gretel* got loose and ran home. I wondered where the boys were. They finally came home towards evening all excited. "We lost the goat!" they cried. I said, "The goat is here, but you have to go to bed without supper for not watching out for her." But this was soon forgotten. There were always bows and arrows to be made, expeditions to be mounted to track wild game (usually pheasants), and if the birds remained elusive, at least water cress could be plucked from the local streams. This we learned could be a most delicious winter vegetable. Then there were sleds that Papa made for them using parts of the old car. And I don't remember any more meaningful Christmas celebrations than those we spent in Karuizawa when we had almost nothing but the Christmas spirit and all the presents we gave were hand made. Christmas Eve was always a

Snow at the entrance to our Karuizawa House.

special celebration. Papa and I decorated the tree. The children all had to be washed and bathed. Each had to prepare a verse, or song, or special contribution. Then the door was flung open and to the singing of Christmas carols all were allowed into the living room. What great shining eyes, as they saw the candles burning on the tree, and the few sparklers we had carefully saved for the occasion. Those were the best Christmases. We had so little, and so much to be thankful for.

There were also darker moments. One of our neighbors in Karuizawa was

Mama and children in homespun sweaters resting and singing on one of their treks.

Mr. Engel. He had been a businessman in China before coming to Japan. He was a very lonely man and used to come just to sit in our living room. On one of these visits he told us that the Japanese thought him to be a spy. He had been arrested and tortured by the Japanese military police. And he was very fearful of being arrested again. We comforted him as much as we could. But one morning when the children were going to school they found him hanging from a utility pole. He had committed suicide. We never knew the full story behind Mr. Engel's death, but we were saddened by the tragedy.

By the end of 1944 and into 1945 American bombers regularly flew over Karuizawa. They often bombed Yokogawa and Maebashi which were not far away. Usually we would be awakened by the air raid sirens in the middle of the night, and then we would all have to get up and go down to the bomb shelter which was out in the garden away from the house. It was cold and dark out there with the potatoes, cabbages, and carrots. I remember that Fred particularly disliked being awakened in the middle of the night and taken to the bomb shelter. After a number of such nighttime trips, he announced one evening, "I don't want to go to the bomb shelter anymore. If I have to die let me die in my bed!" Often we could see the planes flying at very low altitudes over Karuizawa with their bomb bays already open. When they bombed the railway facilities at Yokogawa we could feel concussions from the bombs going off. Karuizawa was never bombed directly, so we remained safe from the fire storms that were destroying much of Japan. As mentioned above, one of the worst of these took place on March 10, 1945, when a large part of Tokyo was destroyed by B-29s. Papa was in Todoroki that night. Somehow he managed to get to Omiya the next day and made it back to Karuizawa. He told me the fire of Tokyo burning was so bright that night that one could read a newspaper outside our Todoroki house. It was in this air raid that so many Japanese lost their lives. We knew a German couple who owned a beautiful house full of expensive oriental carpets. When they were told to leave Tokyo they refused. Both were killed that night as their house and carpets went up in smoke. How terrible war is. Not long thereafter our house in Todoroki was also bombed but the Lord protected it. The first bomb fell just outside the special alcove off the living room where I did my sewing, and it landed directly on top of one of Papa's gooseberry bushes. Gooseberries had to be kept in very soft soil, so the bomb simply buried itself and did not explode. The second bomb fell to the rear of the house and landed on a cement surface setting the side of the house on fire. Fortunately our White Russian engineer and his wife, with the neighbors, were able to put the fire out using the sand Papa had so wisely placed around the house. We were thankful that our house survived the war.

In May of 1945 we got news of the German surrender. This news did not come as a surprise to us, but many of the members of the German community were very angry at Hitler, and I know of some who took his picture off the wall, threw it on the ground, and trampled on it. Now many of the Nazi's became quiet. Others in the community were hopeful that they could go home. But there was no way for them to leave Japan. When the Japanese did nothing to make this possible, they were disappointed. As for the Japanese, they were really mad at the Germans for surrendering. They said they would never surrender. But we knew that they, too, were at the end of their power. Many people were starving, and all longed for the war to be over.

Atomic bomb destroys Hiroshima Aug 6, 1945.

By the summer of 1945 the situation in Japan was quite desperate. Okinawa had fallen by the end of June. Now only an invasion of Japan itself lay ahead. In Karuizawa, too, security was tightened. Troops were regularly stationed in town. What few of us realized at the time was that the Japanese planned to make their last stand very close to where we were located in Nagano Prefecture. The Emperor's final bunker complex had already been constructed near Matsushiro. And this certainly meant that we were close to being in harms way. There were rumors of various types. Some were quite ominous. One proposed sending the whole German community to Hokkaido to get it out of Karuizawa. Later my Jewish dentist told me one day, "Mrs. Notehelfer, did you know that your name and that of other missionaries and the Jews was on a list of persons to be given over to the Russians if the war had gone on longer and the Russians had invaded?" I told him that I did not know this. Praise the Lord!, I thought, that he protected us from such a fate. I was also glad that I knew nothing about such things at the time. We had enough to worry about in keeping life and limb together.

Then August came. July and August are often the best months in Karuizawa. When the rains have gone the air is usually clean and crisp. It rarely gets really hot in Karuizawa, but during these summer months it was nice to set the table in the garden and eat outside. Sometimes we would put large metal basins full of water out on the grass in the sun. By afternoon they would be pleasantly warm for the littlest children to play in and bathe. But now there were even fighters flying

81

overhead. Soon we heard truly startling news. We no longer had a radio, but Karuizawa had a car with a loudspeaker that went around making public announcements. On the seventh this car broke the news that the whole city of Hiroshima had been destroyed the previous day by a small bomb. There was no mention of an Atomic bomb. Everybody wondered how this could have happened, that a whole city could be destroyed by a single bomb. Everyone talked about it, but no one understood it. When Nagasaki was destroyed three days later, we were all appalled. We hoped the Japanese government would come to its senses and bring the war to an end. There were, in fact, rumors that the government was making such efforts, and we were really hopeful that the war would end before more lives were lost. But none of us could be certain. There were still those who called for a final battle. The military wanted all Japanese to fight to the death. Civilians had been training with bamboo spears, and many of the hills had been tunneled out with caves for a final stand. We sensed that if Japan were invaded the carnage would be truly ghastly.

On the morning of August 15th we were told by a public announcement that we were all to go to the Mampei Hotel to hear a special radio broadcast from the Emperor himself. We were surprised by the announcement that the Emperor would speak. This was quite unprecedented. We took the family to the Mampei Hotel and listened to the broadcast which was aired precisely at noon. This was the first time that the Emperor had spoken to the nation, and all Japanese, as well as we foreigners, were curious to hear him speak. His voice was very high-pitched, and I could not understand everything he said. I did hear him say, however, that the Japanese people had always obeyed him and that he expected them to obey him now. Then he said that the war had not gone to Japan's advantage and that Japan could no longer resist. While he never spoke of surrender, we knew that he was ending the war. All those present understood that Japan was accepting defeat, and that the Emperor would not call for a final battle. All through the speech, and even after he finished, no one said a word. There was a cloud of silence that fell over the whole audience. For the first time I saw Japanese cry in public. Tears rolled down many faces. No one spoke a word. All left very quietly. We too walked back to our house, and even we were stunned into silence. It took some time for reality to sink in. The war was finally over. There was a profound sense of relief. Not just for us, but for most of the Japanese we knew.

As we looked out of the windows of our Karuizawa house that August afternoon, suddenly the garden seemed brighter. We thanked God for bringing us safely through this difficult period in our lives. The war was over. We did not know exactly what lay ahead, but we were willing to be optimistic. The world we knew in Japan and Germany lay mostly in ruins, but out of ruins new seeds of hope and promise could sprout.

**Chapter Eight
Recovery**

Bombed out Tokyo with rubble and shacks.

Finally the war had ended. But what would Japan be like hereafter. Destruction was everywhere. I remember standing in Tokyo and looking in all directions with nothing to be seen but a few cement walls and brick chimneys. The rest was a complete wasteland. Every house as far as the eye could see had been destroyed. Not only were the cities in ashes, but the Japanese people were close to starvation. While bombs no longer rained from the sky, hunger and disease now stalked the land. For Japan the winter of 1945 was even worse than that of the previous year. The people were fearful about the Americans coming. Many thought they would treat them badly.

When General MacArthur and his forces landed, Japanese closed off their houses with the wooden shutters they usually used only at night or during Typhoons. All young women were hidden away deep inside the houses. Only a few daring children were willing to approach the soldiers. How surprised people were when the Americans smiled at them, and those passing through on trains threw chewing gum and candy to the children.

American troops soon arrived in Karuizawa. One of the military-government teams that administered rural Japan was to be based there. The occupation was also concerned with screening the German community in preparation for its repatriation to the homeland. None of us had an idea of what the Americans would do. I remember that Papa, who was always cautious by nature, thought it best to shave off his mustache. He also threw out all the German marching records we had. We sometimes liked to play these on our hand-

American troops arriving in Japan.

wound Victrola. Papa was fond of music, and he was an excellent *zither* player. During the war his caution had worked on the other side. We never kept a radio, for example, for fear that even a receiving set could be misinterpreted by the wrong people. Karuizawa had several excellent hotels and golf courses, so there were also many American soldiers who came there strictly for rest and recreation. All these facilities were taken over by the American army. In our family, too, it was the children who met the first Americans. Bill was particularly curious and intrigued by the soldiers and their uniforms. He was a gregarious boy. Jeeps just fascinated him, and he often got the soldiers to give him a ride. I recall, he brought home the first chewing gum. A stick of Orbits. We had never seen chewing gum and didn't know what to do with it. Was one to take a little piece, chew it a while, and swallow it? Bill soon instructed us on how to properly "chew." But chewing gum was not a part of American culture I cared for. It made me think of the goat. Why should people chew like goats? Hershey Bars were a different matter. I always loved chocolate. One day one of the children told me that Bill had tried to drive a Jeep and had been terribly scolded by an American soldier. He was only eight at the time. That night, when I gave him his bath, I asked him, "Bill, how does one drive a jeep?" He said, "Well, there is this thing you turn, and the motor starts. Then there is the pedal you push in. You push a stick forward, let out the pedal, and it just goes." Those were years when Bill was into lots of mischief.

The arrival of the Americans was one thing. But at the same time the German community still remained in Karuizawa as well. We went about our lives much as before. By 1946 I had a serious goiter problem and through a German doctor I consulted in Karuizawa I was referred to Doctor Schröder,

American and Allied troops on the Parade Grounds before the Imperial Palace in Tokyo, July 4, 1946.

who was with the German Navy. After an examination he told me that unless I had an operation I would die. He said that if I could come to Hakone, where he was interned by the Americans, he would be able to operate on me as he had a clinic there. That was a very hard decision to make because of the children. We had six children. The youngest, Peter, was only two, and I didn't know

The woods near Hakone.

whether I would come home again. Hakone was some distance from Karuizawa. Papa and Tante Adelheid said they would take care of the children. After we had laid everything in God's hands, I went to Hakone to have the operation. But Doctor Schröder could not operate on me right away because my red blood count was too low. For a week he gave me special liver injections to build up my strength.

The day before I entered the little hospital for surgery, I went into the woods and prayed. I asked God to take care of me and my family and the expenses of the operation. We had almost no money at the time. Doctor Schröder thought the operation would take about two hours, and he gave me enough anesthetic for this duration. The surgery was complicated and a local had to be used because the doctor needed to be able to speak to me during the operation, and I had to talk to him because he was operating so close to my vocal cords. After two hours he told me that he had been able to remove the goiter only from one side. The operation was only half done, and he would have to sew me up and operate again at another time because he could not give me a renewed dose of the local anesthesia. I said to him, "Doctor, you have opened me up, please finish the operation." He said, "Do you think you can stand the pain?" I said, "With God's help I can stand it." He continued to operate, but one of his assistants passed out, and he said to the other, "If this woman can stand the pain, you must endure as well." I managed to hold out until he was sewing me up, then I asked him if he was finished. He said, "Just two more stitches." When he finished he carried me upstairs in the Japanese house in which his clinic was located, put me on a bed, and ordered one of his assistants to stay with me all night. If any change took place, he wanted to be called immediately. Early the next morning he came to see me. With tears in his eyes he said, Frau Notehelfer, I stopped believing in God, and on the ship coming to Japan I threw my Bible into the sea, but yesterday I saw God in the

Hakone with Lake Akashi and Mt. Fuji. This is where Mama went for surgery.

operation, and I need to get a new Bible."

It took me four weeks to recover. One day when I was getting a little better I looked out of the window of the little hospital. I saw an American soldier being carried in. He was badly injured in a jeep accident and required immediate attention. Dr. Schröder took him in and helped to save his life. A few days later an American officer visited Dr. Schröder and I heard him thanking the Doctor for all he had done for his fellow American. I saw them from my window as they walked out together still carrying on an animated conversation. Then the American officer and Dr. Schröder warmly shook hands. I thought why do people have to fight? Here is an American officer and a German navy doctor shaking hands over a life that has been saved. How much better the world would be if we spent time trying to save each other's lives rather than taking them.

A little later Papa came to pick me up. When we asked Doctor Schröder for the bill, he charged me for nothing except the food I had eaten. I was still weak, but full of joy that I could return to my children. The doctor told me to go home and eat, so that I could recover my strength, but when I returned to Karuizawa there was little food, not even flour was left to make a sauce for the vegetables I cooked. I went to a neighbor who worked for the Embassy and asked whether they could give me some flour. They kindly did. A few days later some American soldiers came and brought us food. From then on, we got help from the Americans. Thereafter Christian soldiers often came to visit us and many of them became good friends.

We also received some relief food. This usually came in the form of canned goods. Each family got so many pounds per member. I remember there were tins of all sizes and shapes. The problem was that the cans were all unmarked. None of us knew what was in them. They were simply shiny tins. This led to some curious meals. We had no refrigeration, so whatever we opened we had to eat. There was a lot of shaking of cans to see what was inside, but this was no guarantee. We ate whatever came out. I remember once there was a very large tin. It was full of turkey drumsticks. We had no idea what turkeys were. But we were firmly convinced that everything in America was larger than life. Looking at those drumsticks we marveled at the size of American chickens. Nothing in our chicken house could compete with them! Sometimes we encountered strange foods. Once we opened a tin of olives. We didn't know what olives were and thought they were grapes that had gone bad. We threw them out.

With more food available my health gradually improved. Soon I was back in my element. We continued to entertain our American guests. It was also at this time, in the fall of 1946, that Richard Neumaier, a Liebenzell Missionary from Truk, came to stay with the Lang family in Karuizawa. Mr. Neumaier had been badly treated by the Japanese, and the Americans had sent him on to Japan because they were worried about his emotional state. He recovered nicely in Karuizawa and sometimes came to our house for dinner. While there he met Adelheid Zilly. Both returned to Germany the next spring. None of us had any idea at the time that Adelheid and Mr. Neumaier would be married and eventually have seven children of their own. Oh! How I used to say to Adelheid, who was rather easy going, "What you need is a strict man and six children!" But God blessed them and they had a wonderful family and ministry. Much better than my own.

We stayed in Karuizawa another winter, the winter of 1946-47. In February of 1947 the majority of the Germans living in Karuizawa were repatriated to Germany. They were allowed to take only a small amount of luggage with them. This meant that much had to be left behind, and we inherited some of these things. The children, especially, got many toys. Missionaries, unlike other Germans, were given a choice. They could return to Germany, or remain in Japan. We decided to stay. By late summer the rest of the Germans went home. This meant that the German school was closed. This confronted us with some difficult de- cisions about the children's educa- tion. They were too old to enter Japanese schools. But there were few alternatives. We also wanted to leave Karuizawa and return to Tokyo. But the

Joe Losacco and Tom Watson helping us move back to Tokyo from Karuizawa.

Timothy Pietsch is seated at the far left of this gathering of Scandi-navian Alliance and Liebenzell Missionaries in 1941. The others are from left to right are: Joel Anderson, Pastor Hertel, Oba Sensei and Bernhard Buss.

couple that lived in our Tokyo house, the White-Russian engineer and his wife, needed to find a new place to live, and that was not easy in a city that was almost totally destroyed. Finally, by late spring of 1947, our Tokyo house was once again available to us.

Two American ser-vice men, Dr. Tom Watson and Joe Losacco, helped us with the move back to Tokyo. Both had been very kind to us in Karuizawa and provided us with food. Now they brought a large six-by-six army truck on which they helped us pack all of our belongings, the children, and even the chickens, and we drove to Tokyo. Driving through Japan was still an adventure. We had so many flat tires on that trip that when we crossed the final bridge into Tokyo we had only one good tire instead of two on most of the back wheels. The dust was also so terrible that we could hardly breathe in the back of the truck. But all this mattered little. We were all glad to be back in our Tokyo home.

It was at this time that Timothy Pietsch returned to Japan and was looking for a place to live. Timothy Pietsch was an American missionary. We knew him from before the war, when he had been working in Tokyo with an American board, The Scandinavian Alliance Mission. Because housing was so scarce he asked if he could live with us. He had been in our house briefly in the late 1930s before his marriage to Helen Dozier. They had left Japan not long before the outbreak of war. When we went to the United States in the fall of 1947 he and his wife took over our house, and for a time we lived in his house

Bill with Jeep in Todoroki.

in Turlock, California. But this is getting ahead of things. In 1947 he returned alone because missionary families were not yet permitted into Japan.

Tim Pietsch was something of a character. He was very good at Japanese, and he liked to play jokes.

Open air church service at Shibuya Station during the American Occupation.

He used to tell the most fantastic stories. One of these was that he had been returned to Japan by submarine, shortly before the surrender, to bring the war to an end and to prepare for General MacArthur's arrival. The children would listen to these stories wide-eyed, and he was most entertaining. He also remembered that I had once stood up for Hitler in the late thirties when he visited us, and now liked to tease me by putting his comb under his nose to look like Hitler's mustache, and laughing uproariously. Sometimes I got quite mad at him! He used to keep boxes of Hershey bars under his bed, and the children hadn't seen candy for many years. Yet he was not very generous in sharing these. Since I was cooking, washing, and ironing for him, I said to him one day, you can pay me a bar of chocolate for every shirt I wash and iron for you. He said that would be fine with him and gave me a box of chocolate bars which I divided among the children. Then the rainy season came and all his chocolate bars mildewed and had to be thrown out. That made me really mad!

Tim Pietsch also had a jeep. The children were crazy about jeeps in those days. All wanted to go for rides. But he would take them for a ride only if they washed his jeep, and then he would drive around wildly showing off the power of his American vehicle. After one of these outings to wash the jeep in the Tama River it wouldn't run anymore. It seems sand got into the transmission. He was quite scared, because the jeep belonged to the mission, and it took a good Japanese mechanic who lived a block away to take the transmission apart and put it together again. He usually paid for things in food and old clothes, of which he had a large supply. The mechanic was happy to get the food at a time when most Japanese were still hungry and trading their precious kimonos and possessions for food so that they could survive.

A part of the American Occupation's policy for Japan was to democratize the country. One aspect of this policy was to restore religious freedom.

Timothy Pietsch and David Johnson visiting the site of the bombed out Nakano Church in 1947. Only the baptismal font remains in the field of vegetables.

Missionary activity was now strongly encouraged, and the Japanese Christian church, which had been subjected to many pressures during the war, once again flourished. Major American church groups concentrated their attention on Japan. To those in the church the democratization of Japan went hand in hand with the Christianization of the country. There were also members of the Occupation who supported such efforts. One reason that we, as German missionaries, were allowed to remain in Japan was this concern. The emergence of new Christian institutions, such as International Christian University in Mitaka, was a further expression of this effort. But there were also many others. To get a better sense of what opportunities now faced the church, many American missionary boards and societies dispatched representatives to Japan. One of these was Dr. David Johnson, the Director of the Scandinavian Alliance Mission. We had worked closely with this mission board in the 1930s, and Tim Pietsch had returned to Japan under its auspices. Dr. Johnson arrived in Tokyo in the summer of 1947. Tim Pietsch took him all around Japan in his jeep. At this time the Japanese were very open to the Gospel and they had many excellent meetings. In fact, Pietsch took Dr. Johnson on such a whirlwind tour of the Japan field that poor Dr. Johnson found it hard to keep up in the heat, and on one occasion fainted. When I scolded Pietsch for trying to do too much with the Director, he replied that he just wanted to show him how difficult missionary life in Japan was. Still, we had a blessed time with the General Director and were really happy that he visited us. Papa and the children spent part of the summer back in Karuizawa while I took care of Pietsch and the Director. Later the Scandinavian Alliance Mission was to be renamed The Evangelical Alliance Mission (TEAM), and it was under this board that Papa and I returned to Japan after our stay in America.

My health was still not fully recovered. At the same time no new educational opportunities, other than the American Army schools, seemed to be available for the children. We did not like the idea of sending them to military schools. Still we wanted them to get a good education. With Japan largely destroyed it seemed unlikely that private schools, such as the American School in Japan, or the Canadian Academy of Kobe, could be restored in the immediate future. Then too, Papa and I had never been away from Japan on furlough. It now seemed appropriate to consider such a possibility. But returning to Germany was out of the question. The first letters from our families in Germany did not reach us until 1946. I remember they were delivered through the Red Cross. The news they brought was deeply disturbing. Papa's father and mother had both died in the war. I had lost two brothers, and the remaining members of my family were largely bombed out. Returning to Germany would only add to their misery. We therefore thought of going either to Australia, or to the United States, rather than Germany. The Liebenzell Mission's New Jersey farm for missionaries on leave seemed to present an interesting possibility. But getting a visa to go to the United States in 1947 was no easy matter.

Through Timothy Pietsch we came to know General William K. Harrison. He was a fine Christian man of broad vision who served under MacArthur. We invited him to our home and I cooked him a good dinner. Pietsch gave us all the food we needed for the meal. I remember the General came with his wife and chauffeur. He said to me, "Wherever I am invited, my chauffeur is also!" We enjoyed the visit. Then he invited us to their house for a wonderful dinner that was served by two orderlies. The Harrisons helped us a great deal with food and clothing. It was also through the General's good offices that we were able to get a visa to go to America. Years later, I remember, he played a leading role in the truce talks that ended the Korean War.

Before leaving Japan we returned to our church work in Todoroki. The people were unusually receptive to Christianity and we held meetings at our house and helped Pastor Sugihara build a new church. We no longer had to report to the police and were free to interact with our neighbors and friends without police interference.

By the fall of 1947 arrangements had been completed for us to go to the United States. Again my life started on a new course. I was forty-four years old; Papa was forty-eight. We had six children, and were going to a country we knew little about. We had few friends in America. There was one distant aunt in New Jersey, but her son had been killed in the war by the Japanese and she had no sympathy for missionary work. I knew that everything would be new and different. Once again I asked the Lord to go before us. We were so busy making last minute preparations, getting our vaccinations, X-rays, and health certificates that there was little time for contemplation. Still, there were a few last minute considerations. One day Tim Pietsch said to me, "Are you going to go to America with hair like that?" I said, "Well, is this impossible?" He said, "American women always have their hair nicely done." I said to Papa, "I will go and have my hair done." So I went to the beauty parlor for the first time in my life. But when I came home, I looked at myself in the mirror. I saw a different woman, and I said, "That's not me!" I quickly took a comb and redid my hair in the old way. I said to myself, "America will just have to put up with me as I am."

Finally the day of our departure arrived. Mrs. Harrison drove us to the pier in Yokohama. I remember she gave me a purse and a pair of white gloves so that I would arrive in America in style! We boarded an empty refrigerator ship, *The Flying Dragon*, that had brought food for the Occupation. As our freighter moved out of Yokohama harbor we passed the American liner, *President Harrison*, that was bringing Mrs. Pietsch and their children back to Japan. Our timing could not have been better.

The Japanese have a saying that if you see Mt. Fuji when you leave Japan you'll return, if you don't you won't. There was no Fuji in sight the day we left, and I wondered whether this was an omen. The reason soon became only too clear. As we headed out into the open sea, the ocean became extremely rough and we skirted the tail of a typhoon. None of us lasted on deck for more than a few hours. Soon we were all forced below. I was always a poor sailor, but this was one of the worst trips I have ever taken. Our ship was completely empty and rode high in the water. This meant that in the giant seas the whole

back of the vessel would lift out of the water, and the screw would start to accelerate. When we went down again the ship would shudder. Bill was the only one who wasn't seasick. When I went to check on Fred after a week, he was lying on his bunk still wearing the same clothes in which he had left Yokohama. I can see Rosalie lying on her bed saying, "I will never go to America! No, Never!" Even the crew was seasick. Often we heard great crashes from the galley as plates and crockery were smashed. Although there was plenty of food, none of us could think of eating. Just

Bill and Fred on the freighter to the U.S.

the smell of bacon rising from the galley was enough to bring on nausea. Fred was so traumatized by the smell of bacon that it took six years for him to recover. I never could get him to eat bacon in America. Finally, after a week, the seas calmed and we started to feel better. From then on the trip was pleasant. There was lots of ice cream aboard ship, and the children just loved ice cream. The only other passenger traveling with us was a very kind gentleman who worked for the Bear Line and enjoyed playing with the children. John shared a cabin with him.

Entering Under Golden Gate Bridge.

Shortly before our arrival this man presented each of the children with a crisp dollar bill. Now they, too, could arrive in America in style!

On October 31st, 1947, our freighter pulled underneath the Golden Gate Bridge. It was early in the morning and the bridge was spectacular. It towered over us, a glorious spectacle of red steel. I had never seen anything like it. Even more stunning was the city of San Francisco which sparkled like a white jewel in the morning sun. Everything seemed so neat and orderly, so clean and well maintained. As the tug boats pushed us toward the wharf we could see the people going to work. There were cars and trucks everywhere. We were all excited to be in America. Only little Peter seemed a bit upset. Looking down on all the cars from the ship, he announced with disappointment, "No jeeps, only staff cars."

Chapter Nine
America

The "Immigrants" in Chicago in December 1947.

Arriving in San Francisco was quite an adventure. We didn't know anyone in the city, but we had written ahead to the mission home in Oakland. This was a place where missionaries going to the Far East often stayed. We thought that someone from the home would come to the pier to welcome us. But when our ship docked there was no one to be seen. I thought of my arrival in Japan from Truk. But that time there had been plenty of people to welcome me, only no Papa. This time there was no one.

We waited and waited, but no one came. All of our luggage was unloaded from the ship and our suitcases and trunks now sat on the wharf. There was lots of noise and activity as the ship prepared to take on new cargo. The cranes from the ship were whirring. Little vehicles were racing about with pallets of cargo. The children watched with interest. But still no one came. We waited more than six hours, and didn't know what to do. Then a truck driver came over to where we were standing. He said, "I've been watching you for hours. Where are you going." We told him we were missionaries and were waiting for people from the mission home in Oakland to pick us up. He said, "Did you phone them?" We hadn't even thought of the telephone! He asked me whether we had the home's phone number. I told him that we didn't, but that we had the address. He asked for the address and went off. After a while he came back and said, "There seems to be no one home." Then he asked us, "What are you going to do? Are you going to sit here until night comes? Or shall I load all your things on my truck and drive you over to Oakland?" We thanked him for his kind offer and said that would be wonderful. So he loaded our luggage on his truck and put the children in back with the suitcases. Papa, Peter, and I rode in front with him.

The truck driver took us across the Bay Bridge, the other of the two great bridges, and we were able to look down. It was our first aerial view of America. What a spectacular sight the city and bay provided! The late afternoon sun was now behind us; the city ahead was all lit up. We marveled at the landscape, the bridge, and the people. It was just beautiful. Then we drove into Oakland. Our driver had some difficulty finding the mission home. The street, Ronada, on which it was located, was only a few blocks long. He went into a gas station to inquire and was told it was just around the corner. Not long thereafter he stopped and said, "Here we are!" I looked up and saw a beautiful house on a slope. It was surrounded by geraniums. I said, "That's too beautiful to be the mission home." The driver replied, "Well, this is Ronada 1, the address you gave me!" I said, "Let me go up and see if we are right." So I climbed up the little slope between the geraniums. The house had a big door and a door knocker—there was no bell. I knocked with the knocker. A young man opened the door and I told him that we were the Notehelfers from Japan and were looking for the home of the Scandinavian Alliance Mission. He said, "This is it. Your room is ready for you upstairs." So I waved to Papa and the driver to come. Papa and the driver unloaded our things. He charged us twenty-five dollars for bringing us over from San Francisco, which we thought was a lot of money, but we were really thankful for his help and could hardly imagine what we would have done without him. He was a real angel of mercy.

Upstairs in the mission home was a large room with eight military beds in it. Before the mission bought the home, it had belonged to a Christian order of young men called the Navigators, and several of them were still living in the house. The young man who greeted me at the door was one of these. When I asked him why no one had come to the ship, he said the Jensens who usually ran the home, had gone to New York for a wedding and had forgotten to leave instructions about our arrival. It was now close to evening, and we had not eaten since breakfast. I asked him where we could get some food. He said there was a kitchen that we could use. But we had brought nothing in the way of groceries, so I asked him "Where are the stores?" He replied they were downtown, and told me the bus that stopped just across the street would take us there. For groceries he recommended the Safeway Store. So just before six we caught the bus and asked the driver to let us off near the Safeway Store. He kindly did. Once off the bus, we noticed that the streets were full of children and adults, all dressed up in the strangest outfits. Many were wearing masks. There were devils, and goblins, and all kinds of strange characters, some in white sheets. We stared at them and wondered what a

Safeway Store on Grand Avenue in Oakland.

95

peculiar place America was. I stopped a man and asked, "Why are people going around like this?" He said, "Well Lady, its Halloween!" I said, "What is Halloween?" He looked at me with a quizzical look, and then blurted out, "Lady! Halloween is Halloween!" So I still didn't know what Halloween was. I had heard that America was a little crazy, but this was even crazier than I expected!

We went into the Safeway store. This was the first time we had been in an American supermarket. What a sight! We were surprised to see the extent and variety of the goods for sale. By the end of the war, Japanese stores were entirely empty. Here there were shelves and shelves of good things. The children thought we could just fill our cart with all the things that interested them. I said, "No, you let Mama and Papa choose, and you look around." So they did. Bill went to the bakery section of the store. There in one of the glass cases he saw a beautifully decorated birthday cake. Ann's birthday was just two days away. He came running over to me and said, "Mama can I buy that beautiful cake with my dollar?" I said, "No, Bill, we will buy some flour and I will bake a cake." "But you can't make such a beautiful one," he said. "No," I replied, "but it will taste good." He was so disappointed that I wouldn't let him buy that beautiful cake for his sister.

When we finished our grocery shopping we left the market. Across from the Safeway was a bakery that sold large loaves of French bread. I said to the children, "You wait here with the groceries, Papa and I will quickly cross the street and buy some bread. When we came back from the bakery, I saw Bill standing there with a big white box, and his face was shining! I said, "Bill, you didn't buy that cake anyway, did you?" He said, "The lady from the store came out and said to me, 'You want that cake don't you!' I said, 'Yes!' She said, 'Give me your dollar.' So I gave her my dollar. And she brought me the cake and gave me all this money!" I looked as he held out his hand, and there, in his palm, lay two fifty cent pieces. The lady must have watched us and thought these are displaced people; I will help this boy get his cake. How kind and generous she was. What a charming introduction to America. This experience typified so much of what we encountered in the United States.

On Sunday we wanted to go to Church. We asked one of the young men in the home, whether there was a church nearby that we could attend. He said the Jensens always went to the Covenant Church which was not far away. We had never heard of the Covenant Church. When we inquired how to get there, he suggested we take the bus and ask the driver to let us off at the Covenant Church on Fifth Avenue. So we took the bus. A few stops after we got on a couple joined us. They looked at us and said, "Where are you going?" I said we are going to the Covenant Church but we don't know exactly where it is.

They said they were members of this church and would show us. The couple's name was Norman and they brought us to the church. We later became life-long friends. The usher seated us in the second pew from the front. People could not help but look at us and wonder who we were. Even the Pastor noticed us and said, "It seems we have some strangers in our congregation this morning, will you tell us where you are from?" So Papa stood up and said that we were German Missionaries working in Japan and that this was our first visit to America." Hearing this, the church got quite excited about us.

After the service a woman from the church came up to me and asked, "Do you know a missionary named Mary Juergensen?" I said, "Oh! Yes. We know the Juergensens." They had, in fact, been very close friends of ours in Karuizawa. Mr. and Mrs. Juergensen had been American Pentecostal Missionaries to Japan. Their two daughters, Mary and Agnes, had gone to Japanese schools and were fluent in the language. Mr. Juergensen died in Karuizawa in the late 1930s and Mary, Agnes, and their mother returned to the U.S. before the war. During the war we lost all contact with them. I had recently prayed that I might somehow find them again in America. And here was a lady saying to me, "Mary is staying at our house right now. If you have time please come over this afternoon. We will pick you up in our car." So we went that afternoon and had a wonderful reunion.

The Oakland Covenant Church was very generous to us. The members of the congregation took us in, gave us food and clothing, and helped us in many ways. Again it is interesting how God works. None of us could have known at the time that my son, John, would one day become the Pastor of this church.

We stayed at the Mission Home until Thanksgiving. This allowed us to become acclimated to the American setting. Papa and I also made several trips. One was to Los Angeles where we spoke to a German congregation. There we also had a chance to spend a little time with old friends. Among these were the Carlsons whom we had not seen since 1941. They had been members of the Scandinavian

Mr. and Mrs. Juergensen (far left) in Karuizawa with the German Missionaries.

97

The California Zephyr.

Alliance Mission and worked closely with us before the war. Thanksgiving, I remember, was a very festive affair at the mission home. For the first time we had roast turkey with all the trimmings. Now we came to understand what a turkey was. Later we were to move to Turlock in the San Joaquine Valley of California. Turlock liked to describe itself as the "Turkey Capital of the West." There we had some really spectacular Thanksgiving birds!

After Thanksgiving it was time to go East, first to Chicago and then to New Jersey. When we left Japan we had formally agreed to exchange houses with Timothy Pietsch. It was the Pietsch house that eventually took us back to California, but at the time it was occupied by a missionary from South America who had an invalid sister. At the same time, we were still uncertain about our future work in Japan. Given the Liebenzell Mission's financial circumstances in Germany following the war, it seemed unlikely that it could continue to support us. One reason for our journey to the United States was to consult with its American branch to see if U.S. sources of funding could be provided. Meanwhile a decision to transfer us to the Scandinavian Alliance Mission was being considered by both boards. We knew that shifting boards would mean some adjustment for us. The Liebenzell Mission had provided financial support for us from general funds raised by the mission. By contrast, the Scandinavian Alliance Mission, and its successor TEAM, were faith missions in which missionaries raised their own support from independent churches. These funds were then channeled to each missionary through the mission's headquarters in Chicago. We didn't know which of these options would materialize, but we realized that they presented clearly different paths for our future. If we became part of the Scandinavian Alliance Mission we would have to settle down in the U.S. long enough to create a network of churches that would support us. It also seemed appropriate that if American churches supported us we should become American citizens and that required a longer stay in the United States. If our

98

German board succeeded in raising the needed funds, we could return to Japan within a year. Under such circumstances, our visit to the U.S. would constitute little more than a normal furlough. We trusted that God would show us the way and help us to make the right decisions, for we knew that much would rest on these decisions and that they would have important consequences for us and our children.

We took the train from Sacramento to Chicago. It was early in December. The train was the California Zephyr and it followed a beautiful route through the Sierra Nevada mountains. It had several observation cars from which you could look out on the passing scenery. As we came through the mountains, and also in the high desert, there was already snow on the ground. This was our first long train trip with the children and they were very excited about seeing America. What impressed me the most was the wide open land. In Japan, and even in Germany, there was nothing like it. Japan's narrow valleys and limited plains were intensely cultivated. In Japan there were people everywhere. As the train sped through Nevada, Utah, and Wyoming one saw almost nothing but wild, uninhabited land. One saw neither people nor signs of civilization. At the same time, the vistas were truly spectacular. Looking out at all this wide open space was almost overwhelming. Even in Nebraska and Iowa, where there were many farms and farm communities, the scale of everything was so much larger than what we were used to. When I returned to Germany in later years, my German friends often spoke of Americans as people who liked to speak in a big way. I would always reply, "Have you seen America? When you see the size of their country you can get an idea of why they speak in such a way!"

The train had a nice dining car. We had packed some of our own sandwiches for the trip, but we also took several meals in the dining car. The porters and waiters were all blacks. I remember they were very kind to the children, especially Bill. Bill liked tea. And he would go to the dining car to get a cup of tea. We never had lemons in Japan. So we always drank our tea clear with sugar. The black waiter offered Bill a slice of lemon, and milk for his tea. Bill took both and put them in his tea. But by the time he returned to his seat the milk had curdled. He was convinced that there was

Mama, Rosalie, Anne-Marie and Fred having tea in the dining car.

99

something wrong with his tea so he took it back. The waiter gave him another cup. Again he offered him lemon and milk. And again Bill did the same thing. I don't know how many times he did this, but finally the waiter explained to him very politely that one couldn't put both milk and lemon in one's tea without having it curdle. "Both are offered to allow you to have a choice," he said, "so you must choose one!" Thereafter Bill took his tea with lemon and sugar.

We arrived in Chicago in the second week of December. The Scandinavian Alliance Mission provided us with a place to stay. I was happy to see David Johnson again. We wanted to get the missions advice about our future. So we had a meeting with the whole board and told them about our life and work in Japan. The board included not only the Director, David Johnson, but also the former Director, T.J. Bach, who was now Emeritus, and the Assistant Director, Mr. Mortenson. They listened to what we had to say and were very kind and supportive. They advised us to continue with our plan to visit the Liebenzell Mission in New Jersey. They thought that if the Liebenzell group in the United States could support us we should stay with our former board. If not, they would be prepared to take us on as missionaries, and would introduce us to various churches that supported their work in Japan. We felt at ease about this decision and left Chicago for New Jersey.

The Liebenzell Mission's farm was located at Schooleys Mountain. This was a rural spot in the Northwestern part of New Jersey not too far from the Delaware Water Gap. As the name implies the farm was literally up on a mountain. On one side, four and a half miles to the West lay Hackettstown, where the High School was located, and where we often went to shop. Two miles to the East was a small rural town named Long Valley where the elementary school was situated. The farm was managed by Mr. and Mrs.

Zimmerman. They came from China, and because they could not go back, they were asked to direct a branch of the Liebenzell Mission in America. Mr. Zimmerman was a very hard worker, and demanded that everyone should work as hard as he. The farm was run communally, and there

The Liebenzell Mission's Schooley's Mountain Headquarters in New Jersey.

100

were several good sized houses on the property. We shared one of these with missionaries from China, the Kamphausens, who also had six children. They later moved to Chicago.

Our arrival in Schooleys Mountain was just before Christmas. This was our first Christmas in the United States, and it was the first time in more than five years that we could buy the children Christmas presents. How full of goods American stores were! What a difference from Japan! Like other holidays, Christmas was celebrated communally at

Tree downed by ice storm.

Schooleys Mountain and all the children sang "Glory to God in the Highest" in five or six different languages at the gathering of the group. Then we had our own family Christmas. Again I saw those shining faces and bright eyes as the children were allowed to open their gifts. I can still see Fred sitting on the floor with his Erector Set, which was the Legos of its day, making all kinds of contraptions. He just loved to build things. For me Christmas was always a time of reflection. I would think of the past, of my family in Germany, which I had not seen in almost twenty years, and of old friends. It was also a time for giving and sharing. We knew that Christmas would not be easy for our relatives in Germany. I hoped that the large package we sent off shortly after our arrival would reach them, if not for Christmas, at least for New Year. I also thought of the Christmases we had spent in Japan during the war, when we had so little, and how blessed we now were with ample food, clothing, and housing. I was beginning to feel much better physically, and found my energy restored. How much we had to be thankful for.

We had lived through several severe winters in Karuizawa, but the winter of 1948 in New Jersey was really something! Early in January we experience one of the century's great storms. It was a blizzard that brought not only snow, but freezing rain that formed into fantastic layers of ice. Each branch, and every electric wire, was covered with more than an inch of ice. Outside our house stood a great oak tree. It must have been more than a hundred years old. The night of the storm John and Fred were sleeping in an upstairs corner room next to this tree. In the middle of the night there was a great crash. The children's first response was that the house had been bombed. There was no electricity so we couldn't see exactly what had happened. When we finally got a flashlight and looked into the room where the boys had been sleeping the whole corner of the room was crushed to a few feet above Fred's bed. No longer capable of bearing the weight of the ice, the great oak had split in two and one half had come down on the house. The next day we could see how truly lucky the boys had been. A few feet more and they would have been killed. We thanked God for his protection. The storm finally abated and when the sun came out the whole world was turned into a fairyland. I have never seen anything like it. Everything was covered with ice, and sparkled with fantastic colors. The ice created a series of prisms that gave off colors of every description. It was truly beautiful!

The storm did so much damage that it took weeks to recover and get life back to normal. Without electricity, we lived, as we sometimes had in Japan, with kerosene lamps. The children did not go to school because the school busses could not run. John and Anne commuted to the High School in Hackettstown, as did Bill who attended the Junior High School. They were sorry not to be going because they liked their schools very much. But the same could not be said of Fred and Rosalie, who were hardly sorry. They went to the elementary school in Long Valley, and there was nothing nice about their school. The anti-German prejudices of the war years were well established in Long Valley, and our children, whose English was still limited, were made the target for these prejudices. In Fred's case, especially, there were classmates who regularly baited him and picked fights. Name calling, which included invoking Hitler and the Nazis, was not uncommon. Often this turned into physical attacks. The situation became so serious that Fred's teacher would keep him in during recess and lunch hours. Even getting from the

schoolhouse to the bus could be traumatic. This was not a positive environment, but we could do little to change it.

When spring came we discovered that the setting of the farm was really quite splendid. The area was surrounded by

One of the farmhouses at Schooley's Mountain.

lovely fields and meadows. There were woods nearby and everything suddenly turned green, leaving behind the winter drabness. At the edge of the woods we found wild strawberries that made a wonderful jam. When spring turned into summer, there was lots of work to be

Family portrait at Schooley's Mountain New Jersey, 1948.

done. We helped in the fields, particularly in filling the large barn with hay. All of us pitched in. The work was often hard, and John, in particular, worked long hours with the other boys to bring in the hay. Everyone was so proud when the task was completed. This was shortly before we left. Two days after our departure the barn was hit by lightening and burned to the ground. All our hay and hard work went up in smoke. I remember how badly John felt when we got the news.

By summer of 1948 it became clear that the Liebenzell Mission could not raise the money for our return to Japan. So we wrote to the Scandinavian Alliance Mission and formally asked the board to accept us as missionaries. They were happy to do so, and even provided us with interim support on a monthly basis until we could raise the funds for our return to Japan. We now were clear on our course of action. The Pietsch house in California would become available at the beginning of September, so we decided to leave New Jersey for the West Coast. As many of the churches that supported the Scandinavian Alliance Mission's work were on the West Coast, this seemed even more appropriate. Once again we packed our suitcases and caught the train across America, stopping briefly in Chicago, and arrived in Sacramento on September seventeenth. At the end of that long rail trip a well dressed gentleman who had been sitting near us came up to me and said, "When you got on the train in Chicago, I said to myself this will be a terrible trip with all those children. I want you to know that I had a most enjoyable time with your children, and congratulate you on how you are bringing them up." In the next few years, as I was struggling with my children in California, I sometimes thought of this man, and said to myself, "If you could only see me now!"

We reached Turlock late that evening. Turlock did not have a railway station with a platform, and we were dropped off on what seemed to us the street. We didn't know where we were. Then an old man, Mr. Olson, came and asked if we were the Notehelfers. We said, "Yes!" He told us he had brought his truck to pick us up. He was a very kind man and brought us to the Pietsch house, which was located almost directly behind his own house on Cahill Avenue. The next day, I remember, it rained. People always say it doesn't rain in Turlock in September, but it did the year we arrived. When we got to the house, we discovered that the people of the Free Church, to which Pietsch belonged, had carefully prepared it for our arrival. The beds were all made and ready for us. When we opened the refrigerator it was completely stocked with food and there was plenty of milk. Even the cupboards had groceries in them. This was truly a great kindness and reflected how the people of Turlock were to treat us in the years that followed. We met with nothing but kindness from the people there.

Turlock was a city of about 10,000 in 1948. It was surrounded by orchards and farms. It had more churches than any other town of its size. When it came to picking a church we therefore had lots of choices. At first we went to the Free Church. But most of the children's friends went to the Covenant Church. So for a time we went to both churches—to the Free Church on Sunday mornings and to the Covenant Church in the evenings. Finally Papa thought it was not right to do this. He wanted us to choose and join only one church. So we had a gathering of the children and each of them voted to join the Covenant Church. We respected their decision and decided to become members of this church. At the time C. Victor Nyquist was pastor of the Turlock Covenant Church. He and his wife Mary were most hospitable to us. In fact, the whole church adopted us and we received the help of so many people that it is now almost impossible to name them all. They displayed to us the true generosity of postwar America and its willingness to take in strangers and help them. For me Turlock served as a kind of oasis. Even now, when I've come back to this town for my last years, the residue of Turlock's warmth lingers like the sun on an Indian summer day. So many of those Papa and I knew have gone to be with the Lord, but I often see their children, and I think of them. Sometimes when I think of the past, they seem to be right here with me. It was a blessed time. I felt so free, and everyone loved us. There was a wonderful group of ladies in the church which I joined. When I wrote to my sister, Walburg, how nice the people were, she wrote back saying that these must be truly "extraordinary" people of a type rarely found among mortals. And so they were. I am so thankful for Turlock.

Chapter Ten
Turlock

Mama as a "Single Mother."

The years in Turlock from 1948 to 1953 were interesting and challenging. I enjoyed the town and its people. What was difficult was the fact that from the end of 1949 to the end of 1952 I lived essentially as a single mother. Raising six children without a father in the home was no easy task. Especially when those children were entering their teen-age years. I remember kind Mr. Olson, our neighbor, coming to me one day, probably after some escapade with the children, and saying in his quiet way, "Mrs. Notehelfer, your children are very nice, but they are like all other children." He was right! During those years my children grew up like weeds. The boys were always into sports. There was baseball, football, and basketball. Which meant that there was usually something flying around the yard. I felt sorry for poor Mr. Olson's windows, and for the barn which stood next to the Pietsch house that served as basketball court, baseball backstop, and the target of many other devices. By the time the boys stopped impaling it with missiles it looked old and tired, and decidedly ragged. I sometimes felt the same way trying to deal with their latest antics. I prayed a lot, and at times I reached for the cut off broom handle I kept in the kitchen closet. The boys remember only too well that I could wield my bat when provoked. Today I would be in serious trouble.

But here, too, I am getting a little ahead of myself. When we reached Turlock in the autumn of 1948 we knew that the Mission wanted Papa to return to Japan as quickly as possible. The board needed his skills with the language and his experience in dealing with Japanese to bring in the large number of new missionaries they intended to send to Japan. But in keeping with the mission's rules, he needed to raise his own support. This meant visiting numerous churches and explaining the work in Japan. Already in the Turlock area we received many invitations for such presentations. We bought

Visiting regional churches in the Turlock area.

an old 1937 Chevrolet and nearly every Sunday visited a different regional church. All the children would come with us, and we would often sing in Japanese, German, and even the language of the South Pacific. One day a friend of ours, Mr. Swanson, announced that we would never be able to go to heaven unless we learned to sing in Swedish. There were many Swedish families in Turlock. In fact, the Covenant Church was originally known as the Swedish Covenant Church of America. So out of respect for Mr. Swanson, and our new church home, we added a hymn in Swedish. Even today we can still sing *"Tryggare Kan Ingen Vara."* Later, in the summer of 1949, Papa and John made a more extended deputation trip to the Pacific Northwest, visiting churches in Washington and Oregon to which they had been introduced by the Scandinavian Alliance Mission.

But raising sufficient support for Papa to return to Japan was no easy task. I knew that even his trip to the Northwest was producing only a small amount of what was needed. In the meantime, Pastor Nyquist felt that our church should make a special effort to help Papa, so he went to a group of businessmen in the church and met with them about underwriting Papa's work in Japan. They agreed to do so. Shortly thereafter, I remember, Wally Lindskoog came to the house. Wally was one of the men from the church who owned a turkey hatchery. He also flew his own plane. Papa and John were still away. What he told me was to tell Papa that as soon as he returned he should get ready to leave for Japan. The church had settled all matters of his financial support. He even offered to fly Papa to San Francisco in his airplane. "Praise the Lord," I said, "Papa will be happy to hear this!" So the biggest hurdle to Papa's return disappeared, and we celebrated our first Christmas in Turlock knowing that he would soon be on his way back to Japan. The ladies of the church held a shower for us. We had no idea of what a "shower" was and the children asked, "Will they pour water over us?" Each received a new outfit and we were all so thankful for this generosity.

My reason for staying behind with the children involved U.S. immigration laws. We had decided to apply for American citizenship. While conditions for naturalization usually required a five years' residency, in the case of members of the Church, one spouse could reside outside of the U.S. for part of this period. This meant that Papa could be in Japan while the children and I remained in America. We would all be eligible for citizenship in 1953 when we completed our five year stay. Thereafter the children and I would be free to return to Japan as American citizens. We knew that the separation that faced us would not be easy. At the same time, we also realized that there was still no adequate schooling for the children in Japan. Moving them again would present its own problems. So there were advantages to staying for a few years in the same place. Turlock seemed ideally suited for such a stay. The Lord had always gone before us in the past, and we now asked Him to lead us through these new circumstances. Papa bought another car, a station wagon, and a wire recorder. The car was for his work in Japan, the wire recorder was the link that connected us on a weekly basis. Trans-Pacific phone calls were out of the question, but those reels of recorded wire crossed the Pacific like clock-work. We heard from Papa once a week. Somewhere I still have some of his homilies to the children. What they liked best was his *zither* playing.

Papa left by freighter on a cold wintry day late in 1949. We all went to San Francisco to wish him *bon voyage*. I still see him standing there on the ship in his leather jacket. I didn't really like leather jackets any more than brown suits, but they were popular at the time. When I look at the photograph of all of us, we don't look that different from the family that arrived from Japan two years earlier. We still looked like typical immigrants. But seeing the pictures that follow, I realize how much we changed in the next four years. As the photos show, we all went through a gradual, but distinct, Americanization. Of course America, itself, was changing rapidly during these years. A world of

Papa playing his Zither in Japan.

radio was turning into a world of television. War in Korea, followed rapidly on the heels of the communist seizure of power in China. Asia was becoming more important and also more troubled. I think we occasionally worried as much about Papa as he worried about us.

But life went forward and a family of children turned into one of young adults. Speaking quite frankly, America influenced me as much as it influenced the children.

One of our neighbors, who was a nurse in the Turlock Hospital, came to see me one day. She said, "Mrs. Notehelfer, do you work?" I said to her, "I don't know what you mean. I work from morning till night!" She said, "I don't mean that. I mean do you work for money?" I said, "Do you think I would be able to do this?" "Sure," she said, "You can work in our hospital." I had learned nursing in Germany, and I thought I could work as a nurse's aid. But I was afraid of my poor English. So I said, "Can I work for half a year as a dish washer, while I learn more English?" She said, "I'm sure you could!" So she introduced me to the hospital manager and I started as a dish washer for six months. At the end of this period I was promoted to nurse's aid. I really loved my work in the hospital as an aid, and I worked very hard to do a good job. My one condition was that I should be home on Saturdays and Sundays to be with my children. So every weekday I went to the hospital and worked. I remember my pay was one dollar per hour. And I even managed to save a little of this money.

After I had been working in the hospital for a while, one of the chief surgeons called me into his office and said, "Mrs. Notehelfer will you tell me the secret of the pills you give to our patients." I was taken aback. I said, "I have no special pills. I don't give the patients any medicine, except what is prescribed for them!" He said, "Oh, but you do!" "Nobody can cheer them up the way you do!" I said, "That is just the joy and peace I have with my work here." There were many people who needed help, and I was pleased that the Lord could use me to help them. I remember a woman who was extremely agitated and constantly in tears. She was convinced that she had cancer. I reminded her that her biopsy was scheduled for the following day. I agreed to pray with her and placed her in God's hands. She calmed down and was able to sleep. The results the following day were negative and she went home joyously. Years later I sometimes encountered her on the streets of Turlock and she always thanked me for the help I gave her that evening.

There was another difficult case. We had a patient who was quite wild. In fact, he was so out of control that he had to be restrained with a straight-jacket. I was asked to watch him one night. But I agreed to do so only if the straight-jacket were removed. I didn't like the idea of straight-jackets. The nurse said this was strictly doctors orders. I told her to call the doctor and ask if I could stay with him without the straight-jacket. The doctor told her that if I was prepared to face him without restraints, that was acceptable to him, as long as I was aware of what I was doing. I went in to see the man and had the jacket removed. I also had all of his clothes taken from the room. That left him with only his robe. Meanwhile, I told the staff that all the doors leading outside of the hospital were to be kept shut and locked. Then I took some old sheets and tore them into long strips. I brought them into the room with the man. At first he was glad to be released from the jacket. But then he began to speak quite excitedly about having to leave the hospital and go home. He got up and started for the door. I said to him, "It is cold outside tonight, and you have no clothes. How can you go home like that." He said, "But my clothes were right here!" I said, "But I don't see any here now." He looked around and was a little perplexed. I suggested that he use the strips of the sheets I had brought to make some clothes. Then I showed him how to wrap the strips around his legs. From the legs we moved the wrapping process further up the body. This was slow work and took him hours, but finally he was all wrapped up. Now he announced that he had to go, and once again started for the door. I said to him, "But you have no hat, and it is winter." He felt his head. I said, "Let's make a hat!" So we experimented with more strips of sheeting how one could make a hat. This also took a long time. Finally we produced an acceptable hat. Now he wanted to leave again, so we walked out of the room into the hospital corridor. Despite my instructions, someone had left the emergency doors open. I saw that he noticed they were open. They led directly out of the hospital. Suddenly I had to think fast. I asked the patient whether he had received his medication to take home with him. He said, "What medication?" I said, "Didn't the nurse give you some medicine to take with you?" I told him we would have to check on this. He would not be able to go home without medication. I quickly went to the nurses' desk and told them to close the doors, and that one of the nurses should bring a few aspirin tablets to the patient's room. I told the man that we would have to return to his room and wait for the medicine to be brought. This he did. When the "medicine" came, we started off again, but the doors were now all closed. We walked about for some time trying the doors, but none would open. I explained that they would be open again early in the morning. It was now late at night. I also told the man that it would be much better to get some sleep before morning came. He was now quite tired and agreed. So we went back to his room and he fell asleep. At seven the next morning, when my shift was over, he was still sleeping soundly. I wonder what my replacement thought of him all wrapped up in sheets?

Dealing with patients was sometimes easier than dealing with the children. I wish there had been some good "sheets" that I might have used to wrap them up. I certainly needed as much strategy. And there was no going home the next morning. I don't think the children were unusual. As Mr. Olson said, they were just children. But they were heading into those years when any parent knows they become exhausting. I always believed in clear and well defined rules. Children need these. When the family was out in public, the children knew that any misbehavior on their part would not bring a public reprimand, but that a certain look from me meant they would hear from me later. In typical German fashion we emphasized courtesy and a respect for others. On the whole, the children were very good about such things, and people often complimented me on their conduct. John, in particular, was older than his years, and in Papa's absence took on the role of father. Some kidded him about his seriousness, and called him "Gramps." He had gone to German schools longer than the rest of the children, so it took him longer to take on American ways. Once, I remember, we invited a family of missionaries from Africa to dinner. They had a six year old girl. After watching John for a while she asked him, "Are you the father of this house?" He was a little embarrassed and said, "No, I'm too young to be a father." John was clearly older than his years. To some degree this was true of Anne-Marie as well, and when I worked she often had to take over family cooking responsibilities. Bill and Fred, the next two, were a different matter. They had lots of friends, and their birthday parties were often lively affairs, but they were always into something.

One day I had a report from a neighbor that he had seen Bill and Fred and some of their friends on the roof of our house puffing away on cigarettes. That required a good thrashing. On another occasion the boys came home from a fishing outing with over a hundred striped bass. I didn't know what to do with

John as "Gramps."

all the fish and gave some to the neighbors. Dear Mr. Olson came and said, "I think the boys have been fishing in the wrong place." I asked, "What do you mean?" He said, "These fish look like they came from the hatchery." The boys had caught them in the river all right, but they were nearly all undersized! That required a serious warning. Then the boys decided to raise their own chickens. That was something! We had a barn, but we were in the city. When they couldn't sell the chickens they decided we should eat them. Now they turned butchers. Fred would tie a string around the chicken's neck and pull it forward over a wooden block; Bill held the feet of the chicken and cut off its head with

Fred--baseball by the barn.

a hatchet. Sometimes the boys would let the chicken go and it would fly or run about wildly without its head. They thought this amusing, but I had to tell them that this was not the way to butcher chickens. Another time they decided to enter a bottle cap contest. Whoever found the most bottle caps from a certain bottler would win a bicycle. They didn't win the bicycle, but they won the second prize which was a B.B. gun. I hated guns and had a strict rule about them. So I made them take the gun back, and they managed to trade it for the third prize—a baseball glove. Fred became an avid model airplane builder, and loved to run his engines. They made more noise than today's leaf blowers. I sometimes wonder how the neighbors put up with that. Even little Peter came in one day with a badly burned finger. When I treated it and asked him how he burned it, he replied that he had been trying to make a fire in the barn. I could see the barn going up in flames! This gives you an idea why I prayed a lot and kept that broom handle in the closet!

I don't mean to give the wrong impression. The children all had their chores and they worked very hard to help us to live together. While Papa was away I continued to send almost monthly care packages to our relatives in Germany. They all had to be wrapped, taped, tied with string, and addressed. It was Bill and Fred's job to do the wrapping, taping, and tying. I still see them sitting there making those parcels. Even Papa, who was an expert when it came to parcels, couldn't have done a better job. The children all loved their schools.

How different they were from New Jersey. On the West Coast there were few feelings about Germans and none of the prejudice that Fred and Rosalie had encountered in Long Valley. In Turlock they soon made many friends and their schoolwork was usually outstanding. I never

The neighborhood "gang" at one of our birthday celebrations.

111

tried to push the children, and I emphasized only one rule: that whatever they did, they should do it to the best of their ability. If they did this, they had no reason to be ashamed, no matter what the outcome. John was a particularly good student. He was already a sophomore in High School when we arrived in Turlock, and he was soon made the treasurer of his class, and later elected class president. Anne was also an excellent student. By the time we left Turlock, John had won a scholarship to Wheaton College near Chicago, and Anne had just been accepted there as well. Fred had graduated from his Junior High School as valedictorian.

Nor was I the only member of the family who worked. All of the older children had jobs. John had a very nice position helping with sales at the Turlock Toggery, a men's clothing store. He was now a very smart dresser. How little he resembled the boy who had gotten off the boat four years earlier. Anne was a regular baby sitter for a whole series of families. Bill and Fred both got up very early in the mornings. Bill delivered milk for a dairy and Fred had two paper routes. Fred also cut lawns and raked leaves. During summer vacations most of the boys worked picking peaches, berries, or apricots. In the fall they spent weekends at Wally Lindskoog's hatchery, punching holes into cardboard boxes used to ship turkey chicks. In later years they worked in a local cannery. Even Rosalie helped to sort apricots for drying. While Peter was still too young for a real job, he and some of his friends would go to one of the local packers of cantaloupes and get seconds. These they peddled around town for ten cents a melon. All the children became self reliant and earned their own money. They each had their own savings accounts at a local bank. I told them that any money they earned they could keep for themselves. America quickly turned them into entrepreneurs. Bill even bought his own car when he was old enough to drive. A 1939 black Ford convertible. How proud he was of that car! John spent some of his money on clothes, which he always bought at a discount. And Fred was constantly at the Gatewood's hobby shop buying another airplane kit or engine. Rosalie's weakness was dolls. She had quite a collection of them. I still see her with all her dolls on the bed, instructing them that she was "going out shopping" and that they should "behave" while she was away. How often our words come back to haunt us through our children!

Within the family I tried to keep us on a clear course between our German heritage and the American environment in which we found ourselves. This was not always easy. Particularly for the girls. In their case I was far stricter and more protective than with the boys. At the same time they were also influenced by their peers who came from different backgrounds. Parents of their friends were often more lenient than I was. This could lead to tensions. I remember once Anne asked if she could go to a slumber party. I said, "No!"

She told her friends what my response was. So they came and said, "Please Mrs. Notehelfer, let Anne come." Again I said, "No!" Then Anne said to me, "Mama, do you really know what a slumber party is?" I said, "Yes, you wear sloppy dresses, you let your hair hang down, and you do not care for anything good!" Then all the girls laughed and said, "Oh! No! We eat together; we sleep together; and we have a really good time." I finally said, "O.K., if this is true, Anne can go." Anne packed up her things and reported the next day that she had a wonderful time. We were still poor, and there was not much money for new clothes. Rosalie was too young to feel peer pressure in matters of dress, but Anne did. I remember she once came to me and said that all she ever got was hand-me-downs. All her friends had parents who bought them new clothes. She never got a new dress. So I quickly took her down to a dress shop and bought her a new dress. One she chose herself. And she felt better. Years later in Japan, I remember, Rosalie admired a beautiful dress in a Japanese boutique. She wanted me to buy it for her, but I told her it was too expensive. She suddenly looked at me and said, "No wonder there are so few missionaries, when they can't even afford to buy their children one nice dress!" It was not easy being a missionary's daughter.

Church remained important to us. I still think with pleasure about the fine group of young men who were John's age, and about one older man, Dad Stubbs as everyone called him, who spent much of his time encouraging and leading them. Out of that group came an outstanding set of ministers and businessmen. At a time when Papa was absent, I was especially thankful for this peer group, and for a man who was willing to serve as surrogate father for many of the boys. I know this did much to shape John's later life and his decision to go into the ministry.

While we worked and studied hard, our life in Turlock had other dimensions as well. We often got into that gray 1937 Chevrolet with its dents and went for rides in the countryside. This included trips to Yosemite National Park with its spectacular scenery, and visits to parts of California's "gold country" that was not far distant. There were picnics and lots of invitations from people we came to know. For the children there was usually summer camp which took them to Mission Springs, not far from Santa Cruz, where

Taking a drive in California's "Gold Country" in the 1937 Chevy.

Mama with her "Bavarian Chicken" as it appeared in the Turlock newspaper.

Papa and I lived many years later. This provided some relief from the summer heat of the valley. Occasionally we went there as a family and stayed in a cabin for ten days. "Gramps" was a good driver and he saw to it that his siblings behaved while they were in the car with him. All the children had large groups of friends with whom they played. Like most teenagers there was a lot of strange music, at the time played on small vinyl records. It was not music I liked, or understood. We never had a television set, but some of the children's friends did, so there were invitations to spend the evening and watch. But there were also things I didn't approve. Guns and comic books were two. And I didn't want the children to stay out late. We had clear rules on this, and a strict curfew. If the children were not home by eleven the door was locked. A blanket and pillow were put on the door step. I had to exercise this rule only once when Bill failed to return home on time. But the children were growing up fast. I remember one spring John, Anne, and Bill all went on their first date to a church party that was held at prom-time. They were quite excited. Each dressed in a special way, and the boys bought corsages for their young ladies. As they were leaving and looked so adult, I suddenly burst into tears. John stopped and said, "What's wrong?" I told him between my tears, "I just realized that each of you will marry Americans not Germans!"

I always enjoyed cooking. Often members of the church brought us food. This was particularly true at Thanksgiving. Many of Turlock's farmers prided themselves on their turkeys. The birds they brought were spectacular in size and weight. That made for grand feasts. I even appeared in the Turlock newspaper one day for my cooking. Not for turkey, but for chicken. We sometimes ate what I learned to cook as Russian Chicken, which was a kind of chicken dish with rice, vegetables, and cheese. When I told the newspaper reporter that the dish was called Russian Chicken he looked at me in an odd way. He didn't think the name would do. So we decided that my "Russian Chicken" should be transformed into "Bavarian Chicken." In the midst of the Cold War the people of Turlock were not prepared to eat a Russian dish—even if it had been invented under the Tzar. I chuckled to myself over human foibles and sent a copy of the article to Papa, wondering what his family in Munich would have thought of this "Bavarian" dish.

In 1952 Timothy Pietsch moved out of our Todoroki home into a new house he built in another part of Tokyo. He wanted to lease his Turlock house to a retiring military officer. So in keeping with our original agreement I looked for a new house. I found one for rent on Fourth Avenue that was comfortable and convenient. We moved to our new home that summer. Ever since my days in Mannheim I had always wanted to buy a nice carpet. In fact, when I first came to America, I found it very difficult to walk on people's carpets with my dirty shoes. Coming from Japan, where one always took off one's shoes in the house, walking on carpets with one's shoes seemed very strange to me. Carpets were valuable and should be taken care of. So after saving a little of my own money from my job at the hospital, I bought a lovely carpet for our new living room. I remember how pleased I was when it arrived. But the carpet later became a problem. Papa did not believe that missionaries should have nice things like carpets. He felt that this would be detrimental to our missionary work. And so he wouldn't allow me to take my carpet back to Japan. I finally had to sell it. I could never understand Papa's reasoning on the carpet, especially when Japan itself changed so much after the war and carpets were often found even in Japanese homes.

Still we were all happy to have Papa return to the family just in time for our Christmas celebration in 1952. We had a lovely tree, as always, and he brought lots of interesting presents for the family. The children were growing up fast, in fact, the older ones were no longer children. In looking at our Christmas photo that year I realize now that this was one of the last times we spent Christmas to-gether as a family. The following year Papa and I, and the three youngest of our brood, Fred, Rosalie, and

Christmas 1952 with Papa back from Japan and Annie Erikson (left), Mama's friend from the hospital.

115

Peter, spent Christmas on the ship a few days out of Guam on our way back to Japan. John and Anne were in Chicago at college. Bill was in Milwaukee. It was not until 1959, the year John announced his engagement to Miriam Cover, that we again celebrated Christmas together. Even then Bill was away on military service with the Army in Germany.

When I think of the year 1953 it is still largely a blur. There was so much to do and so much activity. We hoped to leave for Japan by fall. But there was a good deal that had to be done

Anne, Gilbert Moody, and the Yamamotos in 1957.

before we could go. Once again the Covenant Church agreed to underwrite a part of our support. There were also generous individuals, including Sam Yamamoto, a fine Christian of Japanese heritage, and Gilbert Moody, a lawyer who had become a close friend of the family, who offered their personal support. The Scandinavian Alliance, or what was now renamed the Evangelical Alliance Mission's annual meeting was held at Winona Lake that summer. We drove East for the conference. There were many missionaries from around the world in attendance, and I felt both intellectually and spiritually stimulated in hearing about their work. We had decided that Fred, Rosalie, and Peter should return to Japan with us. John and Anne were at college. But this left the question of what to do with Bill? He expressed a wish to stay in America, but the question remained where? We were concerned about a proper home for him. Then a German-American couple in Wisconsin, Bill Scheiterlein and his wife, offered to take him in for his final two years of high school. They had a daughter, but always wanted a son. Mr. Scheiterlein ran a car dealership and Bill was very fond of cars. We felt the Scheiterlein home would provide him with the warmth and discipline he needed, and finally agreed to leave him there. Bill was a hard worker. He had a lovely voice. And he loved sports. In Milwaukee he became an all-city basketball player. Still, I know that his years in Milwaukee were hard. I was never entirely at peace about him at the Scheiterlein's. They were more than generous in taking care of him, and they were truly fine Christian people, but I knew from my own early years that living with others was never like living at home. I still sometimes think we should have taken him with us to Japan. I prayed for him day and night. Then one night the Lord told me to be still and leave the boy alone. He assured me that he was in His hands and would turn out all right. This gave me peace about Bill's future.

Late that summer we went to San Francisco and were formally naturalized as American Citizens. I had been studying carefully for my examination, and I recall the judge asked me a number of questions about the American government, which I answered to his satisfaction. Papa also seemed to satisfy the judge and he congratulated us on becoming American citizens. I thought about the past five years and how much generosity we had been shown in America. I also thought of my children, two of whom were able to go to college, and the opportunities that stood before them. I felt both proud and thankful that the Lord had led us to this country. At the same time I was ready to go back to Japan. I felt my life divided into three parts, and three identities. There were my German roots, and my family still in Germany. Then there were my years in Japan and my love for the Japanese people and God's work there. Finally, there was that third of me that was now formally American, and that represented the future of my children who would always reside there.

In the fall of 1953 we made a final trip East, visiting a variety of churches and speaking about our work in Japan. We visited John and Anne in Chicago and saw Bill in his new home in Milwaukee. Peter went with us. Fred and Rosalie remained in Turlock. Then came the final push to pack and get ready for Japan. The church held a big farewell party for us and people brought us all kinds of things they thought would be useful in Japan. We still needed to take a good deal of our own food, so there was a lot of buying and crating, including a new refrigerator and washing machine. I remember that when everything was ready there was a whole truck-load of barrels and crates. One of the members of the church kindly took them to San Francisco. Now it was time for us to say our final goodbye's. A group of friends came to the pier to watch our Bear Line freighter pull away from the wharf on December 10th. It was a cool but sunny day. As our ship made its way towards the Golden Gate Bridge, the sun moved behind it. The bridge was completely silhouetted and dark so that we could not see its color. Then, when we passed under it, and came out on the Pacific side, we could see it behind us wonderfully lit up in the rays of the setting sun. I thought of our own golden years in America and of the great kindnesses we had received there. I also thought of the challenges that lay ahead. Once again my life confronted change. In twenty four hours I would turn fifty. I always thought this would be something to celebrate. But in the rush to leave there had been no time. Now we would be alone heading out into the Pacific. Still I was thankful. I had spent five years in Canaan, the land of plenty, and was about to return to a land that I had last seen in ashes. I had to leave half my family behind. The words of the song that had been sung at our parting suddenly came back to me as if they echoed off the beautiful bridge, "God be with you till we meet again!"

Chapter Eleven
Japan Again & Germany

When we left San Francisco on December tenth we thought we might be in Japan for Christmas. But one of the interesting things about traveling by freighter is that you never quite know when or where you will arrive. At the last moment our ship was loaded with the Christmas mail for Guam. So rather than take the usual northern route across the Pacific, we headed south. Before long we could see the Southern Cross at night. We could also see flying fish, and some of these landed on deck. Now I felt I was in the *Nanyō* again. We crossed the International Date Line on Christmas day. Going from East to West you loose a day. This meant no Christmas, but the Captain made certain that we all got to celebrate our lost Christmas with a festive dinner, and we had our family Christmas on the twenty-fourth. We didn't arrive in Agana, Guam until two days later. I thought of all those families whose Christmas cards and parcels were still in the hold.

Guam was delightfully warm. The red hibiscus was blooming profusely everywhere and one really had a sense of being in the tropics. Our car was unloaded to get at the rest of the cargo. This meant we could use it, so we drove around the island and visited various beaches. In getting ready to go to Japan we had worked continuously with almost no time off that summer. Now we were presented with a Christmas gift. A week on Guam with nothing to do. What a pleasant vacation! The island still showed some of the scars of war, but nature was rapidly covering them. Guam in 1953 retained the quiet, almost sleepy, quality of the South Pacific islands I had experienced earlier on Truk. To be certain the U.S. Navy was there, and we saw some jeeps and cars, but life for the natives was still simple, and I thought of my years on Mortlock. How things have changed since then. Guam is now full of hotels and tourists. Modern life has caught up with the South Pacific. Today the Liebenzell Mission flies its missionaries to the islands where I was stationed by plane from Guam. I think of my boys and their canoe. Now I would be arriving on distant atolls like Etal in a float plane.

From Guam we headed north towards Japan. The weather changed and a cold wind now blew on deck keeping us inside. We reached Kobe at the end of the first week in January. Here, too, the most obvious scars of war were gone and there was a great deal of new construction. Already the stores and arcades were filled with goods, particularly those catering to foreigners who visited the port. I was fond of Kobe. Like Yokohama it preserved more of an international flavor than other Japanese cities. I looked at the people. They still seemed poorer than in the 1930s, but they were all busy and active. Many of the clothes they wore were old and worn, but they were clean and neatly pressed. I noticed that nothing was wasted. I observed a

Guam reminded Mama of Mortlock.

man picking up all the dropped cigarette butts on the street and carefully preserving the tobacco. There were a few beggars, but they were mostly veterans in their white clothing and caps. It was really a pity to see these men, who had often lost a limb in the fighting, sitting on the streets, with a small plate of ten yen coins before them playing their doleful harmonicas. Few people paid attention to them. I thought of those proud soldiers who had lined Meiji Shrine in the forties. How they had been cheered when they went off to war. Now they were like the memory of a bad dream that everyone wanted to forget. For Papa these were familiar sights, but for me and the children, it was our first real look at the new Japan that was emerging after the war. As we walked down the Kobe streets, a suicide occurred right before us. A man jumped out of a high-rise building. A crowd quickly formed. The police covered the body with a blanket. I don't think I ever saw a man kill himself like that. Sometimes I had been on a train in Japan when someone had jumped in front of it, but as a passenger I had never seen the body. I thought of the hopelessness that this man must have felt, and the need for God's message of hope and love that could turn around lives. Suddenly the mission ahead seemed once again clear. So much remained to be done!

We reached Yokohama a few days later. Our ship did not dock at the pier and we had to unload all our goods into a lighter while we took a water taxi to shore. Yokohama was already so rebuilt that it was hard to recognize. At the time of our departure bulldozers were razing what was left of the destroyed buildings. Here was a whole new city. A few of the old buildings were still standing near the waterfront, but they had been rebuilt on the inside; the rest were largely new. There were many freighters in the harbor, and much truck traffic ashore. One sensed that the Japanese economy was improving and that goods were beginning to be sent abroad again. In the shipyards near our landing point several large new vessels were under construction and there was noise and activity everywhere.

When we left Japan the U.S. Army had been prominent. There were always military personnel to be seen, particularly in Yokohama, but this was now all changed. Once again Japanese officials were in charge. The San Francisco Peace Treaty had been signed between the United States and Japan in 1951, and in April 1952 Japan became an independent nation. By the time we arrived in January 1954 the American presence was largely confined to military bases that had been agreed to in the Mutual Security Treaty that joined both nations. The officials, I must add, were extremely polite and courteous. We passed through immigration and customs without any difficulties. Our arrival in Yokohama was greeted by a group of old friends who welcomed our return, and by evening we found ourselves back in our Todoroki home. The house was little changed and the neighborhood still looked much the same. I suddenly felt quite at home again. Almost as if I hadn't been away for five years. The next day we had a great winter storm and there was heavy snow on the ground. I remember Papa ordered Japanese noodles, *soba*, from the local noodle shop, because our stove was not yet up and running. How good those steaming hot noodles tasted as we looked out over the snow in the garden.

The snowstorm that welcomed us back to Todoroki.

We soon readjusted to life in Tokyo. The children entered their new school, the American School in Japan, which was located in Naka-Meguro, only four stops by train from Jiyūgaoka towards Shibuya. It was just the

120

end of the first semester and I remember the children had to struggle a bit to make up for the time they had lost in packing and travelling to Japan. In those days the American School was small but very good. The children soon got over the problems of their initial adjustment and made many friends. There were excellent teachers at the school in the mid-1950s, and they were dedicated to furthering the preparatory educations of their students. I always attribute Fred's matriculation at Harvard College in 1957 to the hard work of his teachers. Peter loved to sing, and was in a series of school musicals. Mr. Berger, one of his teachers, strongly encouraged the

Peter, Rosalie & Fred at the American School.

development of his voice, and when Peter graduated in 1961 he received a scholarship to attend the Julliard School of Music in New York. Rosalie finished her high school work in California, in 1959, when we were home on furlough, but her preparation for college at Westmont in Santa Barabara was also largely established during these Tokyo years.

Japan had certainly changed since the prewar days. Mission work was now much easier, and soon we once again had meetings in our house. Papa continued his work with the Todoroki church and with the church he had helped to establish at Kitazawa during the Occupation years. The mission continued to rely on him to find housing for new missionaries and to see them settled into Japan. T.J. Back, the former TEAM Director, once referred to him as "a missionary to missionaries." And this he was. I also returned to Japan with new ideas. The role of women, I noticed, was changing. The kimono clad retiring housewife whose life had been confined to home and family in the 1930s was undergoing significant changes. The war had propelled Japanese women into more public roles and aroused a great curiosity among them. This curiosity took new dimensions in the postwar years. Certainly a genuine interest in the West now stood at a peak. And even in my neighborhood I sensed a renewed interest in Christian ideas and values. My own experiences in the United States had given me a new vision as well. So I though of a way to reach these women around me that could utilize my

Mama with her cooking circle ladies on an outing.

skills. I had never mastered Japanese to the degree that I could intellectually convince them of the truth of Christianity. But I was a good cook, and I knew that the women of the neighborhood were interested in Western cooking so I began to organize a cooking circle that allowed me to reach many of the new arrivals who moved to Todoroki in the postwar years. Through this circle I was able to help a surprisingly large number of women, who came not only to cook, but to study the Bible and to share their family concerns with me. What fun we had, and what fellowship! I can still see them sitting there in my kitchen and dining room, Mrs. Akagi, Mrs. Kato, Mrs. Tsukuda, and several other ladies, all of whom became active Christians, and virtually all of whom were instrumental in leading their husbands and children to become believers as well. Of course I continued to work actively with Papa in the churches we built, but I always felt that this was my own special work that the Lord gave me in Japan. I also had many meetings for students in our house that focused on the English and German Bible.

Just before I left America, I was presented with a real surprise. In Turlock I had come to know an elderly lady, Mrs. Moody, whose son was a lawyer. I used to visit her regularly, and we sometimes spoke of our families and childhoods. She knew that I had not seen my mother since 1930. One day her son asked me to check on the cost of flying home to Germany. I paid little attention to his suggestion. But he repeated it. Then his mother said to me, "Didn't Gilbert ask you to find out how much it would cost to go to Germany?" I said, "Yes, but I didn't know if he meant it." She said, "When my son says something he always means it!" I was quite ashamed. At the same time I was excited. The thought of going home was wonderful. I said to Papa, "Can you ask about the cost?" He smiled at me, and said quietly, "We are now getting ready to go to Japan. We need you to go with us. This just won't work. You have to forget about Germany." I knew he was right. I started packing. Then one day out in the garage, a thought flashed into my mind. "Perhaps Mr. Moody would be willing to pay my way from Japan to Germany." I tried this out on Papa. He once again smiled in that quiet way, and said, "Do you know how expensive it is to fly from Tokyo to Frankfurt! You must be a little crazy." I replied, "It wouldn't hurt to ask." "If you are daring enough," he said, "then please do." I screwed up my courage, called Mrs. Moody and told her my idea. To my surprise she said without hesitating, "Oh, sure, that will be all right with my son. Go ahead and plan your trip." Now I was really excited! I looked forward to seeing my family again! I finished my packing for Japan with new joy.

Shortly after arriving in Japan, Papa did not feel well. He needed a hernia operation and I thought I would not be able to leave for Germany in the near future. I therefore put my plans on hold. But he recovered quickly and the doctor assured me that he was all right. Knowing that he felt better, I asked Papa to inquire at the Pan American office about the airfare to Germany. He reported that the trip would cost $1150. I said, "Papa this is too much money. I never had a thousand dollars in my life. Spending that much money on me is not right!" So I wrote to Mr. Moody, and told him to forget the trip, it was just too expensive. He wrote back, "Dear Mrs. Notehelfer, I didn't ask you for advice, I asked you how much it costs!" Then I heard nothing further, until one day a telegram arrived at the house. It was from the Pan American office in Tokyo and said, "Your roundtrip ticket to Germany has been paid for in full. Please come to the office to make your reservations." What a surprise! So on May ninth of 1954, Mothers Day I remember, I got on a plane at Tokyo's Haneda Airport bound for Germany. It was now twenty-four years since I had seen my mother and sisters.

Mama leaving Haneda Airport on her trip to Germany in 1954.

The trip is still clearly etched on my mind. This was the first time I had ever gone by air. The plane was a Pan American round-the-world clipper. We left Tokyo in the middle of the night. What a sight the city was as we climbed. The lights looked like a fireworks

123

display, only stationary. It was truly spectacular. Soon we were flying in the dark. By 5:30 the sun came up. I could see lots of clouds. Breakfast was served at 7:30. Flying in those days was still romantic and there was some elegance even in coach. My breakfast was not only delicious, it was beautifully served. How different from today's planes. We landed at Hong Kong at 9:30 in the morning. I had been worried about becoming airsick. But flying was much better than being on the ocean. Nothing like the sailboat on Mortlock.

In Hong Kong we were taken by bus to the Peninsula Hotel. We had free time until 12:30. I felt a little lonesome, as I knew no one. But there was a very nice Chinese fellow travelling to Bangkok who asked me if I would like to go downtown with him. I was glad for the invitation. Hong Kong in 1954 was quite fascinating. In those days it was known as the "Pearl of the Orient" and the "Riviera of the East." The old and the new appeared to blend harmoniously in the city. Handmade products stood alongside those produced by factories and machines. You could get anything you wanted. My eyes caught sight of a little girl about six or seven who was sitting with her grandmother on one side of the street stitching a lovely embroidery. It was a joy to see how those little fingers mastered the needle. She made such beautiful stitches. The stores downtown were filled to overflowing with splendid products from all over the world. I thought, "No wonder all the wealthy people go to Hong Kong to shop! Here those with money can find anything they want."

Mama being served dinner aboard the airplane.

At one-thirty our plane took off for Bangkok. The clouds on this part of the trip looked like a great white snow-field. They were so bright that looking out the window hurt one's eyes. Some clouds looked like great volcanoes that rose higher and higher. I wondered how our plane could cut through them. But we landed safely at Bangkok. Bangkok was hot, 106 degrees, and I thought of Truk. While we were having refreshments in the airport, I had a chance to chat with four or five young Americans. An English lady listening to what I said to them of God's care, told me that her husband had been killed in the war by the Japanese and that she had been robbed several times. She wondered if God was watching over her as well, given everything that had happened to her.

From Bangkok our plane headed for New Delhi. Around me sat six young Indian girls on their way to school. They were all from upper-class Indian families. One was the daughter of the Indian Ambassador to England, another was the daughter of an Indian foreign officer in Bangkok. Most were being separated from their families for the first time. They were rather blue and I tried to cheer them up thinking of my own early days away from home. As we flew over the Indian Ocean the sun dressed the clouds in beautiful purple and pink robes. Then, as it began to set, it seemed to form a golden door that made me wonder what heaven must be like. I thought, "Oh! What magnificent beauty is all round us!" We reached Delhi late that evening and the girls got off. They had smiles for me and said "We love you," as they left.

We flew on to Karachi which we reached in the wee hours of the morning. I only recall that it was stiflingly hot and sultry. Everything looked awfully dirty. Some rather rough-looking Pakistani men got on the plane on their way to London to seek work. It was obvious that this was also their first flight. I had to show my neighbor how to put on his seat-belt. He didn't speak much English, so I spent my time looking out the window at the scenery below. Our route next took us over the Persian Gulf. Not long thereafter the steward announced that we were flying over the Garden of Eden. I looked down. All I could see was a desolate and bleak looking landscape. Flying over Syria I knew we were close to Israel, and I thought of all that I had read about the Holy Land. Our next stop was Lebanon. We landed at Beirut, which is beautifully situated on the Eastern edge of the Mediterranean. But we stopped only long enough to refuel. Then it was off to Istanbul. When I was a child we called it Constantinople. Looking down from the air, it reminded me of San Francisco which is also built on hills. After landing our passports were carefully inspected by the Turkish officials. They were fierce-looking men who reminded me of my childhood picture books. I had always feared Turks as a child. Now, even their language struck me as rough and harsh.

Finally we were off again. In the distance I could see the Danube. As children we had sometimes swum in this beautiful river. Soon I could look down on the little villages of Yugoslavia lit up in the light of the setting sun. Before long the steward announced we were over Belgrade. I knew that we were now close to home. It took only a couple of hours for us to reach Germany and land at Frankfurt. My whole trip from Japan had taken less than

Mama Leaving Munich for Switzerland on her trip to Germany.

forty-eight hours. How different from the three weeks it took me to reach Japan in 1930.

At the Frankfurt Airport I went through immigration. What an odd feeling to return to one's native country as the citizen of another land. This was only the second time I had used my American passport. It still gave me an odd feeling, especially here in Germany. But I had little time for sentimental thoughts. As I entered the waiting room someone was already calling my name. Several people were waving in my direction, but I didn't know who they were. Then I spotted Tante Lydia among them. She quickly introduced me to the others. These included Papa's brother Hans and his sister Emmi. I had never met them before, although we had corresponded for years. They had kindly come all the way to Frankfurt to welcome me.

The next day began a three month flurry of activity that took me all over Germany and Switzerland. Starting in Frankfurt with Tante Lydia and her family, I went on to Mannheim to visit my Aunt. I thought I knew the Mannheim station and its exits from my earlier stay there, but to my surprise I could not find the exit I wanted. It no longer existed, having been bombed away in the war. Finally I made my way out to the right spot. There I saw two men standing in conversation. I recognized one as the preacher of the church that I used to attend. I stood nearby waiting for them to finish speaking. But they kept right on. Finally one of them said to me, are you looking for someone? I smiled and said, "Mr. Staeger, don't you recognize me!" He said, "No, I really don't. Who are you?" I replied, "I've just come from Japan." "Oh," he said, "You are Mrs. Notehelfer! We are here waiting for you." The other man was the father of one of my fellow missionaries on the South Pacific. He had a car and took me all over the city.

From Mannheim I went back to Frankfurt and flew to Stuttgart, where my sisters and their families were waiting. We drove to Ulm. The drive took about three hours. It was delightful. Nature had put on her most beautiful garments for me. Everywhere the fruit trees were in bloom, the flowers were splendid, and the birds were singing. It was spring, always one of the most beautiful seasons in Germany, and it felt so good to be home after twenty-four years. The following day we went to Bernstadt. How shall I describe the joy

I felt at seeing my mother again. She had been blind now nearly thirty years. At first we could say little and simply cried together. But soon mother was her old self. She took me by the shoulders and said, "What is the matter with you anyway? Couldn't you bring your husband with you? He has been away for twenty-five years. Don't you think he would like to come home too! Poor fellow! If you couldn't bring him, you should have stayed with him. Don't you think so?"

Well, I didn't think so. I told her I was glad I could come. For missionaries, I assured her, it was not so strange to be separated for a while. I said, "next time, he may come, and I may stay at home!" This seemed to comfort her and she was truly glad to have me home. I only felt bad that there was not more time to spend with her. There were so many visitors that it was hard to have private moments. I also was called away for many meetings.

I was surprised that Bernstadt had changed very little in the years of my absence. The first evening the young people came with their brass band and played all the songs they knew for me. Then the women came, the ones with whom I had gone to school forty years earlier, and every one brought a little present. They were gaily dressed in the familiar village costume, still worn by the older women on special occasions. In the skirts of this costume there is a big pocket which is covered by a large silk apron. All of a sudden they reached into these pockets and brought forth the presents. I inwardly smiled at the gifts. One gave me ten eggs. Another some sausage. Then there was also

Bernstadt in 1954.

127

Liebenzell Mission House.

butter from a third, and a piece of meat from another. We talked till well past midnight about all the things that had happened in the years since I had left. The next day the policeman went around with his bell and announced that I would speak that evening. So many came that the church was full to overflowing. Often they would say, "Hello, Rose, How are you?" And I would have to say, "Who are you? I don't remember your name." "Oh, sure you do," they would reply, "We went to school together," or "We used to play together as children." There was a lot of rejoicing on both sides.

Of course I also went to Bad Liebenzell. The mission always has a big conference at Pentecost when six to eight thousand visitors gather there. In 1930 I had been ordained at this meeting, and now it was my privilege to speak about my life and work on the islands and in Japan. I was pleased to see the renewed interest in missions and happy to see the mission once again in good hands and continuing its work at home and abroad. In the wake of my presentation at Liebenzell I was swamped with invitations for speaking engagements. I tried to accommodate as many as I could, but there was little time. Between these meetings, I made an effort to be with mother and family as much as possible, though even here it was difficult to please everyone.

I visited Papa's family in Munich for a week. This allowed me to meet not only his brother and sisters but many of the friends with whom we had corresponded for years. It was certainly a pleasure to put real faces to the photographic images with which I

Mama traveling with her niece Marga.

had lived for a long time. On the fifth of August I said goodbye to those dear people in Munich. Many of them came to the airfield to see me off on my way to Switzerland. I spent some time in Zurich and at Beatenberg on the Thuner Lake where I attended a missionary summer conference. I also had a chance to get

Zurich, Switzerland.

together with an old friend from Truk. My schedule was arranged to have me leave Zurich for Rome on the tenth of August, but when I went to the Pan American office to confirm my flight I was in for a big shock. The company claimed they had no record of my reservation, which I had made in Munich at the end of May. The staff insisted that there was no record of my booking. Moreover, the young lady at the office told me that there would be no possibility of getting a flight before October. I could hardly believe my ears. But she insisted that this was true. What was I to do?

Faced with this dilemma, I decided to return to Bern and the mission home in which I was staying. At first I thought there is nothing I can do but wait. Then I realized there was something more that I could do. I decided to pray. I told the Lord that I knew that he could find a way for me to return to Japan before October. And I trusted him to do so. I also decided that if I had to wait, it would be best to return to Germany. So I went once more to the Pan American office in Zurich to tell the company that if there was no flight open in the next few days, I would go back to Germany. Just as I was telling the young lady at the desk of my decision, the phone rang and she answered it. The call was from a man who had booked a flight from Frankfurt to Hong Kong on the fifteenth of August. He informed the office that he would have to cancel his reservation. "Praise the Lord," I said, "he has answered my prayers." So I back-tracked to Frankfurt and caught the plane for Hong Kong on the fifteenth. The route we flew was the reverse of that by which I had come, and I managed to reach Hong Kong by the afternoon of the seventeenth.

Because food was still so expensive in Japan, Papa and I had planned for me to buy food in Hong Kong and bring it to Japan by ship. Unfortunately the ship on which Papa had booked reservations for me departed from Hong

Kong the day before my arrival. The Apostle said "Give thanks to the Lord for everything," so I did, especially for bringing me back safely. A German missionary lady who worked with the blind in a special home in Hong Kong was waiting for me. She took me to her mission compound, where I saw the impressive work in which she was engaged. I was wondering how I could book passage to Japan, when the following day I met a pastor and his wife from the Swedish Lutheran church, Mr and Mrs. Anderson, who were visiting their children in Hong Kong. They told me they were going to Japan on a Norwegian freighter that Saturday, the twenty-first of August. I immediately called the shipping line and was told that the ship was all booked. The agent told me, however, that there was one man who was still uncertain if he could go. I asked the Lord to take care of this matter, and he did, for the next day I got a phone call asking me to come down to the office at once. When I arrived I heard the good news that I could have the cabin, as the original passenger had cancelled. Once again I thanked God, and quickly arranged for the delivery of the food I had purchased.

We left Hong Kong as scheduled on the twenty-first. The Andersons were pleasant travelling companions and we had a wonderful trip to Japan. The weather was perfect. It was the smoothest sea voyage I have ever taken. On August twenty-sixth we reached Yokohama. There Papa awaited me. I introduced him to the Andersons who were going on to the United States. Then we arranged for the transportation of my shipment of food and went home to Todoroki. Fred, Rosalie, and Peter were still in Karuizawa, so the following day I went up to the mountains to see them. What a joy it was to be back together again. And what an adventure I had been through.

My mother died a few years later and I was so glad that Mr. and Mrs. Moody had made it possible for me to see her one last time. We often forget the burden that distant mission work imposes on families, and on those who remain at home. Growing up without relatives in a foreign land, is the price we demand of our children. Missionary children are often fiercely independent. Many, as was true of mine, go on to important public careers. But they rarely develop the kind of close ties that my fellow villagers and family had in Bernstadt. I realized that in one way what had happened to me, was also happening to my children. While I remained close to my family, that closeness was affected by distance. It was only wonderful moments like the one I had just experienced that allowed me to break through the effects of time and space that increasingly separated us. When I think about my mother's questions about Papa today I sense that she saw this in me. I too had become independent in my own way. When I saw in my children the same qualities, it gave me the sense of looking at myself in a mirror. I sometimes wished that things were different. But our life experiences mold each of us in different ways.

A Paper Theater, or *Kamishibai*, man telling his story to children in Tokyo.

Chapter Twelve
A New Work

After my return from Germany, Papa decided to start a new work near Mizonoguchi. He still enjoyed interacting with rural people. New opportunities presented themselves in the Tama River valley. This region had once been largely agricultural, but was now being urbanized by Tokyo's postwar expansion. Todoroki itself reflected the massive growth that marked the age. What had been a quiet rural setting with a few modern houses before the war mushroomed into a major residential district. New houses were built all around us, and many newcomers moved into the area. Denenchōfu, Jiyūgaoka, and Todoroki became preferred addresses for Tokyo's upwardly mobile professionals. Before the war, the little blue and yellow train that ran through the town terminated a few stops beyond Todoroki at Mizonoguchi. In those days Mizonoguchi had served as the last urban outpost. Beyond it there were only small villages. But as the population of Tokyo began to push out from the center, the railway was extended and soon stretched well beyond the Tama River. Improved communications began to open up new sites for Tokyo's land-hungry citizens. The district we selected for our postwar efforts was therefore interesting in that it still retained its rural roots but was rapidly being transformed into one of Tokyo's outlying suburbs. The people we encountered there were also a mixture of former agriculturalists and more recent urban dwellers. The mix proved to be a positive one. There was a

Papa using *Kamishibai* with children in the 1930s.

genuine openness to new ideas as the arch conservatism of the traditional village gave way to urban intellectual patterns. Christianity was often welcomed as part of this changing environment.

In 1956 we began the process of building a new church at a small town named Shinjo in the Tama River valley. As in previous instances Papa and I began with the young people of the region. We often used *kamishibai* to reach the children. *Kamishibai*, literally means "paper plays," or a "paper theater." This type of storytelling was extremely popular in Japan just before and after the war. What it consisted of were pictures mounted on cardboard sheets that went into a wooden box open at the front. As the first sheet was removed, the next scene was revealed. Stories might include as many as ten to twenty scenes. In the days before television, children just loved to gather for such presentations. In many parts of Tokyo there were professional *kamishibai* entertainers who gathered children together, told them stories, and sold them a few candies while the narrative was in progress. These men often went around on bicycles, and mounted their wooden stage on the back. Even before the war Papa thought that *kamishibai* could serve as an interesting way to reach children. Immediately after the war he had a Japanese artist, Mr. Yoshioka, produce a series of delightful illustrations for Bible stories. I recall that the stories dealing with Noah's Ark and Moses were always in high demand.

Kamishibai scene of Baby Moses being discovered in the basket by the daughter of Pharaoh painted by Mr. Yoshioka.

Papa also held street meetings, and we often used our tent. Sometimes, the more traditionally minded villagers opposed our meetings. I remember on one occasion Papa set up our tent in a village near a hospital. The day before the meetings were to open the tent lay on the ground. Someone had loosened all the ropes and broken the main poles. Papa and his Japanese assistant worked hard to fix the poles and put the tent up once more. To assure that this would not happen again he slept in the tent that night. The meetings started on schedule and were well attended. On the third or fourth night, a young man came forward. He said that he had a confession to make. He was opposed to Christianity, and when he saw the tent go up and heard that meetings would be held there, he decided to take matters into his own hands. He loosened the ropes and knocked the tent down. But when it was put up again and he saw that many people attended, he became curious. Hearing the singing he decided to come in. After listening the first night he returned. Hearing the preacher for three nights, he realized that he had been wrong, and wanted to let us know that he was sorry. He even said that if we wanted to call the police and report him, he was prepared to face his punishment. We had no intention of doing so, and gave him a

Bible and prayed with him. Later he became one of the most faithful members of our new church.

Mama and a group of children at a tent meeting in Shinjo.

With time we hoped to find a more permanent site for our expanding church, but there were few available buildings. One particularly cold and windy day Papa and his assistant were conducting an open air service. A man watched them. After the meeting was over, he came to Papa and said, "It is awfully cold out here. Wouldn't you like to use my Judo hall for your services in the future?" Papa and I were delighted with his offer, and so for several years we had our meetings in this man's Judo hall. But before long the Judo hall became too small for the number of people attending, and we needed a larger space. We wanted to build a church building in Shinjo, but we just couldn't find an available piece of land. The region was changing rapidly and land was much in demand for housing. Few landlords were willing to part with their land as they saw prices increasing rapidly. So the door remained closed in Shinjo. But not long thereafter we heard of an opportunity in the town of

Nakahara which was not far from Shinjo. In fact, in Nakahara we were offered a building that had a prominent local history. It had started as the town's fire station. Later it served as its Police Headquarters. And finally it had been the telephone office. Papa and his co-worker did a wonderful job in rebuilding the existing space into a very handsome meeting hall. The people from Shinjo were happy to have a new church home and all attended our services at the new site. We used this building for years as our church. Indeed, our new church was still located there at the time of our departure from Japan in 1965. It was only after we left that the congregation was able to purchase its own land and build a new church building at Shibonoguchi— a church that remains active to this day.

While I worked with Papa in our new church and shared his concerns for finding a new home for our congregation, missionary work for me involved more than buildings and meetings. Of course I knew that these were necessary, but for me God worked in people's lives. People came first. Even when it came to matters of faith, I always thought that belief was a very personal thing. I could show others the way, and I could pray, but they had to follow their own path. God had to do his work in their lives, as he had done in mine. I still remember a woman in Todoroki who demonstrated this to me. One night, it was still hot, and we had recently returned from Karuizawa. I had all the windows of the house open. In the middle of the night I heard a woman sobbing. She was crying bitterly. I got up and went to the window. The sound was coming from just beyond our back yard. I awoke Papa and said, "There is a woman out there crying, can I go and look after her?" Papa said, "You can't go at midnight to other people's houses, wait until tomorrow!" I stayed where I was, but I started to pray for this woman. I said, "Dear Lord, if I can be of help to this woman, send her to me." Early the next morning, just after breakfast, two women came to the house. I recognized one of them. She attended my Bible class. But I didn't know the other. I opened the door and welcomed them. The lady from my Bible Class, Mrs. Kato, said "Mrs. Notehelfer may I introduce Mrs. Aoyagi to you, she is the wife of a professor who teaches at a Tokyo university." I bowed to her and said, "Oh, where do you live?" She said, "Right at the end of your back yard. We just moved in this summer." I said, "How interesting. Last night I heard a woman crying bitterly nearby, do you know who that woman could be?" She started to cry, and said, "I am that woman."

We had been standing in the entryway. I opened the door to our living room and said, "Please come in. You see, I prayed that God should send you to me. You are clearly in need of help." She then told me how hard it was to live with her husband. He drank a good deal and when he was intoxicated he would beat her, and often ejected her from their house. Last night he had been drinking, and had hit her, and thrown her out. When I heard her, she had been out in her back garden crying. I asked her whether she was a Christian and knew that God could help her. She said no. So I asked her to come to the house every day. She came each morning at ten and we started to read the Gospel of John together. She was very open and interested in what we were reading. When we reached the sixth chapter of John, I got rather scared. In this chapter Christ says "I am the bread of life" and "you must eat me." How was I to explain this to a woman who had been raised in such a different culture? I told her that I could not meet with her on Monday, because this was the Mission's day of prayer, which we always attended, but that I would see her again on Tuesday. "In the meantime," I said, "Please read the sixth chapter of John while I am away."

We prayed for her at our meeting. She came the next day, Tuesday, and I saw right away that something had happened to her because her whole face was shining. She said, "You know, I was reading this chapter and the Lord Jesus said in it, 'I am the bread of life!' I know that bread is made to be eaten. If I leave it sitting on the table it is no use to me. So, I said, 'I have to take the bread. I have to believe in Jesus Christ!' And I started to pray that the Lord should really take me in. It was as if an electric shock went through my whole body. I knew that Jesus Christ was real. My heart was filled with joy and peace. I no longer fear my husband."

From that day on she set aside an hour every evening when she would sit down with her children to read the Bible and pray. One night her husband came home and saw them sitting there praying. He became very angry and picked up the lid of the brass kettle that was on the *hibachi* to throw at her. But just as he was about to throw the lid, he suddenly dropped it and clutched his hand. A bee had stung him in the hand. The pain caused him to drop the lid. The next day his hand was so badly swollen that he had to go to the doctor. In the evening, when he came home, he brought his wife flowers for the first time and asked her for forgiveness. From that day forward he never harmed her again. Later the family moved to Okinawa, and I heard little more about them, but it was wonderful to see how God worked in their lives and helped her to overcome her problems with her husband. They were a happy family thereafter and I was truly thankful. I never heard her cry again.

With the growth of the city, new families regularly arrived in our neighborhood. One of these moved into the house that had belonged to the Nakamura sisters in the late 1930s. The new family's name was Akagi. Mr. Akagi was an executive in the Japan Express Company, Japan's leading transport firm. Mrs. Akagi was a high level flower arrangement teacher in the modernist Sōgetsu school of flower arrangement developed by Teshigahara Sōfū. They had three children, two sons and a daughter. Like most Japanese families, the Akagi's wanted their eldest son, Kenichi, to attend a first-rate university. This meant placing well on the notoriously difficult university entrance examinations. Kenichi was artistically gifted, like his mother, but had difficulty with English. So Mrs. Akagi came to see me one day to inquire whether I might be able to help Kenichi with his English. I agreed to do this. Kenichi regularly came to the house and I went over some readings with him. Then he became a regular member of my Bible Study class that included a number of university students. A little later Kenichi told his mother that she should attend my ladies meetings.

While I had set up a new series of meetings in Shinjo, I also continued my earlier ladies circle in Todoroki. At first Mrs. Akagi thought that due to her very demanding schedule she would have no time for these meetings, but after attending a few, she became really interested and came on a regular basis. One day I spoke to the ladies about prayer. I said that it was wonderful that we have a living God who hears our prayers and knows our needs. "Last Wednesday," I told them, " I was so very tired, and I went into my kitchen, and I said 'Oh, God in heaven give me strength so that I can make it through this day.' And God gave me new strength. I had two meetings that day and I came home so happy and full of joy for the strength He gave me." A few days later, Mrs. Akagi came over. I was out in the garden. She hugged me, which Japanese almost never do, and said, "Oh, Mrs. Notehelfer, it works! It works! I said, "What works?" "Your prayer," she said, "it works!" "My prayer?," I asked, not certain to what she was referring. "Have you forgotten what you told me?," she said, "How you went into your kitchen and lifted up your hands in prayer to God. Every morning, when I get up, I go out on the balcony of our house, and I lift up my hands and say, 'You true and Living God, You God of Mrs. Notehelfer, help me for today and give me strength for today. And I get the strength, and I am not so tired any more, and I am really happy!"

Thereafter she became a central figure in my ladies circle.

Mr. and Mrs. Akagi.

She started to read the Bible with her other children and asked us to pray for her husband. He was away from home a great deal due to his official duties and often had to live away from the family for considerable periods of time. This life of separation was hard on Mrs. Akagi and the children. But through her and her son's efforts he too became a Christian not long thereafter. Kenichi graduated from Japan's Fine Arts Academy. Her husband was soon reposted to Tokyo. And with time the whole family became a pillar of our church. I still remember that when I left Japan in 1965, it was Mrs. Akagi who dedicated herself to carrying on my work with the women's circle. There is nothing that could have made me happier. Above all, I was pleased when the work, we as outsiders started, was taken over by the Japanese themselves. This was always our goal in the churches we established. Missionaries by their very nature can serve only as temporary sojourners. The seed may be planted by them, but the tree that forms from it must have its roots in domestic soil. Still the world we live in is truly diverse. Kenichi later came to the United States, married a lovely American girl, and works as a designer in the computer industry in Colorado today.

There was another neighboring family that also showed me we are only the catalysts in the process by which God works. Just to the right of the path that led to our front door stood a large field. This was usually used by one of the local farmers to grow vegetables. In autumn there were often heads of cabbage growing in this field. Before the war we had been surrounded by such truck-farm patches, but many of them were now surveyed and staked-off for new houses. One of these was built right beside our front driveway in this field. We didn't know who the owners were, but when the house was completed and the family moved in, the first thing we heard were Christian hymns being sung by two girls. The family's

Student Meeting at the Todoroki House.

137

My Ladies gather at our house in Todoroki for Christmas.

name was Kobayashi. Mr. Kobayashi had been the captain of a Mitsubishi Line freighter. He had recently retired and decided to settle in Todoroki. The girls singing were Yasuko and Kazuko, two of Mr. Kobayashi's daughters. They were both Christians. There was also a son Toru, and another daughter Akiko. Toru was very interested in English, and like Kenichi, came to my Bible classes. One day Mr. Kobayashi came to the house. He told me that he wanted to send Toru to study in the United States, but that Toru needed a sponsor in the U.S. He asked whether I knew a person who could act in such a capacity for his son in America. I told him that we might be able to arrange for such a sponsor, and wrote Gilbert Moody our lawyer friend in Turlock. Mr. Moody was happy to serve as Toru's sponsor, so the young man went to the United States and entered the University of Washington in Seattle. While at the University of Washington he attended a Christian student group and became a believer. Shortly thereafter he wrote to his father of his conversion to Christianity. Mr. Kobayashi brought me Toru's letter and it was clear that he was quite disturbed and angry. He said to me, "I didn't send my son to the United States to have him become a Christian, I sent him to become a good businessman!" I said to him, "Mr. Kobayashi, you have no right to talk like this, because your son really belongs to God, and doesn't belong to you. If he becomes a Christian you can be sure that he will also become a good businessman!"

But Mr. Kobayashi didn't speak to me for a long time thereafter. He was mad at everyone, including me. Then one day half-a-year later he came to the house. It was spring and he asked to borrow our wheel-barrow. He wanted to prepare his garden and needed to haul some earth. I went to the garage to get him the wheel-barrow. Then he suddenly said to me, "Mrs. Notehelfer, I am so sorry that God hates me." I said, "Mr. Kobayashi, you don't even believe in God, how can a God who doesn't exist hate you?" "Oh, no," he said, "deep in my heart I do believe there is a God, but He hates me." I said, "How do you know that God hates you?" "Well," he said, "Every plant, I plant, dies. But when my wife plants it, it does beautifully." "Every seed I put in the ground, fails to sprout! If my wife plants it, it does well!" His wife had come to my Bible Class and had also become a Christian. I said, "Mr. Kobayashi, are you in a hurry? Can you come in for a moment." He said he had time and came into the house. There I read him from Romans Chapter 8, where God says we have all failed and have come short of his glory. And then I read to him from the third chapter of John, substituting Mr. Kobayashi's name for "the world" as I read, "and God so loved Mr. Kobayashi..." He quietly stood up and tears were running down his face. Then he said, "Mrs. Notehelfer, that is too good for me." The next day he came and asked me to give him a New Testament. He wanted his own copy of the Bible. Thereafter he studied the Bible day and night. His wife said to me, "He constantly studies the Bible and makes hundreds of notes." Not long thereafter, I went over to visit his wife one day. While I was there, Mr. Kobayashi suddenly came into the room where we were sitting. His demeanor was entirely different. He was full of joy. And he said, "Oh, Mrs. Notehelfer, for the first time in my life I have peace with God and peace with man." Later that summer I saw Mr. Kobayashi in his garden with some beautiful zinnias he had grown. It seems that even nature and Mr. Kobayashi had come into harmony again.

While many of our neighbors, and some of the members of our new church in Shinjo-Nakahara, reflected the more open values that permeated

Shinjo Church Congregation.

Yone Otomi.

postwar Japan, a number of the Japanese we dealt with in our church experienced severe tensions between their new Christian commitment and the traditional Japanese society in which their family and friends remained rooted. Here I often think of Yone Otomi who was from Hokkaido. Her father was a Buddhist priest and Yone grew up in a strict Buddhist household. From her early years she set out on a spiritual quest, and after a rather troubled childhood, she came to Tokyo to study nursing. She saw nursing as a way to help people. She liked her new profession. At the same time her dedication and hard work made her well-respected among her colleagues. We first met Yone when we had tent meetings in Shinjo. In fact, it was at the same meetings near the hospital that I mentioned earlier. We invited all the nurses to attend those meetings. Yone was one of the nurses who came. Earlier she had been given a Bible by a patient. She had been reading this Bible, so when she came to our meetings she already knew a good deal of scripture. Soon she became a Christian and joined our church. She was always such a cheerful member of our congregation.

Then one day she came and asked us to pray for her. She told us that her father had requested her to return to Hokkaido. He planned to turn his temple over to a young priest and intended to marry her to him. Yone now found herself in a difficult position. She knew that in the traditional society in which her father lived, his request was tantamount to an order. At the same time, she also knew that she could not marry a priest and remain a Christian. She suddenly felt torn between two worlds. After praying with us, she screwed up her courage and went home. There she quietly spoke with her father, telling him that she was a Christian and could not marry his successor at the temple. She spoke with such conviction that the whole family was impressed. Her father said to her, "You may return to Tokyo, but I no longer regard you as my daughter!" Yone was both happy and sad. She had prevailed as a Christian. But she had deeply hurt her father. Her Christian faith had severed her family ties. Later she went to a Christian college and married a preacher. She remained a cheerful person. But I often thought of the sacrifices that individuals are called upon to make in following their faith. I wondered if Yone could return home after twenty-four years, as I had, and I tried to imagine what such a return would be like.

While my church activities occupied a good deal of time, I also had my family to look after. Half of our children remained in America. Those were not yet days when a trip across the Pacific was quick and easy. Neither we, nor they, could afford to fly home, even in the summer. So I felt rather separated from the three older children we had left behind. We tried to keep up a lively correspondence, and I knew my children were in God's hands. I also realized that each of them had set out on his and her own spiritual journey. John had graduated from Wheaton College and decided to become a preacher. That was a special joy for Papa and me. He was now attending Fuller Theological Seminary in Los Angeles, and Anne, who had also gone to Wheaton wanted to pursue a nursing career. She was studying nursing in Chicago. Bill had completed high school in Milwaukee and had decided to perform his military service right after graduation. He was with the Army in Germany. It was interesting to see his response to living in his native land. He was not yet clear on what he wanted to do. I think his years with the Scheiterlein's in Milwaukee had not been easy for him. He was always a gregarious boy, but like many a teenager he wrestled with his identity. In one sense the Army was good for him, it allowed him to come to grips with himself in a structured environment. I think my children will agree that I rarely gave them advice. Of course I prayed a lot. But I knew they had to find their own way. In 1957 Bill was twenty, a good age for a boy to become a man. That was also the year Fred graduated from high school. Papa and I wanted him to go to Wheaton. But Fred was always different. He had done very well at the American School and had served as president of the student body. He liked to study and to paint. And he pursued

In front of the Imperial Palace in Tokyo with Fred, Peter, and Rosalie.

his own vision, which was to go to either Stanford or Harvard. One day, I remember a thick envelope arrived for him from Harvard College. To our surprise, and his pleasure, he won a scholarship to attend this fine university. I was never entirely sanguine about his choice, but he was clear on what he wanted to do, and I accepted his decision. I still am not quite sure about his faith, but I have come to accept the fact that not everyone can travel the same path in the same way. God works differently in different people's lives.

Fred's departure in the summer of 1957 meant that only Rosalie and Peter remained with us. I was not yet aware of the effect that my dwindling family would have on me. But I remember that when we packed Fred's trunk and put him on the freighter for San Francisco there was already a sudden pang of loss. Two years later, when we were home on furlough, we left Rosalie to start her college education at Westmont in Santa Barbara. Returning to Japan in 1960, only Peter was still with us. A year later, even he had graduated from high school and had left us for the Julliard School of Music in New York.

While my church-work was expanding, my family was rapidly disappearing. For me life in Japan had always focused on both components. So much of what we had been through involved our children as well as our congregations. What I had not realized was the degree to which one sustained the other. My home and family had served as a warm refuge from the storms and tensions that had buffeted us during the war years. My family had also provided me with the social environment that sustained my need for contact with others. Now my world was changing. My children were leaving one after another. No matter how hard I threw myself into my missionary activities, I could never quite overcome the sense of loss. Papa may have had similar feelings. He seemed to become more solitary during those last years in Japan. I always had to have people around me. He was able to draw on some inner source of strength that was fed by solitude. I was just the opposite. One reason my ladies circle became such a joyous group, and so important to me, is that I treated it as if it were my new family. Still, I knew, even then, that as wonderful as these women were, they could not take the place of my children. I devoted myself to my work as never before. How often we substitute action for thought. Doing replaces being. When I left Japan for furlough in 1958 the complex emotions that swirled about me were still largely undefined. The full force of what lay before me remained dormant. It was only after my return in 1960 that I faced the maelstrom.

Chapter Thirteen
Sunshine and Clouds

I was hardly aware of what lay ahead as our Italian passenger liner left Yokohama on the twelfth of May 1958. We had been granted a year of furlough. Papa and I felt that it would be nice to return to the U.S. by way of Europe. This would allow him to see his family again. He had gone to Japan in 1929. It was nearly thirty years since he left Germany. Thirty years is a long time! It had been my privileged to go home in 1954, but this was to be his great trip. For all of us it proved to be a sunny interlude.

But the sun was not shining the day we left Yokohama. It rained so hard that our friends could not stand on the pier and hold the usual farewell streamers. Saying goodbye without that colorful ritual seemed odd. Our ship stopped in Nagoya and again in Kobe. In Nagoya we visited the Noritake China factory, and from Kobe we managed to get in some sight-seeing that included Osaka Castle. Kobe showed how far Japan had come since our return in 1954. The port was now bursting with activity, and a quick trip to the Daimaru Department Store for some last minute gifts confirmed that there was no shortage of goods for all shoppers. We left Kobe on the evening of the seventeenth. This time there were thousands of streamers of all colors and many colored balloons were released as we pulled away. It made our departure very festive.

We stopped in Okinawa only long enough to take on forty passengers, Japanese farmers bound for Brazil. Many of their fellow villagers came to see

Hong Kong.

them off. The scene was moving and full of tears, as friends wished them well and *bon voyage* to their new homes and lives. We were soon at sea again. The weather turned hot. Peter and Rosalie started to complain, and Papa said, "Oh! It's hot!" every five minutes. I wondered how they would have liked the Mortlock Islands!

For me this was another new adventure. In 1930 I had taken the train across Russia. Just four years earlier I had flown home by way of India and the Middle East. Now I was about to retrace much of my aerial route by ship. For Papa it was also a new experience. He, too, had come to Japan by way of Russia. It was eleven thirty at night when we made our next port of call, Hong Kong. What excitement! There were lights everywhere and the city looked like a thousand Christmas trees. We stayed at the Lutheran mission home. Papa and Peter had suits made. The tailors were excellent and they could finish a complete suit in two days. Everything in Hong Kong was amazingly cheap. There were plenty of tempting things sold on every corner. Only Rosalie couldn't find anything she liked.

From Hong Kong we sailed towards Singapore. The sea turned rough. There were heavy rains and wind. We seemed to have caught part of a typhoon. I was once more thoroughly sea-sick, just like on the schooner out of Truk, but at least I didn't have to roll around the deck. Our cabin was pleasant and air conditioned. Before we reached Singapore the sea became a little calmer. Singapore, itself, was very warm and unkempt. We took a taxi to town shortly after our arrival, but it was so dirty that Peter and Rosalie asked to go back to the ship. The following day we visited the botanical garden, which

Orchids in the Singapore Botanical Garden.

144

The *Victoria* in Colombo harbor.

was famous for its orchids, and had a pleasant time capped off with coffee and sandwiches at the Princess Hotel. We were served outside on the veranda. I guess we didn't look the Princess type, at least no one offered to seat us inside. For me Singapore lacked the charm and fascination of Hong Kong.

Our ship stopped briefly in Ceylon, now Sri Lanka. We managed to take a tour of the island by taxi. The Ceylon zoological garden was then quite famous, but when we reached its gates we were disappointed to discover that we could not enter because of some recent confrontations between the English and native speaking populations. There was little we could do, so we consoled ourselves by buying some Ceylon tea at a dollar a pound, and Rosalie finally found something she liked—a nice bracelet.

Our ship, the *Victoria*, reached Bombay on the afternoon of June the eighth. I remember it was Sunday. Earlier that day we had held services in one of the ship's lounges. There were a number of missionary families aboard and we soon came to know each other. Several of us got together that evening and went sight-seeing by horse and buggy. Our destination was the hanging gardens on the other side of the city. As we drove along the shore we saw people, people, and people! I always thought that Japan was crowded, but nothing can match India. The hanging gardens were beautifully lit up in the evening, and from their terraces we overlooked the city with its thousands and thousands of lights. It was quite spectacular. We drove slowly back to the ship and went to bed after an enchanting evening. The next day we were nearly left behind in India. We had gone to town and asked our taxi driver to take us to the Victoria Gardens and the zoo. Unfortunately it was soon eleven, and our ship was scheduled to sail at eleven-thirty. We asked our driver to hurry, but he was more interested in running up his meter. By the time we reached the pier the tourist gang-plank was already up. The ship was on the verge of leaving. We raced for the first-class gangway and made it just in time. Peter had remained on board. He saw himself sailing for Europe alone! We could imagine being left behind in India

Karachi.

with its teeming crowds of unemployed which filled its streets and parks. Poor souls!

We docked in Karachi two days later. It had been hot there when I had landed by plane four years earlier. Now it was even hotter. We walked about a bit and watched the unloading of a whole train, some twenty-five cars in all, from a Norwegian freighter that tied up right behind us. The train had been built by the German firm Hoffman von Braunschweig. The following morning we went to town by horse and buggy, and I thought, "Oh! how poor the people live here!" There was so much mud and dirt, and the people seemed so poor. At the same time everything was much more expensive than in Hong Kong. The city was divided into three quarters, the English, Chinese, and Indian. The Indian section was clearly the poorest.

We arrived at Aden on June fourteenth. A taxi driver drove us to town, if one could refer to it as "town." It was six miles from the port. A terribly dirty place. We didn't even buy a souvenir. On the way back we asked the driver to stop at the cable office so we could send a wire to Mr. Moses at Suez who was arranging our trip to Cairo. The driver waited, brought us back to our ship, and charged us seven U.S. dollars. I said five dollars was enough. But he insisted on seven. The police came and said that we should pay him five dollars and five shillings. We gladly accepted this compromise. By the following day our ship was sailing up the Red Sea. Here, too, it was very warm. The water was a bluish-green and quite calm. We seemed to be surrounded by schools of fish that jumped out of the water, glistening like rainbows, then they would dive down again. It was a beautiful sight. There were also sea-eagles that flew close to the ship. The landscape looked awfully barren. In the distance we could see the mountains of Sinai, but we never could figure out which was Mt. Horeb. Finally on the evening of the seventeenth we landed at Suez.

I had always wanted to visit Egypt and the Pyramids. It seemed appropriate that our guide's name was Moses. We started out by driving through the desert for nearly two hours. Then we came to Cairo. I was surprised to see such beautiful buildings and such clean streets and gardens. On nearly every street corner, and at every gas station, there was a large picture of Nasser. Suddenly there seemed to be police everywhere. We were whistled to a halt. The reason for the excitement was that Nasser, himself, was coming. Soon we saw his car. The city was all decorated for a visiting prince who was with him. Our driver joked by saying that even Nasser had come out to welcome us. We went on to see an old palace with its harem. Both were still in use. But these old buildings were surrounded by beautiful new mansions built in 20th century style with all the modern comforts. Thereafter we visited one of the largest museums of the world. What we saw made me think of the story of Moses and the Palaces of the Pharaohs in which he was brought up. I was intrigued by the sarcophagi and the whole ritual of mummification. The multiple caskets were really something. Then there was also all the food, ornaments, clothes and other objects that were placed beside the Pharaoh, including many precious silver, golden, and gemstone ornaments. Even his favorite wagon was there, although there was no sign of the horses for it. There were also three-hundred-and-sixty-five servants—one for every day of the year. They were all there in stone, painted with their appropriate colors of rank. Looking at the coffins within coffins, Peter said, "Even if he tried to come back, how could the Pharaoh make his way out of so many coffins?"

After the museum we went to see the oldest mosque. It was magnificent.

There was an enormous room covered with Persian carpets and lit up with seventeen hundred beautiful lamps and a large crystal chandelier. All around were the most beautiful stained glass windows that sparkled like diamonds. The inside of the room was handsomely painted, and the acoustics were amazing. There was a "secret"

Rosalie on a camel near the pyramids.

147

room that was made entirely out of alabaster, and our guide said we should make a special wish when we entered. He always spoke of the light that came to the people from Allah through his great prophet Mohammed to open the hearts of the blind. And I thought of our own mission to bring hope to the hopeless.

After a bite of lunch we drove to Giza where the pyramids are located. Soon we could see them towering on the horizon. The camels were lying there in a long row ready to take us for a ride. We climbed up on their backs, but when they stood up one had to hold on for dear life not to be thrown head over heels. Still we had loads of fun watching each other riding along the hill to the pyramids. How many thousands of slaves had given their lives in this desolate place, just to fulfill the ambitions of a few men. After seeing the pyramids we went back to Cairo, had tea in a little garden restaurant, and crossed the Nile to drive further on the other side of the Suez Canal. This was a lovely ride and we saw many country people working in the fields, plowing with wooden plows that were pulled by water buffaloes, just as in ancient times. Camels and donkeys were carrying the harvest home. Water was still being pumped using great water wheels that were turned by camels or buffaloes. Most of the people lived in traditional mud houses. On both sides of the road were great eucalyptus trees that provided a beautiful shade. To the right of the road was a small canal that provided water for the thirsty animals. Of course, without irrigation, nothing could be grown here. We could see some ships moving up the Suez Canal and wondered if the *Victoria* had already gone by. Then we crossed a bridge where the Nile flows into the sea. To the right the water is salty, and to the left it is sweet. Our guide told us it never mixes together. By eleven we were back on board our ship which had arrived just an hour earlier. What a day! How much we had seen and heard! How interesting it was to put what we had seen in the perspective of the scriptures we knew so well that dealt with the life of Moses and his fellow Israelites in this ancient land.

Soon we were at sea again, this time in the Mediterranean. We stopped briefly at Crete and then sailed on for our destination. On the evening of the 20th we had the Captain's dinner. It was very festive and there was a dance afterwards. While some danced the night away, we decided to go to bed. We knew we would be passing through the Straits of Messina early the next morning. We wanted to see this, so we were on deck not long after sunrise. It was a little hazy but we enjoyed the beautiful sight. On the right was the coast of Italy; on the left Sicily. In the distance we could see Mt. Etna. Two hours later we passed the volcano, Stromboli, which greeted us with a light cloud of smoke coming from its large crater. We wondered how people dared to build their houses on the slopes of this dangerous mountain.

On the twenty-second of June we arrived at Naples. It was quite a sight, but we were looking less at the scenery than for Bill, who was to meet us at

Papa with his sister Emmi, Mama, Peter, Rosalie, and Tante Anni, arriving in Naples.

the ship. Yet, no matter how hard we looked we couldn't find him in the crowd waiting for the ship's arrival. Soon we saw a group of people waving in our direction. There stood Papa's brother, Hans and his wife Anni. Beside Anni we could see Papa's sister Emmi. They had kindly brought the new Opel station wagon Papa had ordered to Italy. While we were waving to them a steward came up to us with a telegram. It was from Bill. His plane had been grounded at Wiesbaden. Poor fellow, he was still stuck in Germany and would not be able to join us in Italy.

What a joy it was for Papa to see his brother and sister again after so many years. The next day we made an outing to Pompei with Hans, Anni, and Emmi. We had a most enjoyable time together examining the excavations and ruins of this ill-fated city. I remember I was struck by the lovely Roman baths that the houses had. Onkel Hans and his wife were going on to Capri so we decided to have a farewell lunch together. We parked the car just around the corner from the restaurant. When we returned after our meal the car was in the process of being burglarized. The thieves had smashed the little front window and had already taken our typewriter, projector, and Rosalie's camera. Had we not returned when we did they would have taken all the rest. We called the police. I remember saying to the Italian officer that we had lived in Japan for thirty years and had never had anything stolen from us. He looked at me and smiled. Then he said, "I am afraid that Italy is not Japan!" He advised us not to leave anything visible in the car, not even a newspaper. Of course, nothing

With the pigeons in Milan.

was done to catch the thieves.

Despite this experience we had a wonderful time in Italy. Our first stop was Rome. I was always fascinated with Rome's classical history, and I hoped to see many of the old monuments. We stayed in a very pleasant penzione. The landlady had two sons, one of whom was lame, but he was a fine pianist and we enjoyed listening to his music. The other son served as our guide and took us all around Rome. We saw most of the important places from the coliseum to the catacombs. There were so many splendid churches and so much to see and do. Late one afternoon our guide took us up Mt. Garibaldi to a beautiful park that overlooked the whole city. He told us to sit still on one of the walls of the park, and wait until it got dark. Slowly the lights below us started to come on one after another and in a little while the whole city sparkled before us. It was really lovely.

From Rome we went to Genoa, taking in the Leaning Tower of Pisa on the way. Then we drove on to Milan. The cathedral in Milan was really spectacular, particularly the stained glass windows in which, I believe, one could see almost every Bible story illustrated. The colors of red and blue, and red and purple, were truly stunning. By evening we drove on towards the Swiss border. We were thinking of where to stay, when Rosalie reminded me I had promised to buy her a purse in Italy. So we stopped and Rosalie bought her purse. At the store I asked if there was any place in the area where we might spend the night. The proprietor told me that a German woman had just opened a penzione not half a kilometer away. We drove to where he had indicated and found a large house, but no sign. When I started toward the house a woman greeted me in *Schwäbish*, saying "Are you looking for something?" I said, "Yes, a German Penzione," She said, "Come in, Come in." They had just been licensed and still waited for their sign. The house was immaculate. We had dinner up on a veranda from which we had a marvelous view of Lake Maggiore. Mrs. Bretzel's *Schwäbish* dialect made me feel right at home.

The next day we started into Switzerland heading for Interlaken. I was struck once more with the beauty of this country. We had to cross two passes. One was

At the top of the Grimsel Pass in Switzerland.

the Furka Pass. We went higher and higher, right into the snow. It was foggy all around. Even in the afternoon it was already getting dark. We hoped to see the glacier and walk on the ice. Everything was snow and ice. Papa was worried about leaving the car for fear the coolant might freeze. Then suddenly the sun came out and everything was lit up in a rosy light. It was really beautiful. It was both scary and beautiful. We came down the mountain on a narrow road. It was already towards evening. In the valley we saw a nice hotel, but we thought it would probably be too expensive for us. We stopped anyway. A boy came out and asked if we wanted to stay the night. We asked how much it would cost. A room with cold water was sixteen marks and one with warm water was twenty. But after consulting with his boss he offered us the room with warm water for sixteen marks, which was only five dollars. We decided that this was fair and far better than driving through the mountains at night. We had a pleasant stay at Gletch. The next day, after a nice breakfast, we crossed the Grimsel Pass. The weather was clear and we had a wonderful view of the mountains covered with snow.

The country above Thuner Lake.

The Grimsel Pass was not as steep as the Furka Pass and we had a smooth drive down to Interlaken, and then along the Thuner Lake and through the valley to Bern. At Bern we stayed with an old friend from Truk. Her husband had died, but she was most kind and hospitable. She was particularly good to Rosalie. I hoped to see an old friend in Frutingen who was originally to have gone to China with me many years earlier. Unfortunately she had to be away, but her brother-in-law ran a small hotel, and she arranged for us to stay there a week. All of us had a nice time relaxing and hiking in this region above Thuner Lake. From there we drove to Germany.

We went directly to Munich. I remember we arrived in Munich towards evening, just as the sun was setting over the city. Munich looked so beautiful, and Papa got so excited. I never saw him so exited in all my life. We stayed at his sister Emi's. The next day Papa's family had a party for us at a large restaurant. All the relatives came, big and small. Each greeted us, and we had a lovely time together. The following Sunday we were invited to speak at Papa's church, where he had been associate pastor for two years before going to Japan. It was a great joy for him to meet again some of the young people he had shepherded so many years ago and see that they remained faithful members of the congregation. One of Papa's friends, Frau Kopfmüller and her husband owned a department store. For years, while the children were growing up in Japan, she had sent us clothes and other supplies for them. Now she decided to treat us to a two week stay at a lovely hotel in Ammerland on the Starnberger See. She even invited Bill to join us. It was truly a wonderful two weeks. Only poor Bill, who was so happy to be with us, soon had to

Beautiful Munich, Papa's home town.

return to Bremerhaven because the first Lebanese crisis had broken out and all American troops were ordered back to their bases.

We left Munich on the first of August. It was hard to say goodbye to Emmi. It was hot and a great thunder storm developed as we approached Ulm. Fortunately we reached my sister Walburg's house just before the storm broke. This was Papa's first chance to spend some time with my family. Both of my sisters, Walburg and Gretel, treated us royally. Gretel's idea of entertainment was always food. Papa, for his part, enjoyed eating, so they soon had something in common. The trouble was that Gretel cooked enough for a dozen people and we were only four. But she had a good heart and we enjoyed her hospitality. We called on friends and relatives all around and made some lovely trips. One, I remember, was to the Bodensee on an absolutely perfect day. We held a meeting with the evangelical community in Ulm, and I managed to see most of my old friends. It was a real joy to be with them, if only for a day or two. Of course we also went back to Bernstadt to visit, and showed slides in the Church there of our work in Japan. It was all too short, and soon we had to bid my family farewell.

On our way to Liebenzell we stopped off in Dettenhausen to see Adelheid Zilly who had spent the war years with us in Japan. She had married Mr. Neumaier, who was now the pastor of a large church, and Adelheid was the mother of seven children. I thought of the days when I told her that she needed six children of her own. What a fine mother she had become! We had a delightful visit with her and her family and reminisced about those earlier days.

At Liebenzell they gave us a great welcome. What a pleasure it was to meet all the old friends again. How good it was to see dear old Pfarrer Hertel. He was still full of enthusiasm for the work of the mission, and our old teacher, Herr Heinzen, with his big heart for God's work and his children. As a result of our visit we were extended many invitations to speak. Going to one of these meetings from Bad Liebenzell, we returned quite late. We had forgotten to take the house-key with us and all the doors were shut. We tried to throw small pebbles at the windows of the rooms where Peter and Rosalie were sleeping but they didn't wake up. Finally we had no choice but to spend the night in the car. Neither of us slept very well. We were happy when the house was opened in the morning. I thought of the rule I had created for my children in America. If they did not return by eleven, I put a blanket and pillow on the doorstep for them and the door was shut. For the first time I had a sense of what it meant to be locked out!

We finished our German stay with a visit to Mannheim and to Bad Wimpfen where we spent some time with Tante Lydia. We had five meetings in one day at Bad Wimpfen, which may have been a record for our trip. But being with Lydia Becker was a true joy. From there we went on to Heidelberg and northern Germany. Our ship was scheduled to leave for the U.S. from Amsterdam. Tante Emmi and a niece came to Holland to say goodbye. Papa and Peter took a day off to visit the World's Fair in Brussels while we remained in Amsterdam. Amsterdam in 1958 was already full of hippies. It was a far cry from the Amsterdam I had known earlier. It was dirty, and we were really astounded by the degree to which it had changed. Much of the student unrest I was to see again in Japan was already apparent here. It was clearly a new world, the world of the sixties, that already dawned before us. Our ship, the *Bismark*, sailed for New York towards the end of August. It was a lovely vessel and the journey to New York was smooth and pleasant. Tante Emmi generously paid for our passage home, and we were sad to say goodbye to her after such a happy and eventful stay in the country of our birth.

Fred and Anne waited for us at the pier in Brooklyn where we docked. Anne had a friend, Ruth Landis, who invited us to stay with her family on their farm near Doylestown in Pennsylvania while our car was unloaded and properly processed. The Landis farm was located in the heart of Amish country in Bucks County, and Ruth's family was wonderfully generous to us. It was apple season, and Papa and Peter helped with the picking. Fred and Anne's schools were about to begin, so they had to leave. We wished them well as they headed in different directions, Fred by bus to Cambridge and Anne by plane to Chicago. Finally the car was ready, and we thanked the Landises for their hospitality. Papa and the three of us began our drive West. Poison ivy and poison oak were always Papa's enemies. While working on the Landis farm he had picked up a serious case of poison ivy. In Chicago, I remember, we had to see a doctor who provided him with medication that alleviated his terrible rash. From there we drove west as quickly as possible.

With Papa in Turlock in the fall of 1958.

Peter and Rosalie needed to enroll in school the following week. We therefore drove directly to Turlock and arrived there safely in the middle of September.

The first part of our furlough had been both exciting and fulfilling. Seeing members of our families again after so many years was richly rewarding. Our trip to Germany had been a truly sunny time. Everything had gone well. It felt good to be back in Turlock. Papa and I were happy in our work. We had a lovely fall. After all our traveling it was nice to stay in place for a while. The church rented a house for us on Florence street. That Christmas all the family gathered in Turlock, only Bill was still in Germany. It was truly a joyous occasion, made even more so by John's announcement of his engagement to Miriam Cover.

If 1958 had been a sunny year, 1959 seemed to usher in gathering clouds. This is not to say that there were no bright and happy times during this year. On July 19th John and Miriam were married in Modesto. What a lovely event this

John and his bride, Miriam Cover.

was! The wedding was in the garden of the Cover home which was beautifully arranged and decorated. We thoroughly enjoyed Miriam's parents and the extended Cover family which warmly took us in and made us feel at one with them. This was really special. Both John and Miriam were dedicated to their Christian calling. Papa and I were very proud and happy for them.

I first felt the clouds gather in January when we went to pick up Anne after her graduation from West Suburban Hospital and Wheaton College. She had completed her five year program early in 1959. Anne was now not only a registered nurse, but possessed her bachelors degree as well. How proud we were of her achievements. The graduation ceremony was held in Chicago. The Losacco family, whose son we had come to know in Japan, generously offered to put us up while we were there. We helped Anne pack her things, and wanted to leave for the West Coast as soon as possible. But the weather was not propitious. Winter in all its fury was only too evident. We prayed for a break in the storms so that we could start. Finally a more favorable weather report convinced us to set out. We began our drive in the rain, but not far from Bloomington, Illinois the rain turned to sleet. Then suddenly the whole road turned to ice. Papa couldn't manage the car any more. I remember Anne saying, "Papa where are you going!" Then I cried "Oh, Lord, Help us!" The car left the road and rolled completely over ending in the center divider of a four-lane highway. When it came to a halt all the windows were gone and the entire roof was crushed. The car was lying on one side. Anne looked out the back window and tried to call for help, but all the cars on our side just drove past. Then a man on the other side stopped. He came over and helped to pull Anne from the car. Next he called the police. Fortunately none of us seemed to be seriously hurt. The police came and took us to a nearby Salvation Army home. In fact, they helped us to get all of our luggage to the home, before they called a wrecker to tow the car to a garage. The car needed a completely new roof, but because it was an Opel it was not easy to acquire the parts in the U.S. In the end the garage had to literally rebuild the old one. This took a long time. We spent another three weeks with the Losaccos. How kind and generous they were towards us. For Papa and me it was really a terrible time.

Then in March Papa and I went on a speaking tour to Washington State. We had meetings in several places and were in Walla Walla when I became very sick. I vomited nothing but gall. The people we were staying with called a doctor. He said I needed an operation right away, but I didn't want an operation from this doctor. The doctors I trusted were all in Turlock. So I told Papa I wanted to return there. We drove the night through, but at about midnight I had such pain that I couldn't stand it any more. Papa took me to a motel and put on hot compresses. Finally we reached Turlock. When Anne saw me, I was all yellow. She said, "You have to go to the hospital right now!" I went, but they couldn't operate immediately because my gall bladder was so inflamed. I also had a serious fever. Finally after waiting three days, the doctors operated. Praise the Lord, the operation was successful! I was soon on the road to recovery.

Unfortunately I was not familiar with our new house on Florence Street. One day I opened a door that led to the cellar; I still don't know how it happened, but I fell down the steps and broke two ribs. That took me back to the hospital, and while they didn't keep me long, it took time for my broken ribs to heal. There was considerable pain, and I just didn't feel good.

All this took place in the spring. Summer brought the pleasant respite of John's wedding, but by early fall it was Papa's turn. One morning he got up and didn't feel well. He vomited. I saw him standing there as if he had another hernia. So I ordered him right off to see our doctor. The doctor instantly confined him to the hospital and arranged for an operation. This was not Papa's first hernia operation, but this time after the surgery was finished the surgeon came to me and said, "We nearly lost your husband today. He seems to have a serious breathing problem. We need to have him checked out by a specialist." The specialist found that papa had a deep goiter around his windpipe, and so he was kept in the hospital for a second operation. We were all happy when the second surgery was successfully completed and Papa was once again improving. But he, too, was feeling his age. For both of us the bright colors of the previous year seemed to be giving way to more somber tones.

All this was very confusing. We were scheduled to leave for Japan that fall. For a time I wondered if we could make the passage we had booked on a Japanese freighter back to Yokohama. Fortunately by November we were both feeling a little better. Still there were further problems. One day Peter came to me and said that he thought we would have to go back to Japan without him. He was in trouble. He had thrown eggs at a car belonging to the father of one of his classmates. The police had been called. He was certain he would be arrested. I told him to go instantly to the

Peter and Mama returning to Japan in 1959.

man and apologize for his act and provide restitution. He did this and the potential vandalism charge was dropped. Even in Turlock the restlessness of youths seemed all pervasive. In a way, I was glad to hear that a definite date for our sailing had been set. But at the last minute the port of embarkation was changed from San Francisco to San Diego. Friends offered to drive us to San Diego. Even here the was a glitch. We had been given several smoked hams to take to Japan with us, and these were in our refrigerator. Somehow we started out without them. Driving down the highway towards Los Angeles I remembered that we had forgotten the hams, and we had to drive back to retrieve them. Despite all this, we somehow made it to the ship on time.

Given the incidents that had befallen us that year, we were thankful that our trip across the Pacific proved to be smooth and uneventful. Shortly before Christmas we arrived at our Todoroki home. The odyssey of traveling around the world was now complete. Happy to be back in Japan, we celebrated a quiet Christmas. Still, coming back to Japan presented new challenges. Japan was changing. That New Year marked a new decade. At home things were also different. Peter was the only child to return with us. Somehow the house seemed awfully empty. Although it was filled with a lovely Christmas tree, and the beautiful decorations that Papa and Peter put up, our home seemed strangely barren. Despite the many Japanese visitors who came to welcome us back to Japan, and despite the flurry of church activity that accompanied the season, I felt a growing inner void that expanded within me. I was somehow looking for the lost, but I didn't know how to find it.

Chapter Fourteen
Facing Myself

Much of my life had involved struggle. My early years. My time in the South Pacific. The war years in Japan. None of these had been easy. I had often faced challenges. I had even wrestled with God for little Lotte's life on Mortlock. There had been plenty of hard times. In most of these, the forces I struggled against were a part of the environment in which I found myself. I always felt that God was there with me. I firmly believed that in the stillness I could hear those inner voices that sustained me and provided me with direction. My anxieties had come from the world outside. Even in my most difficult moments I had learned to maintain a degree of cheerfulness. How unprepared I was for my next challenge—a struggle not with the world beyond, but within myself.

Our return to Japan at the close of 1959 seemed to open a new door in my life. I sensed a kind of restlessness within. 1960 was also a year of great unrest in Japan. I observed this even among the students who came to my English and German Bible classes. For most Japanese the war had now faded into the background. On the one hand, there was a renewed sense of national pride, but on the other, there was also what seemed to be a collective soul searching about the direction Japan should take. Much of this involved Japan's relations with the United States. The U.S. Japan Security Treaty, which the Japanese agreed to in 1951, gave the Americans the right to station troops in Japan on an indefinite basis. We had a number of friends among these troops and knew several fine army Chaplains. At the same time, many Japanese peace activists, labor leaders, and left-wing students were increasingly opposed to the American presence. They didn't want Japan to become an American military base in the cold war struggle with Russia. Several incidents involving American troops and Japanese citizens occurred and aroused a public outcry. An effort to expropriate landowners to expand American bases was also thought unfair.

The Prime Minister when we returned to Japan was Nobusuke Kishi. He had just been elected the year we left on furlough. I know my students didn't like Kishi very much. They said he had served with Tojo during the war, and didn't trust him. One student, I remember, called him a "fascist." Many labeled him "undemocratic." There was something about his way of doing things that did not sit well with the younger Japanese. But it was the treaty with America that became the biggest problem. In the two years we had been away, the Japanese tried to negotiate a new treaty. It seemed that the proposed treaty was better for Japan, but there were those who wanted no treaty at all. Many socialists in the Diet were firmly opposed to

Students and workers carry effigy of Kishi. Sign says, "Foreign Aggression."

the new treaty. The majority party in the Diet was, however, the Liberal Democratic Party that Kishi headed. Kishi invited President Eisenhower to Japan in June to commemorate the signing of the treaty. The trouble was, it soon became May and the treaty was not approved in the Diet. On May 20th Kishi's party passed the treaty in a late night session, while the other Diet members were not present. To those Japanese who already doubted his motives, including most of my students, Kishi's tactics confirmed the belief that he was undemocratic and could not be trusted. The result was a period of intense public turmoil.

There were suddenly massive rallies everywhere. I never saw so many people in the streets. The usual labor union people were joined by large numbers of students. For the first time I heard the word, *Zengakuren*, the Federation of Student Organizations which appeared in the papers almost every day. The militant students entered the Diet and clashed with the police.

A female student was trampled to death. This led to larger crowds. Everywhere there were anti-American slogans, such as "Yankee go home!" James Haggerty, President Eisenhower's Press Secretary, who came to Japan to prepare for the President's visit, was mobbed and held hostage in his car for a time. In the end, the Eisenhower visit had to be cancelled because the Japanese government could not guarantee his safety.

Snake Dancing zengakuren students outside the National Diet.

My, those crowds were something! Often there were blocks and blocks of "snake-dancing" students in long columns. We tried to avoid going out as much as possible, but one couldn't help but feel intimidated by the demonstrators. In all the years I had lived in Japan I never saw people so unruly. And there were literally millions of them. Nor were they just the usual red flag-waving leftists, but many were everyday Japanese. Even housewives joined in to oppose Kishi and the Americans. When I asked my students about this, they assured me that it was really Kishi more than the Americans they disliked. I remember a cartoon showing a Japanese student demonstrator who carried a placard reading "Yankee Go Home!" He had stopped to speak to an American young man and said, "Don't worry Joe, I'll be over for English lessons tonight!" Perhaps this reflected some of the mood. But as Americans in Japan we couldn't help but feel anxious. Living in Japan had always required a degree of caution, but this was something new. While we had been wary of officialdom, whether German or Japanese, we saw ourselves living in harmony with our Japanese neighbors. The shrill atmosphere of 1960 seemed to dampen that possibility.

Kishi resigned in July. But not before a knife-wielding right-wing fanatic made an attempt on his life. Things got a little better under Ikeda, the new prime minister, who restored a degree of order. Still, the quiet of the fifties never returned. Student unrest and public protest soon shifted to the Vietnam War. Here, too, there was a subtle note of anti-American sentiment that even the efforts of the new American Ambassador, Edwin O. Reischauer, whose parents we had known as missionaries before the war and who had taught Fred at Harvard, found difficult to counter. In a more positive sense, what we were experiencing were also the growing pains of the new Japan. Dependent though Japan remained on the United States, it was once again trying to come into its own. Our final years in Japan from 1960 to 1965 paralleled an important part of this maturation process. Starting with the Security Treaty riots, we watched the halting steps as Japan once again reentered the international arena. What began so awkwardly in 1960 was to be transformed into the splendid coming out party of the Tokyo Olympics in 1964. How different the mood was then. Perhaps we sense too little the pains that are needed to turn from grub to butterfly. I sometimes think of myself during these years, and from today's perspective can see how my own experiences mirrored a similar process of change.

How interesting we are as individuals. For years I had lived with my family. The house had always been full of children. I had been surrounded by noise and activity. All of my children showed strong independent traits, and they could be as unruly as any of their peers. I frequently had to reign them in, and of course Papa and I prayed a lot that they would turn out all right. How often I told them, "Children be quiet!," so that I could read or study while they were their usual rambunctious selves. Even in recent years, while the size of the family had declined there had been lots to do. I sometimes hoped for peace and quiet to focus on my own preparations or study. But all this suddenly changed.

I didn't sense this so much in 1960. In one respect that year put off my having to face myself a little longer. Peter had returned with us and was in his senior year at the American School. He liked to sing and was in a number of school musical productions, including the Mikado, which he enjoyed. Fred had decided to spend a year at International Christian University to study Japanese. He lived in Mitaka during the week, but was often home on

weekends. So there was still lots of activity at home and we went on a number of outings together.

Peter graduated from high school in June of 1961. Shortly thereafter we saw him off for Julliard in New York. Fred stayed on for part of that summer and was

Peter and Fred in 1960. Peter was a Senior at the American School, Fred was studying Japanese at International Christian University in Tokyo.

in Karuizawa with us before returning for his final year at Harvard. It was that fall that I first began to feel deserted. The house was suddenly empty. All my children were gone. I somehow felt that a good part of my life was over. There seemed to be a vast hole that I couldn't fill, and I didn't know what to do about it. Physically I was not well, but the problem went beyond that. I didn't feel good in body and I didn't feel good in my soul. In Tokyo my work kept me busy. I continued with my students and the ladies of the neighborhood. The church at Shinjo welcomed us back and I was also active there. But I just couldn't be cheerful in my work. In June of 1962 Bill married Sandra Ankrum in California. How much I wished that Papa and I could have been there. We went to Karuizawa

Bill and Sandra cutting their wedding cake.

that summer. Papa was already worried about me. I was often tearful and he couldn't cheer me up. Karuizawa was even worse. Perhaps, because I always associated the time there with family and friends. We had so many good times there. Now the cabin was empty and I felt dreadfully lonesome. Its hard to express the burden that was on my heart. I became very depressed and started to cry all the time. One day I stood before the mirror in my bedroom and saw how awful I looked. I hated myself. Then I heard a voice that said, "Stop crying! If you don't stop crying now you will never be able to stop!" I raised up my hands and said, "Lord with your help I will stop crying!" And somehow I managed to stop. Papa watched all this in silence. He felt sorry

for me, but he didn't know what to do.

The next year was not easy. Though I had stopped my continuous tears, I often went for long walks, sometimes into the night. I was wrestling with my change of life, and also with my

Christmas 1961 after Fred and Peter returned to the U.S.

Matsuda Sensei.

sense of hope and mission. What lay before me? Somehow the past seemed all used up, and I didn't know how to face the future. Others weren't able to help, although there were some who tried. It seemed like such a strange reversal of roles. How often I had counseled younger women with their problems. Now I was the one who needed help. One night out on one of my walks I just thought I couldn't make it any more. Then I heard such a clear voice within me that said, "I am the Almighty God, walk before Me and be faithful!" These words gave me new strength. I decided once again to place my family and everything that lay ahead in God's hands. I did as I was told. I started to walk. Perhaps like anyone who needs to learn to walk again my first steps were halting. But gradually I developed a steadier gait, and before long I had regained my sense of balance. The clouds gradually parted and the sun came out again.

I don't know why, but I felt a close affinity with our wonderful preacher, Mr. Matsuda, during those years. He was such a kind man and a great friend and helper in our work. Then he became very ill with cancer. We felt so sorry for him. He was in the hospital for a long time and the doctors gave up all hope for his recovery. The end seemed not far away. His son paid him a last visit, and he openly spoke of his death. He even selected the songs to be sung at his funeral. That night one of the nurses reported that he was dying. But at midnight, when everything in the hospital was quiet, he came to life again, got up, and walked out into the ward. All the nurses were taken aback. Some thought he was a ghost. They called the doctors, who examined him and

Mama addressing a church group in Tokyo.

found a strong heartbeat. A few days later he was released from the hospital and was well again. Not long thereafter he traveled to Germany and Sweden. In Germany he visited the Liebenzell Mission. He served as pastor for four more years. Then one day, I'll never forget, he came to the house and said he was sick again. He wanted to know why God had made him well only to let him get sick again. I had no answer. He was sad to return to the hospital. In the room in which he was placed there was another patient, the mayor of a nearby town. The mayor watched Matsuda Sensei, who read his Bible and prayed every morning. He said to him, "You speak to God as if he were

Opening Ceremony of 1964 Tokyo Olympics.

a friend of yours." Matsuda replied, "He is a friend of mine." The mayor wanted to know more. Not long thereafter he became a Christian. Later the mayor died, but Mr. Matsuda was healed once more and released from the hospital. He returned to his work in our church. Years after we left Japan he died in ripe old age.

I often though of Mr. Matsuda's question of why God had made him sick again. I can only answer that God had a special purpose for doing what he did. Perhaps it was to help the mayor. How are we to know? What I admired about Mr. Matsuda is that he had been asked to walk a far more difficult path than I. He was not always happy about that path, but he walked it with dignity and faith. I had been given the same message, "Walk before Me and be faithful!" In a way that became my text in the years to come.

By 1964 the mood in Japan and my own mood had changed dramatically. The

Anne in Kimono in 1964.

164

Olympics provided almost a complete facelift for Tokyo. The city was greatly transformed. Splendid new buildings were put up everywhere. The Olympic Stadium complex near Harajuku was truly stunning. The games themselves went off like clockwork. The whole nation seemed to have gone on a television buying spree. I think we were now the only family in the neighborhood without a set. During the opening ceremony I had an errand to run and I was struck by how few people were in the streets. Even in the shops I saw everyone glued to the television. The whole nation felt immense pride in this event which was opened by the Emperor. How different from the demonstrations four years earlier!

The Olympics were also a pleasant interlude for Papa and me. Papa's brother Hans decided to visit us for the games, and his nephew Ralf came representing one of the German newspapers as a sports reporter. At the same time Anne decided to spend some time with us in Tokyo. Then Fred came from Princeton where he was working on his doctoral degree to do two years of research in Japan. Rosalie also visited us for the summer holidays. So it was almost like old times. There was lots of activity, many things to do, and much to see. The last two years in Japan were a truly joyous time. I went back to my work with new strength and new hope. And the Lord blessed me in my work with my ladies and the young people.

By 1965 our church was increasingly independent. It was now under the able leadership of a native pastor. We felt it was best to allow the work to stand on its own feet. In keeping with our long-held ideas that Japanese Christians should be in control of their own enterprises we agreed it was time to withdraw. Papa was sixty-six that year. In those days the normal retirement age in the mission was sixty-five. From today's perspective that seems young, but we realized at the time that our work in Japan had been largely achieved and that we should consider leaving for either Germany or the United States. Our decision was further influenced by our Todoroki house

Papa playing the zither in the garden of our Karuizawa house in the summer of 1965.

which stood on rented land. The original lease, which dated to 1938, was for twenty-five years. This had come up in 1963. Our landlord had been willing to make a two-year extension, but as Todoroki was undergoing rapid change and the value of land skyrocketed, he was increasingly reluctant to extend the lease much further. Relocating to another house and starting a new work at our age seemed a difficult undertaking. In the mission, too, the postwar generation of missionaries was now coming into its own. We had become Mama and Papa Notehelfer to many. I was struck one day when one of our younger Japanese commented that Papa spoke such nice prewar Japanese. I suddenly realized we had gone through our life-cycle in Japan. We had seen our youthful idealism take root in the 1930s, had reached the maturity of middle age in the 1940s, and had experienced our prime in the 1950s. While I was fully convinced that God would show us where he wanted us in the years ahead, I felt that my time in Japan was drawing to a close.

I often think about those final years in Japan. Someone once asked me why Papa and I didn't retire in the land where we spent so much of our lives. I'm not sure that I have an easy answer to this question. I think that I would have to say that despite all the years I spent there, I never felt completely at home in Japan. This is not to say that I didn't have Japanese friends, and there was not a sense of Christian oneness that I felt with many of the Japanese with whom I worked and whom I loved and admired. But Japanese society on the whole is hard to penetrate. There are so many unwritten rules and special ways of doing things that for anyone not born into that society mastering them all is virtually impossible. Then the language is extremely demanding. I think when we are young, we are willing to be more tolerant of such differences. We believe that we can overcome them with time. As we grow older we become more accepting, and in one sense pessimistic about the possibility of doing so. For my part, the turmoil I experienced in the early 1960s could, in fact, have been heightened by a growing awareness of this reality. My sense of isolation may have had its roots as much in this recognition as in my family environment. Of course there were also other reasons. I had begun my Christian work in the South Pacific as a "sister." In that capacity I had committed myself entirely to my religious calling. But marriage had given me a family and different responsibilities. My life had become entangled with that of my children. I had come to see my Christian mission as equally focused there. The Lord had somehow led us to America. We had made our interim home there, and my children had all chosen to live in the United States. While I still felt German, I also felt that I was an American. What strikes me as strange about this is that I had lived in the United States only seven years, while I had lived in Japan more that

The mural of the "White Thread Waterfall" Fred painted for our Karuizawa house in 1961.

three decades. Yet, I never felt Japanese to the same degree that I felt American. I suppose in part the answer lies there. Returning to the United States and returning to Germany, were going home. For me Japan could never be home.

The summer of 1965 was a delightful one. Fred and Rosalie were both with us in Karuizawa for the last stay in the old home where we had spent so many of the war years. We had decided to sell the property to a German mission board that worked with women in Tokyo as a summer retreat. While our Todoroki house was torn down soon after our departure, the Karuizawa house still stands. Now it is sixty years old. Last fall, John and Miriam were able to stay there for a few days with their son Tim and his wife, Kim. The pictures they brought back made me feel nostalgic. How tall the trees in the garden have grown! But at my age I know I will never go back. Still, memory is a wonderful thing. It allows us to make journeys we can never make physically. I still can see so clearly the birthday parties we had for Bill in the garden all decked out with Japanese lanterns of every color. In the evening the children would see their friends home each carrying a lantern of their own. It was really magical. In the spring when the azaleas came out and in the fall when the maples turned color there was no more beautiful place. I just loved it there.

The mission held a farewell reception for us in Karuizawa that summer. Many old friends came. The program focused on our life in Japan. It was really well done and showed all the places we had built our churches. So many nice things were said. It was really wonderful. I still sometimes look at the album that was made for us on that occasion and read the kind comments it contains. One, in particular, seems poignant today. On a page of that album my old friend Dorothea Lang, "Mutti" as we called her, penned the following poem in German.

Lebensstürme

Es hat gestürmt, so wild und oft
    Wir haben geglaubt, wir haben gehofft!
Es hat geblitzt, es hat gekracht,
    Wir haben geweint, wir haben gelacht!.
Es hat gedränt, es hat gewankt,
    Wir haben gebetet, wir haben gedankt!
Un d wollt es uns werden zu viel, zu schwer,
    Wir haben geliebt uns nur desto mehr!
Dann wurde das Leben noch einmal so schön,
    Die Sonne brach siegreich aus Wolkenhöh'n,
Dann wusten wir beide, die Liebe wird stark
    Erst durch die Stürme, die greifen ans Mark!

Life's Storms

The storms have come, both wild and often.
    We trusted in faith and sometimes in hope,
The lightning has blazed, the thunder has rumbled
    We've spent time in tears, and in laughter too.
The world has been shaken, our boat has been rocked,
    We sought help in prayer, and gave thanks a lot,
And just when our burdens were heavy and sore,
    Our love for each other expanded the more.
Then life before us became once again bright,
    And sunlight broke through our cloudy sight.
Now both of us know, our love has grown firm,
    Honed by the tempests that taught us to learn.

Mutti and her husband reminded me that I had written this poem for their wedding thirty-five years earlier. She said that she and Ernst had often read it in the intervening years. I had largely forgotten it. But when I read it again, and even as I read it now, I think of how much it echoes the feelings of my own last years in Japan. I had gone through one of my greatest "Life Storms." My boat had been thoroughly rocked. But I had found my equilibrium again, and the sun had broken through the clouds once more. I knew that I would be all right. How much I had learned about myself from that experience!

I still thank Muti for the return of my poem. Years later, in 1996, Muti died in San Louis Obispo, California. Fred and his wife, Ann, drove me to the funeral from Los Angeles. It seems odd to say so, but Mutti's funeral was such a happy event. All of her children were there, and several of the younger generation of the Buss family also came. It was the kind of farewell that was filled with hope and love. For those of us in attendance, Mutti had gone home. It was as if we had come to see her off on a journey that would soon be my own. As we drove back that afternoon I was struck once more by that poem. Just as we were passing Santa Barbara the sun started to set. It was one of the loveliest sunsets I have ever seen. The clouds kept turning every possible color from yellow and pinks to mauve and purple. The sky behind the clouds ranged from cobalt to pale green. It seemed such a perfect benediction to Muti's life. For her, too, the storms were over, and only a beautiful afterglow remained.

The fall of 1965 was a busy time as we prepared to leave Japan for good. Selling, or giving away, the many things we had acquired, but could not take with us, was hard. Harder still were the meetings of farewell we had in our churches. Saying goodbye to so many friends was not easy. At our Shinjo church pastor Shimada and his wife Hisako put on a skit that had me returning at the age of 80 and meeting the children of some of our faithful parishioners. Hisako also impersonated my style of teaching the ladies. I noticed she had a handkerchief in her left hand and constantly dabbed her nose. I was surprised and asked her, "Do I really do that so often?" She replied, "You certainly do." We laughed heartily together over this, and I realized that I still had things to learn. I was always careful to watch my handkerchief thereafter.

We left Japan towards the end of November on a United States Line freighter. It was a rainy day and our freighter was docked at one of the military piers in Yokohama which made it difficult for people to see us off. But this did not stop our Japanese friends. I don't know how many hundreds came to the ship that afternoon, but there seemed to be an endless line. One man even carried his old mother on his back up the long gangplank so that she could say goodbye. There was a great outpouring of affection that one seldom sees in Japan. I remember there was a woman reporter from a Des Moines, Iowa, newspaper aboard our ship. She said to me afterwards, "Who are you anyway? What have you been doing in Japan?" I told her that we had been missionaries in Japan for many years. She had tears in her eyes as she said, "Never in my life have I seen so much love."

It was still raining as our ship pulled out of Tokyo Bay into the Pacific Ocean. Mt. Fuji was nowhere in sight. The old adage may be correct. He who fails to see Fuji when he leaves Japan will not return. I have never gone back. At ninety-three I doubt I ever will!

Mt. Fuji.

169

Chapter Fifteen
Liebenzell

Bad Liebenzell.

I left Japan with mixed feelings. So much of my adult life had been spent there. I could look back on thirty-three years of service, on good times and bad times. God had blessed our work. We and our Japanese believers had held firmly to the rope of faith and prayer. If I felt sorry, it was for those who were not able to share my beliefs in a living God. At the same time, Japan had become a part of me. It had also become a part of some of my children, particularly Fred who made it the basis of his scholarly career. And yet, my other children were all in America. Papa and I had become grandparents twice over. We had still to meet our first grandson, Tim, who had been born during our last term in Japan. While I was sad to leave, I also looked forward to new experiences. So often my life took unexpected turns. When I left Japan I thought that Papa and I were heading for a few quiet years of retirement. A chance to enjoy our children and grandchildren. Little did I realize that a new field of service lay ahead.

Our trip to San Francisco was quiet and peaceful. We stopped in Hawaii for a few days. Honolulu was already decked out for Christmas. It seemed odd to see Christmas decorations in such a setting, but the poinsettias were the most beautiful I have ever seen. They were truly spectacular! We arrived home just in time to spend the holidays with John and Miriam, Heidi and Tim. John had recently taken over the task of building a new church in Los Altos. His home was not far from the church. We spent a lovely Christmas together getting acquainted with our grandchildren.

Not long after Christmas one of the men from John's former church in Redwood City, Carl Johnson, asked if we would like to live in his cabin at Mission Springs. Mission Springs was a conference center set in the woods of the coast-range mountains near Santa Cruz. We had visited there on occasion from Turlock, and Carl Johnson's cabin was idyllically set at the very top of the conference compound. It was built right against the woods. Next to the cabin stood a field that was covered with orange poppies and blue lupines in spring, and a little further up the hill there was an old abandoned vineyard that dated to the nineteenth century. Trees opened to meadows at regular intervals and there were splendid vistas of the surrounding hills. There were many trails that went through the woods, and it was a beautiful place to live and walk. About five or six cabins were located close-by so there was a sense of community without isolation. At the same time there were many birds and other forms of wild life. Once, I remember, a peacock came out of nowhere and decided to live with us. He stayed with us for over a year, until the

The Peacock that came to live with us.

raccoons got him when his feathers were molting and he couldn't fly up to his usual perch in the oak tree that stood before the house. The raccoons were really brazen, they would come knocking on the glass panel doors of the cabin to let us know they wanted to be fed. But this is getting a little ahead of the story. What I wanted to say is that Papa and I fell in love with this place at first sight. It was like a little bit of heaven.

Carl Johnson rented us his cabin at a very reasonable rate and soon we came to know all our neighbors. We thoroughly enjoyed living in Mission Springs in 1966. At the close of that year we went to Vancouver where Fred married Margaret Ann de Lotbiniere-Harwood, "Fred's Ann" as we came to know her. The wedding was just after Christmas and Fred and Ann both came out from Princeton, where he was teaching. Ann's mother and aunt lived in a lovely house overlooking Vancouver harbor and the wedding reception was held in their beautiful home. Not long after our return from Vancouver a letter arrived from Bad Liebenzell. Our former German board asked whether we would consider coming to Germany to serve as "house parents" in their guest house on the Liebenzell Mission compound. In one way, I was surprised by the offer. We had just settled in. Should we already leave again? At the same time both

Fred and Ann's Wedding Reception in Vancouver.

The Liebenzell Mission Complex.

Papa and I felt that this was God's call. We had earlier thought of returning to Germany for a time and here was the perfect opportunity. We prayed about this and felt a clear call to go. So in the summer of 1967 we packed our trunks once more and headed for Germany. This time the trip was quick and by air. We stopped briefly to visit Fred and Ann in Princeton and made a flying-visit to Schooleys Mountain before continuing on to Germany.

Papa's brother and sister met us at Frankfurt. After a few days with them in Munich and a similar visit with my family at Ulm, we went to Bad Liebenzell and our new assignment as "house parents" in the *Pilgerruhe*, or "Pilgrim's Rest," as the guest house of the mission was called. I felt right at home and enjoyed every day. I was very fond of Liebenzell and I loved the people, young and old. I could speak with them in my native tongue. I felt quite liberated. For so many years I had struggled with Japanese and later with English. What a joy it was to be able to communicate easily and without the sense of distance that speaking in a foreign language always seemed to require. Papa's role was that of Chaplain for the guests, leading the morning and evening devotions. I sometimes joined him in this. But usually my job was to lead special groups who were visiting the mission from different places. The mission had a museum which focused on the areas of the world in which it was active—China, Taiwan, Japan, New Guinea and Micronesia. I was pleased to take visitors through the museum and explained to them the history of our work. Of course the islands and Japan were my favorite subjects. On Sundays we were often asked to speak in different regional churches about our work in Japan. So we kept busy and I felt thoroughly useful and productive.

Our "guests" came not only from Germany, but from England, Holland, Switzerland and America. We even had visitors from Japan. Kenichi Akagi, our neighbor's son, and Pastor Matsuda and his wife were among these. From the U.S. came Gilbert Moody and his wife Caroline. It seemed appropriate that they should join us there when Gilbert had made it possible for me to visit my mother in Germany years earlier. We also had visitors from Micronesia. One was Kumo. I had known Kumo when he was only a boy living on the island of Tol in the village of Iau, where his father was the pastor, and Sister Anna Schneider was his helper. It was there that I had studied the local language, and I remember that Kumo came up the little hill where I lived every day with a gift for me—a banana, an orange, or a little fish he had caught. Now after 37 years I got to meet him again as a man. Like his father he had gone on to become a preacher. How happy we both were to see each other!

At Pentecost and again in the second week of September Liebenzell was particularly lively. On those occasions a massive tent was put up and between seven and eight thousand people would gather in the little town for a special set of meetings. The emphasis was on missionary work abroad, and there was always a wonderful choir and splendid music provided by the churches of the region. Many missionaries gathered there on these occasions, some dressed in the costumes of the people with whom they worked, and the meetings were always lively and interesting. We also interacted with the young seminary students who were at the mission. And I often thought of Papa and my own early days at Liebenzell. How different things now were. I can hardly imagine the young women being told today that they cannot speak to the male students. In some ways the world has definitely improved. At the same time, I thought that growing up is never easy. A lot of our struggles are with ourselves. As I saw the young people around me I often thought of my own past.

For me marriage had come by such a different route. I always encouraged my daughters, Anne and Rosalie, to find their own place in life. Anne had become a nurse and Rosalie a school teacher. I even told them, on occasion, "Don't get married!" By that I meant "Don't get married to soon." Find out what you want to do. Then things will work out for you. I remember at Liebenzell a letter came from each of them that seemed rather blue. They noted that most of their friends were now happily married, but that they had not yet found the right man. They sounded rather discouraged and wondered if God meant them to be single. I took those letters and went into our bedroom. Alone before God I spread the letters on the bed. Then I started to pray. I asked God to lead Anne and Rosalie to the right man as he had once led me through such strange circumstances to Papa. Two months later two letters

The family at the time of Rosalie and Anne's weddings. From left to right. Bill and Sandy with Kurt and Erika, Fred and Ann, Karl and Rosalie Meyer, Mama with Heidi, Peter, Papa, John and Mim with Susan and Tim, Anne and Bob Atkins.

were placed on the table before me. They were from Rosalie and Anne. Both contained the happy news that they were in love and would soon be married. Rosalie was engaged to Karl Meyer who worked for IBM, and Anne's fiancé was Robert Atkins, a minister. Both were married within two days of each other in June of 1968. What a joy it was to be there for the weddings.

Soon we were back in the Black Forest at Bad Liebenzell. Then, one day, I had an accident in the little castle where we lived. We had a special guest whose room was on the second floor of the building. I went to take him something. On the way back I slipped and fell down the flight of stairs. My head bumped on every step as I descended, and I didn't come to a halt till I reached the first floor. I didn't break anything, but my neck and left arm hurt badly. The X-rays revealed that I had a pinched nerve in my neck. We went to a specialist in Stuttgart. He took another X-ray and said, I cannot help you, your neck is like glass, if I tried to do anything it would kill you. So there was little hope for relief of my pain. Often during the night I sat weeping in my bed.

Then one Sunday morning I made myself ready for Church, but I couldn't fix my hair because my left arm wouldn't move upward. I had prayed so often that the Lord should help me, but it seemed hopeless. I threw my comb down on the table and said, "Oh! God, if I were you and you were me, I sure would help you!" And with my upset spirit I went to church. The preacher was speaking about prayer. He noted that God often answers our prayers in a way that differed from what we expected.

He told the story of a boy in his area who regularly attended Sunday School. This boy heard his pastor say that we can ask God anything our heart desires and he will hear us. The boy had only one desire, and that was to ride in a car. So he asked God to let him ride in a car. It was summer and school was out; he went with other children into the forest to pick blackberries, but his thoughts were always on the car. While picking berries he put down his pot and once again asked God to let him ride in a car. Not long after his prayer, he heard a car coming up the curving road. He ran out and stood by the edge of the road waiting. The car came, but it did not stop. It had a sun roof which was open. The boy was so mad that he picked up a stone and threw it at the car. In the back seat was a doctor and his daughter. The stone landed in the car near the girl. The doctor was taken aback and ordered the driver to stop and get the boy. When the driver returned with the boy, the Doctor told him to get in the car and take him to his father. He told him, "I have to speak with your father about your behavior, you could have killed my daughter!" The boy said, "My father is not home." "Then take me to your teacher or pastor," the doctor replied. The teacher was on vacation, so the boy took him to his pastor. The doctor said, "Pastor, you have to deal with this boy, he threw a stone at our car which nearly hit my daughter! She could have been seriously injured." The Pastor replied, "I don't understand this; Peter is a nice, quiet boy. I have never heard anything bad about him." Then he asked Peter, "Why did you do this?" "Well," Peter answered, "You told us in Sunday School that we could ask anything of God and he would do it for us. I have only one desire and that is to ride in a car. I prayed for that. Then a car came up the road while I was in the woods picking berries and I thought God has already answered my prayer. I ran to the street, but the car didn't stop, it just kept going. I was so mad that I grabbed a stone and threw it at the car. I didn't mean to harm anyone, I'm really sorry." The doctor was moved by the boys confession and made a sign to the Pastor. Then he said to the boy. "I will forgive you now. Get in my car, I have to visit a patient in the next village and while I am there my chauffeur will drive you

The Schleyerburg where Mama and Papa lived.

175

around." So the boy got the desire of his heart, but not in the way he anticipated.

The story made me think about my prayer and my impatience that morning. In the afternoon we had to go to Stuttgart to speak at the evening service of one of the beautiful churches there. Papa spoke about the story of John and Peter when they saw the lame man lying by the gate of the Temple. Peter told this man, "Gold and silver we have none, but what we have we give to you. In the name of Jesus Christ rise up and walk." And he took him by the right hand and lifted him up and he could walk. At the end of the meeting they asked me to say a few words. I said, "Have you ever been mad at God?" The audience looked rather surprised. "Well, this morning," I told them, "I was mad at God," and I told them the story of my fall and the pain in my neck and arm, and all the prayers I had made, and then the story of the boy and how God had answered his prayer.

At the end of the meeting, when everyone else had said goodbye to us, a woman came and said, "Mrs. Notehelfer, do you have time?" I thought she too might have a special need and said, "Yes, I have time." Then she said, please go into this room, and she opened the door to a special room near by. She said, "Please wait here for a moment, I will be right back." When she came back she said, "Gold and silver I have none, but what I have I give to you. Please lay down on this table." Then she started to massage my body from head to toe, particularly each of my toes in a special way. Two days later she came to Liebenzell and stayed in our guest house. Every day she worked on me, especially on my toes, and she explained that she could not work on my neck, just as the doctor in Stuttgart had said, but that she could deal with the problem indirectly by massaging my toes. After two weeks of her "treatment" I was relieved of my pain and my prayer was answered. Praise the Lord!

On March 23, 1969, we celebrated Papa's 70th birthday together with all

our guests. I wrote a beautiful poem about his life and his sister Emmi gave him a trip to Israel which especially pleased him. One of Papa's seminary classmates was Fritz Noteacker who was a leader in the Friends of Israel, a group that helped build

Papa visits Jerusalem and the Damascus Gate.

houses in Tel Aviv for former Jewish victims of the Nazi holocaust. One of the houses this group built was to be dedicated in the summer of 1969 and Mr. Noteacker asked Papa to be the speaker at the dedication. After the ceremony they traveled all over Israel and Papa came back full of excite-

Mama enjoying one of the lakes in Berchtesgaden.

ment. The only cloud over the trip was the fact that when they went to swim in the Dead Sea, Fritz Noteacker's brother had a heart attack and died. They had to bring his body home in a casket.

While Papa was in Israel, I made a journey of my own. It was much less pleasant. I suddenly felt ill and went to the hospital with a bleeding ulcer. I thought of Matsuda Sensei, who had just recently visited us, and the mayor. In my room was another woman. Just like the mayor she became interested in my faith. Before long she, too, became a Christian. One night a little after midnight the nurse came and woke me up. She said, "Come quickly you have a telephone call from America." I said, "That must be my children." And sure enough it was John and Miriam inquiring how I was doing. That was a real pleasure. Papa soon returned. Needless to say, he was rather surprised and concerned to find me in the hospital. But a few days later I was allowed to go home, and we returned to the routine we loved in the *Pilgerruhe*. Those were really wonderful days.

Although we were in Germany, the children had not forgotten us. Fred and Ann came in the summer of 1969 and we traveled for a few days with them. One of the places we went was Berchtesgaden. I wanted to celebrate Peter's recent wedding to Ellen Wright which we had not been able to attend. Berchtesgaden is a beautiful town surrounded by lakes and hills in Upper Bavaria. It has many fine hotels and restaurants. I decided to take all my U.S. and German cash with me because I wanted to treat everyone that day. The restaurant we selected was lovely and the food was excellent. We engaged in a lively conversation, and when the bill came Papa paid it. I had put my purse on the floor next to where I sat. Then still in conversation we left the restaurant to go to a nearby park to listen to a concert. Some dark clouds moved in and

Mama and Papa in Switzerland.

it started to rain. I had put an umbrella in my purse and when I reached down to get it there was no purse. I suddenly remembered I had left it in the restaurant and we quickly went back, but the purse was gone. In it was all my money and all my precious things! I was devastated and started to cry. Papa tried to cheer me up. I was mad at myself. How stupid of me! I hated doing dumb things. And yet, even at this late age it taught me a lesson. I have always been careful about my purse thereafter, and even now I double check it when I put it down.

Later that summer, after Fred and Ann returned to Princeton and started their cross-country drive to Los Angeles and his new position at UCLA, Rosalie and Karl came for a visit. We went to Switzerland together and had a most joyous time.

The following summer John and Miriam came with Heidi, Tim, and little Susan. While Fred, Rosalie, and Peter, had met their uncles, aunts and cousins, and even Bill had had an opportunity to visit with some members of the family, John had never been to Germany before. The mission gave us a special house to put them up and we had a wonderful time together. We traveled to many interesting local places, and we also took them to see the family. Sometimes going from one home to the next created curious incidents. Traveling with a family, did not always allow us to stay on Papa's strict time table. Both John and Miriam were less time conscious than he. I remember this led to an odd scene at my sister Walburg's home. Walburg was even more "Germanic" about time than Papa! We had been expected for dinner at twelve noon. But for various reasons we were about an hour late. Walburg had cooked a lovely meal and set a beautiful table. When we did not come at twelve, she waited a few minutes and then cleared the table. When we arrived at one, she was surprised but re-set the table and we enjoyed her excellent dinner. Tante Walburg was really quite a character. In fact she still is. At 97 she continues to live in her own home with her daughter Marga. For "fun" she tends an acre of flowers and vegetables. After our return to the United States she annually sent us a box of *Lebkuchen*, a German cookie that is associated with

At Lake Lucerne with John and Miriam's children.

Christmas. The children particularly liked those cookies. Then one year the cookies stopped. The children asked what had happened. I wrote Walburg to inquire. Not long thereafter I received a letter of explanation. In it Walburg stated that she was "on her way to the graveyard" and could no longer send *Lebkuchen*. That was quite a few years ago. In the family this became something of a joke. Now whenever I don't want to do something I should, the children tell me, "Mama, just say you are on your way to the graveyard, and can't do it anymore."

Poor John and Miriam, between the Schwäbish dialect spoken in my family and the Bavarian dialect spoken in Papa's, they had a hard time with the German language. Finally we went to Switzerland where all of us spoke English and they felt better. We stayed with the grandchildren on Lake Lucerne in a lovely inn, while the parents went on to Italy. Every day we made a trip with the children to another of the beautiful places on the lake by boat. The weather was splendid and we all had a good time. When John and Miriam returned from Italy, we traveled a little more in Germany and then it was time for them to return to the United States.

We had now been in Germany for more than three years. I felt very much at home in Liebenzell. I loved the work and the people. But Papa felt it was time for him to retire. He wanted to be closer to his grandchildren. One day he said to me, "Our own children grew up without their grandparents, should this be true of our grandchildren as well?" I agreed that it would be best to return to America. We spoke to the mission about our decision. Fortunately another missionary couple from

Fred and Ann with Peter and Ellen.

The *Vogtland* on which we returned to the U.S. from Germany.

Japan, Hans Meyer and his wife, were willing to take over our positions as "house parents" in the guest house. The mission held a nice farewell party for us. There were many tears, particularly on my part, but I sensed that this was the right thing to do. We visited our families and said goodbye, realizing that this might be the last time we would see each other.

As on so many of our other trips, the journey home was by freighter. The *Vogtland* sailed from Bremen. We stopped at Amsterdam and Antwerp, then sailed on for Le Havre in France. The *Vogtland* was a container ship, so we usually spent a couple of days in port, loading and unloading. In Le Harve we had a chance to see the museum and visit the cathedral. The city had been heavily bombed during the war; so it was nice to see it well restored. We thought how much we had to be thankful for living in an era of peace. Just as we were about to leave we passed the *France*. What a contrast it was to see the *Vogtland* with its eight passengers next to France's largest passenger liner. All eight of us waved and the passengers on the *France* waved back. After leaving Le Havre we made our way across the Atlantic to the Caribbean, stopping at Cartagena in Colombia to take on oil. Then we sailed for the Panama Canal. It was the first time I had gone through this canal. How interesting it was! Our ship was lifted up from one level to the next. Then we sailed through the lakes and descended the other side. Finally we reached the Pacific. The whole operation took nearly twelve hours. Once we were in the Pacific we slowly made our way north towards California, arriving in Los Angeles in the last week of October.

Coming through the Panama Canal.

180

Arriving in San Francisco.

Our ship docked earlier than we expected. We had not been able to let the children know of our new arrival-time so they were not at the pier. Early the next morning Muti and her husband came to pick us up. The Langs drove us to Fred and Ann's apartment near Century City. They, in turn, took us to Altadena to see Peter and Ellen. This was our first visit with our new daughter-in-law. The next day we had a splendid dinner that Ann cooked for all of us at their apartment. Then it was back to the boat and the final lap of our journey to San Francisco. We slipped under the Golden Gate on Sunday morning. It was a cool, crisp autumn day. Anne and her husband, Bob, were waiting for us at the dock. John had recently taken a new church in Minneapolis and was no longer in the Bay Area. Driving to Anne and Bob to their home, it felt nice to be back in California.

When I think about it today, my life consisted of a series of opening and closing doors. It was my nature to go through those that were open and to seek with curiosity what lay beyond. I usually marched firmly across the threshold with little sense of turning back. Papa was more cautious. He often hesitated and deliberated before making up his mind. My style was quite impulsive. Ever since childhood I wanted to know what lay around the next bend, particularly on a road I had not taken before. For me doors always led somewhere. I rarely felt regret for those that closed behind me. Life was a process of moving forward. I spent little time looking back. It was only as I grew older that I began to sense a narrowing of this phenomenon. New doors seemed to open before me with less frequency. And my own pace of passing through them was slowing down. While my curiosity remained in tact, it was harder to generate the physical energy to spurt ahead. In fact, some doors seemed difficult to pass through, as I would soon experience, and having passed through them it was not always easy to get my bearing. In the past I had listened to the inner voice convinced that it would provide me with my marching orders. Once I had them I could sprint ahead. Now I had to learn to listen in a new way. Rather than instruct me in marching forward, it had to teach me to accept things as they are. While I didn't know it at the time I stepped off the *Vogtland* in San Francisco, there was much I still needed to learn. My return to America soon led me to a new understanding of myself. It was a process that began in the hills above Santa Cruz and continues to this day.

Chapter Sixteen
Mission Springs

Not long after our arrival, Carl Johnson informed us that we could once again rent his cabin at Mission Springs. I was particularly happy with this news. Mission Springs reminded me a little of Liebenzell. Like the mission compound in the Black Forest it hosted conferences and summer camps. We could take part in these and help. At the same time its beautiful setting in the hills surrounded by nature, its combination of solitude with sufficient contact with people, and its wonderful fresh air, reminded me of Karuizawa where I had spent so many happy summers. Papa and I knew the children loved to come here for a few days of quiet or family celebrations. For me just about everything in Mission Springs was perfect. I will always be thankful for the years I spent there. They were like a marvelous Indian summer. Papa and I basked in the sunshine of accumulated friendships. We watched our children grow and mature into middle age. And we indulged ourselves in our grandchildren whenever we had the opportunity. What warm memories I have of those years. How hard it was to leave all that behind.

The cabin, itself, was simple and utilitarian. It had a nice fireplace and we used a wood-stove insert for most of our heat. Here, too, I thought of Karuizawa. Papa split much of the fire-wood. I remember that once Bill brought over a load of walnut that included the portions of the tree that had been grafted. Papa, then eighty, was out there with Fred splitting this difficult wood using wedges and sledge-hammers. I don't think Fred could keep up with him. Papa was also a wonderful gardener, and he made not only a beautiful flower garden but a very productive vegetable garden. Some years he fought with the deer for his vegetables, but he usually fenced them out to his satisfaction and we had lovely

Papa watering his flowers.

produce from his patch. The house was surrounded by flowers that Papa planted. It was really beautiful, and people walking by often stopped to admire his work. I cannot remember a time when we did not have a continuous stream of visitors. Many came to listen to Papa play the zither. I usually baked something so that afternoon coffee was a popular occasion. One summer, I remember, I used sixteen pounds of coffee. I think that was a record.

If I liked my kitchen, Papa's favorite place was his workshop underneath the cabin. He was always good at making things and he now produced all kinds of practical and useful things that ranged from stools to flower baskets. He loved to make things for his grandchildren and produced some charming doll houses for his granddaughters. He spent a lot of time down there in his basement and we had a code. When lunch or dinner was ready I would take

Robby votes for Turkey.

my broom handle and bump it several times on the floor. This let him know it was time to eat. Then he would come up for his meal. I think he loved to eat as much as he loved to play his zither. The cause may have been genetic. Even some of the grandchildren appear to have inherited his tendencies. We still joke about Robby, Anne and Bob's son. When he was three or four, I asked him what he wanted for Christmas that year. I saw him thinking for a moment, then a big grin spread over his face and he said, "a turkey!" I could almost imagine Papa saying the same thing. While we laughed over this, there were also less amusing incidents at the cabin. Papa's love of his workshop, nearly did in his love of playing the zither. One day, while using his power saw, he slipped and

Papa in his workship at Mission Springs.

cut off his thumb. I was in a panic. I couldn't drive and none of the neighbors were home. So Papa had to drive himself to the doctor as he was. I went with him. When we arrived the doctor asked us if we brought the thumb with us. *Dumheit!*, in our excitement we had not thought of this. If we had, the doctor would have attempted to sow it back on. Under the circumstances there was little he could do but deal with the stump. It took quite a while to heal. There was a good deal of pain and Papa worried that he would not be able to play his zither again. But somehow he overcame his injury and continued to play well. That was something!

As the years passed we were clearly getting older. One day I looked out the window and saw Papa working in the back yard. He was working very hard and sweat was running down his brow. I went out and said, "Papa, you're working too hard. Who knows, next month Mr. Johnson may decide to live in the cabin again and we may have to move out." He stopped working, looked around and said quietly, "You know, I think one day this place will be ours." I said, "Oh! Papa, we never really prayed for this, let us pray now!" So we held hands in the middle of the garden and asked the Lord, if it were his will, to give us this place for our own. Two weeks later John phoned. He told us that he had just heard from Carl Johnson who told him he wanted to sell the cabin. We asked, how much? Mr. Johnson wanted $34,000 for the house. We thought that was too high and asked whether he couldn't reduce the price a little. He came down to $32,000. We never had much money, but when we left Japan we had been able to sell our Karuizawa house to a German mission board for $18,000. When we first came to Missions Springs that was just the price of a cabin there, but Mr. Johnson did not want to sell his at the time. In the years that followed prices skyrocketed. We didn't know what to do. Once again we prayed. Mr. Johnson told us that he would be willing to carry a partial mortgage on the sale. We talked this over with the children and each agreed to help us with the monthly payments. So through our fortuitous purchase in Karuizawa many years earlier, a few household economies on

Papa's and my part, and the generosity of our children, we paid off the mortgage and became proud home owners in a few years.

We had such wonderful neighbors in the small circle of houses at the top of that hill at Mission Springs. Vi and Ted Martinson, in particular, did so much

The beautiful deck our neighbors built for us.

for us. On one occasion Fred and Ann invited us to Los Angeles for Thanksgiving. Our cabin was built in such a way that there was space for a deck behind the house under the trees, but the deck had never been built. Ted Martinson organized a whole series of our neighbors to do something about this while we were away in Los Angeles. The men gathered and in the short period that we were gone built a splendid deck, with its own flight of stairs in the rear. It was done in a beautiful and most professional manner. Each man contributed his particular skills and the deck was completed by the day we arrived home. It was late in the evening so I did not look out the window that overlooked the deck. The curtains were still drawn. But when I opened them the next morning I cried, "Wow! Papa! Come here and look!" And there was the wonderful deck with benches all around. Both our hearts were overflowing with joy and thanks. The following Sunday we scheduled a party for all our neighbors to express our appreciation. Papa hurried home. He must have driven a little faster than usual that Sunday, because a policeman stopped us. He said, "Do you know how fast you were driving?" Papa looked surprised and said no. The policeman wrote Papa a ticket for $31. We were sorry about that. But it did not dampen the joy of our party that afternoon. Papa never mentioned the incident with the policeman. But the next day we found an envelope in our mail box with $31 in it. With it came a note. It read: "This is for your ticket yesterday." There was no name. But later we learned that it was one of our church members who saw us on our way home with the police car. In order to know the cost, he must have asked the policeman how much the ticket was. How kind the people were to us!

Speaking of church, when we arrived at Mission Springs there was no church belonging to the Covenant denomination in the area. Of course, the conference center had regular meetings in summer and on special occasions, but there was no permanent church in the area. With the expansion of the Santa Cruz region more and more people moved into Scott's Valley, the little town where we usually did our shopping. Without a church, we joined some of our neighbors and friends to form a fellowship that met in each others houses on Sunday mornings. But we wanted more. We thought we could start a new church in the area. We were not alone in this idea, for many of our neighbors and others living at Mission Springs also hoped that a regular place of worship could be found. So we started a Sunday morning service in the old chapel at Missions Springs and invited others to join us. The group that met together was small and informal. On one occasion I was asked to sing a hymn for the group. I told those present that I could not sing. I explained that when I was a seminary student at Liebenzell I sang in the choir. One day the wife of our mission director stopped me and said, "Sister Rose, sing the scale." I sang the scale up and down. She said, "That was all right, but when you are up there with the choir, you bring the whole choir into confusion!" After that I stopped singing in the choir. But I told the people at Missions Springs that I would sing a song for them on Sunday morning as requested, and with Papa's help on the zither I acted out the song, "Trust and Obey." I told them we have two feet to walk. We put one foot before the other. It is the same in our Christian life. Here, too, we have two feet to walk with the Lord—the one is called *trust* the other is called *obey.* My "song" must have made an impression because many later remembered it.

In Scott's Valley there was a tiny wedding chapel, which was a church in miniature. For a time we rented this chapel. We even called a pastor. Soon the space was too small for us, so we moved to the "Barn." The "Barn" was a kind of restaurant that had a big hall for dancing on Satur-day nights. Some of our men had to go early on Sunday mornings to clean it up and make it ready for our wor-ship service. For some time I taught

Mama enjoying her Christmas Tree in the Mission Springs Cabin.

The Scott's Valley Church.

Sunday School there. Then Mr. Olson, our chairman, found a piece of land to buy right in Scott's Valley, and we all agreed to build a church. Ted Martinson, who had built our deck, was a carpenter, and he agreed to direct the construction project. Everyone helped with the labor, and soon we had a beautiful new church. I taught Sunday School there for many years, and held ladies Bible classes on Wednesday afternoons. Vi Martinson, Ted's wife, organized most of these. We had built a number of churches in Japan, but this was the first church we had been involved in building in the United States. The experience was quite interesting. In the United States the voluntary group played a central role, even in the construction of the church building. Self-help remained an essential American theme. Everyone pitched in to make it happen. In Japan things were much more formal. I can hardly imagine the Japanese members of one of our churches building their own sanctuary. When I think about the building of our deck, and our church, I find myself admiring the way in which Americans are able to organize and use individual talents for the public good. So much is accomplished in America through voluntary groups. In this respect Americans seem different from others. The ability to work together in this way is a wonderful American achievement.

Like most American families, our children were regularly on the move. When we returned to Mission Springs John and Miriam had taken a church in Minneapolis. Not long thereafter Bill and Sandy took a pastorate in St. Paul. Then Rosalie and Karl moved to Rochester, Minnesota, where Karl was posted by IBM. Even Anne and Bob subsequently moved to Minnesota where Bob pastored a church in Forest Lake. After finishing his seminary training in Los Angeles, Peter and Ellen moved to Ashland, Oregon where he was Assistant Pastor in a Presbyterian church. For a while only Fred and Ann remained in California with us. The families of the children also expanded. Bill and Sandy had a daughter, Erika, and a son, Kurt. Bob and Anne had

Visiting Ann and Bob, and our grandson Robbie, in Minnesota.

Robert, or little Robby as we called him. Rosalie and Karl adopted a boy, Thomas, and a girl, Corrie. Ellen gave birth to a daughter, Rosie, and a son, Joshua. Only Fred and Ann were childless. Papa and I felt sorry for them. A few years later, like musical chairs, the children all moved again. John and Miriam were at the Oakland Church, Bill and Sandy were in Modesto, Karl and Rosalie went first to Boca Raton, Florida, and then to Mountain View in the Silicon Valley. Peter and Ellen moved to Washington State; then Fred and Ann went off to Japan for two years. Sometimes it was hard to keep up with all those moves.

We benefited from these transfers in that our visits to the children exposed us to parts of the United States we had never seen before. Going to Minnesota was a new experience. There was much to see and do. I had often heard of the Mayo Clinic. Now I had the chance to tour this interesting medical facility in Rochester. It was, of course, wonderful to see and be with the grandchildren and to watch them grow up. Then there were some memorable incidents. While visiting Rosalie in Rochester we experienced our first tornado. We had been through a number of major typhoons in Japan, but this was different. When the tornado warning sounded, Rosalie ordered us to the basement. Karl was not at home. It was funny to see Papa, who was a large man, sitting on the

floor between the two door posts. I couldn't help laughing. Papa, who was always more cautious than I, said to me, "You have no right to laugh! This is serious!" Still, I couldn't help laughing some more. But I asked the Lord not to destroy the town because of my silliness. The tornado did, in fact, come down on the other side of

Peter with Joshua and Rosie in Washington.

the city and caused much damage. I felt sorry for the people. Seeing the aftermath of the storm, I developed a healthy respect for nature's angry forces. Thereafter I had no inclination to laugh when there were tornadoes nearby.

On an outing with Papa along the California Coast.

There were many later trips. To Florida, Atlanta, Georgia, and Westport, Connecticut, where Rosalie and Karl lived in sequence. Up to Washington State to see Peter and Ellen, and later to Scottsdale, Arizona where Bill took a new church. For most of these years John and Miriam lived near us in Oakland. Anne and Bob were still in Minnesota, but they, too, eventually returned to California to a church in Kingsburg. Papa still loved to drive. In the spring we often drove along the California coast and in the fall we went into the Sierra Nevada mountains to see the beautiful autumn leaves. My life in Japan and Germany had conditioned me to think of fall in terms of the foliage. The Japanese had a special term for this—"the flowers of autumn."

Our life at Mission Springs was, as I noted earlier, a kind of marvelous Indian summer. Papa and I grew old together surrounded by friends and living in an idyllic setting. It was as if we were in the midst of the flowers of fall. But just as the first winter winds come and shake that beautiful foliage, and the leaves suddenly fall from the trees, our world began to change in 1983. In the period leading to the spring of that year Papa had several operations. He was now well over eighty years of age and the body was beginning to fail. He still liked to work in his garden, and in the evening we always took our walks

At Rosalie's in Westport with Tommy and Connie Lynne.

together around the neighborhood. June 28, 1983 was a special day. Early in the morning we had a call from the Martinsons telling us that Ted had had a kind of stroke. They called the ambulance but it was too late. Ted died. Papa went over to comfort Vi and to pray with her. In the evening, when we went for our usual walk, we talked about Ted and his work. How true and faithful he had been even in little things. Suddenly Papa began to stutter. I looked at him and said, "Papa, what is wrong with you, you never stutter!" As I said this, I saw his eyes twitching. Then he started to fall. I wanted to help, but he fell on me. I watched him shaking. I knew that he, too, was experiencing a stroke. I looked around but could see no one. So I cried with a loud voice, "Help!" In the Martinson's house the door opened and Vi's daughter-in-law saw Papa lying on the ground. She called an ambulance right away. How glad I was that they came quickly and took Papa and me to the hospital in Santa Cruz.

After examining Papa the doctors did not hold out much hope. The chief doctor told me that Papa had had a massive stroke on the left side of his brain and that his whole right side seemed to be affected. He could not speak. It was a shock to see him so helpless. They phoned John in Oakland and in a few hours he was with me at Papa's bedside. We had Rosalie's boy, Tom, staying with us that summer while Karl, Rosalie, and Corrie were on vacation in Switzerland and Germany. I was glad that we had sent him to John and Miriam's for a few days just before Papa's collapse. We phoned Karl and Rosalie, who were then with Papa's brother in Munich, and they flew home right away. The other children also gathered. I had lots of comfort and help, but it was hard to see Papa suffer. The doctors and therapists did their best. At the start there seemed to be a slight improvement, but then another stroke came that further immobilized him. He was completely paralyzed on the right side and could neither speak nor swallow. We had visited so many people in similar conditions in the past. Papa and I had often discussed our feelings about such an impairment on our part. If we were helpless we wanted no heroics. We knew that God would take each of us home in his own way. To Papa, and to me, it was clear that his final journey had begun. As little as he could do to express himself, he made it quite clear that he wanted no artificial means of support. He continued to pull out even the tubes through which he was fed his oxygen. Disabled though he was, I was amazed by how powerful a man he remained. One night he took the metal railing on his hospital bed and completely bent it over with his left hand.

Incapable as he was of speech, he could still recognize me and the children. One day the boys sang his favorite hymn, "How Great Though Art," and a shine went across his face. We knew he understood. At the same time the nurses had another stroke-patient who was further down the ward. When he heard the boys singing, he started to sing with them. So the nurses came in and asked if the boys would sing the song once more, just for the sake of their patient, who couldn't speak either, but who could sing with the boys. How we wished Papa, too, were able to sing!

In the days that followed, I usually came early in the mornings and spent the daylight hours in his hospital room. I read the scriptures to him, prayed with him, and my heart bled for him. I asked the doctor if I could take him home, and, with the help of a nurse, take care of him. The doctor said, "That's impossible, it would kill you too." He was often very restless at night and I was so grateful that Fred came from Los Angeles and took care of him during these hours. When Fred had to leave, Peter came from Ashland and took his place. How thankful I was for my children.

One day we had a family conference with the doctor. He told us there was no hope that Papa would recover. He also noted that they could not let him die in the hospital; it was their duty to keep him alive. Papa had requested in his living will that he should be allowed to die under such circumstances. We therefore had to make the difficult decision to transfer him to a nursing home. That was not easy, but I respected Papa's wishes. He had stated them so clearly to me before. We therefore transferred him to a nursing home in Santa Cruz. The fourth day after the move from the hospital was the hardest. His whole body started to shake, and I tried so hard to hold him near me. With all my heart I prayed that the Lord should take him home. The nurse gave him a shot toward evening and he quieted down. Anne brought Peter for the night, but I said, "I will not go home tonight because something is going to happen to Papa." But the children insisted, saying that I needed my rest. Finally I agreed. When I reached home I took a bath and went to bed. A few minutes later the telephone rang. It was Peter. He said, "Papa is with the Lord." I quickly dressed again and Anne brought me to the home. For the last time I took Papa in my arms. All the suffering was over and he looked so peaceful. I said, "Thank you Lord!" I knew that Papa was now absent

from his body and present with God. What a wonderful hope we have as Christians.

On the third of August, 1983, we laid Papa's body to rest in the Oakwood Cemetery in Santa Cruz. We held the service in the church in Scotts Valley. All the children were there. Only Bill was in the hospital in Scottsdale with his back and couldn't come. We missed him, as he had such a beautiful voice and Papa had earlier asked him to sing "The Holy City" at his funeral. Peter substituted for him and did a wonderful job. Reverend Wesley Nelson, Papa's friend, was in charge of the service and George Martin came representing the TEAM Mission. He spoke movingly about Papa's work in Japan. John spoke about his life as a father and man of God. Both the Buss and the Lang families sent representatives. The service was a lovely tribute to Papa's life. At the reception we were able to meet again many old friends. I sensed a great outpouring of love and sympathy. After it was over, only the family members went to the cemetery. We sang Papa's favorite hymns as the casket was lowered. I remember, Joshua, Peter's son, who was just six, asking, "Won't Opa be cold down there?" I suddenly remembered my own father's funeral. I had thought the same thing. How much of life is an ongoing circle.

After we finished, the children went home with me. I was glad because I was afraid to be in the house alone without Papa. But life had to go on. The children had to leave, and when the last ones said goodbye, Tim, John's son, came running back, laid his arm on my shoulder and said, "Grandma, remember you are not alone, the Lord has said he will be with you always." How these words comforted me. I felt God's presence and went on with my work in the church . The ladies meetings, in particular, were a great joy to me. Our kind neighbors were always happy to see me and to help me with transportation. Of course I grieved for Papa in my own way. But the children often invited me to their homes, or came to visit me at the cabin. What a wonderful time I had every spring with Rosalie and Karl in Westport, Connecticut, and later in Dunwoody, Georgia. I always came home refreshed in body and soul. On my 80th birthday John and Miriam invited me to their place in Oakland and the ladies from their church held a big party for me. The following year I even made another trip to Germany and had a wonderful time celebrating my 60 years with the Liebenzell Mission. So many friends came out for that event. I also had a warm visit with my relatives. The trip was capped by the arrival of Rosalie and Karl who took me to Switzerland for two weeks. How that trip refreshed my spirit!

I still missed Papa, but just as in my last years in Japan, I heard that voice once more, "Walk before me and be faithful." Again I had to learn to walk in a new way. But by taking one step at a time, by *trusting* and *obeying*, I somehow managed to do it.

Chapter Seventeen

Forget Not His Goodness

My time in Mission Springs continued to be taken up with the church and the conferences held there. This gave me peace and joy. But I found it harder to keep up with the house and garden. I was beginning to sense my age and I felt badly that I could not maintain the garden in the way that Papa had. It lost more and more of its splendor. Some of my children thought I should sell the house and move to the lovely retirement community that the Covenant Church had built in Turlock. A number of my friends had already taken apartments there. But my heart was not in this. I loved the cabin in Mission Springs too much, and there was another thing that troubled me.

Papa and I never had anything we could give the children. We had little in the way of financial resources. Each of the children had worked his or her way through college with almost no support from us. Some had faced considerable hardship in doing so. Now I thought I could leave them something. If I lived in the cabin until my death, the house could go to them. I remember that John and Fred met with a representative of the Turlock Village in the cabin one day, and I burst into tears. Fred asked me, "Mama, why are you so sad?" "Well," I said, "I hoped so much that I could leave you something when I die. If I move to Turlock, that will be impossible." He looked at me and said, "How much did your mother leave you when she died?" I smiled through my tears and said, "One hundred Marks (that was twenty-five dollars)" He replied, "Mama, if you move to Turlock, I think you can still leave each of your children $25." No definite decision was made at the time, but I thought and prayed about this possibility in the months that followed.

In 1986 I turned eighty-three. The older I got the more it became clear to me that I should move to Turlock. So I talked it over with the children and decided to sell the house. Karl and Rosalie went with me to Turlock that summer to make the arrangements. Their son Tom came with us. While we were handling business matters in the office of the Covenant Village, Tom was inspecting the compound in his usual curious fashion. Later he came in and asked me, "Oma, if you move here, will you live here for the rest of your life?" I replied, "Yes, Tom, I think so." He said, "Not for a $1000 dollars would I live here. Look, there are no mountains, no forests, no ocean, there is nothing!" Despite Tom's pessimism the place was really quite lovely. The housing and facilities were well laid out, comfortable, and beautifully kept up. I still think it is one of the nicest facilities of its kind. In any case, I decided to put my name in for a studio apartment. The arrangement was that I would buy my apartment and pay a monthly fee for living expenses. The costs seemed reasonable to me, and I marveled again how the Lord provided. The fact that Papa and I had been able to buy Carl Johnson's cabin allowed my resources to keep up with inflation and now permitted me to make this move to a comfortable retirement community. I had never imagined that this would be possible when we left Japan.

The hardest thing for me was to get rid of all the things we had accumulated over the years. I was moving into a studio apartment. Rosalie and Karl had measured everything very carefully. I knew exactly what I could take. But the basement was full of things. There was junk, and there were fine things. All had to be examined, sorted, and either given away or marked for a yard sale. There were all of Papa's tools and equipment. Barrels full of things we had shipped from Japan, and heavy boxes in which we had moved all over the world. I hauled all these upstairs. I don't think I ever worked as hard. I became physically exhausted. But I think the psychological pain of cutting off my past as I discarded item after item and thought about what each had meant to me was even harder. There was the Lionel train I had bought for the boys in Turlock in 1950. How they had enjoyed playing with it. I sent it up to Peter in Washington. There was a boat Fred had made in Japan; I sent it to Joshua, Peter's son. These were dozens of items like these. One of the heaviest boxes enclosed many of the *kami shibai* plays from Japan that Papa had used for his Sunday School. Fred, still in Japan that year, wanted these, so I put them aside for him. Each of the children had his or her favorite items and I tried to be certain that they all went to their proper destinations. I also put aside some of my most treasured things. Not things of monetary value, but sentimental things. There was a beautiful burled wood plaque that Papa had made in Karuizawa when he had cut his leg with an ax during the war and was bed-ridden for two weeks. He had carved a poem into its surface and lettered it in silver. It still hangs near my bed today. There were also boxes of photographs and slides, albums, and so much of the brick-a-brack all of us accumulate with the years. Each with its own story. Throwing these out or parting with them was not easy. I didn't feel well and went to the doctor. He told me that my blood pressure had gone sky-high. He gave me some medication which I took. I still didn't feel well, but by the grace of God I finished the job. Later, I sometimes wondered how I had done it. I am so glad that I don't have to do it again.

John's wife Miriam and some of my good ladies helped me with the sale. We decided to have it in the midst of September when there was the annual Woman's Conference at Mission Springs. We had quite a lively time and I was glad that many of the things sold. On September 26, 1986, John came with a rental truck and with the help of a friend loaded up my remaining possessions. It was with a heavy heart that I bid my friends goodbye and said farewell to the cabin and Mission Springs.

A German proverb says: There is no bird that will not find its former nest again. We had spent five wonderful years in Turlock as a family. Now I was back again. But this time I was alone, and beautiful as the Village was, and as good as everything looked, I just wasn't at home. When I closed the door of my apartment I felt so alone and homesick. John and Miriam helped me to fix-up my apartment so that it was really lovely. Many of my old friends from Mission Springs who had moved before me showered me with kindnesses. Others whom I hadn't known before were equally loving in their attention. The staff went out of its way to cater to my needs. To be frank, I had no reason to complain. I just didn't feel good. My blood pressure again shot up, and several times I had to be taken to the emergency room at Emanuel Hospital. On one occasion the nurse asked me, "What are you afraid of?" I told her I feared a stroke like Papa's. She comforted me and told me that strokes did not occur in this way. I tried hard to stay calm and overcome my high blood pressure, but it was not easy. My whole system was affected and all the medication I was taking just made me feel miserable.

Then one day I read in Isaiah, "Learn to do good." I realized that I had been doing nothing but feeling sorry for myself. So I started to visit the sick people in Brandell, the extended care unit of

Mama in her Turlock apartment with John, Miriam, Susan and her husband Jeff.

195

the Village. I went twice a week, and when I shared their suffering, which was harder than mine, prayed with them and comforted them, I started to feel better. Once I met an old German lady who still spoke German, and when I started to sing with her the old fashioned German Hymn, *Gott is die Liebe* (God is Love), her whole face started to shine and she thanked me again and again. So every week when I visited her we sang together, till she passed away.

Gradually I made peace with my new existence. The Village staff asked me to take over one of the Bible study groups, which I gladly did, and for many years I was richly rewarded in these efforts. How much we need to be useful, even in our old age. For years I continued my daily walks and I tried to stay as fit as possible. But sometimes my exercising got me into trouble. We used to work-out in the swimming pool. I rather enjoyed this, till one day I went in the pool and somehow I got into water that was over my head. No one else was in the pool. I never did learn how to swim. So I nearly drowned. Someone came along in time and pulled me out of the water. Then they took me to the emergency room. Peter was coming to see me that day. Poor fellow, he had to visit me in the hospital. That evening the children phoned from all over the country. Each of them said the same thing. "But Mama, you should have worn your yellow oil slicker!" How silly of me. I never went in the pool again.

While I was slowing down, I still managed to get out, see things, and visit people. Rosalie and Karl moved back to Atlanta, Georgia from Westport,

Mama at Rosalie's home in Dunwoody.

Connecticut where Karl started a new job. Every year in spring, I took the long flight to Atlanta to visit them in Dunwoody. I just loved the woods in the region with their beautiful blossoming dogwoods. It did my spirit good! Bill and Sandy, with their children Erika and Kurt, invited me to Scottsdale, Arizona. I also went to

Erika and Kurt with Bill and Sandy in Scottsdale Arizona.

visit Fred and Ann, and then John and Miriam in Los Angeles for Christmas every year. What happy visits these were with the children, grand children, and now even great-grandchildren. Fred and Ann always had the most beautiful Christmas trees, and John and Miriam provided our traditional Christmas Eve supper of ham and potato-salad. John had become the Superintendent of the PacificSouthwest Conference of the Covenant Church, a position equivalent to "Bishop" in another denomination. I was proud of him, even though he became awfully busy. Fred had a neighbor who had been born in Japan. Every year he prepared the complex New Year's meal the Japanese serve. How I enjoyed being invited to these celebrations. It made me think of Japan. The other children also asked me to visit them, and I had a lovely stay with Peter and Ellen, Joshua and Rosie, in Washington. Bill and Sandy often came to see me in Turlock. Anne and Bob moved to Kingsburg, just an hour-and-a-half drive away. That was a special pleasure. The love of my family made me feel that I was not forgotten and I gradually adjusted to my new life. I also learned to keep busy. I had always been an avid reader, ever since my difficult childhood years. Now I had ample time to read and I continue to indulge myself in new books. While Papa loved making things out of wood, I enjoyed knitting and crocheting. I don't know how many baby sweaters I have knitted in the last ten years. But I know that at the annual bazaar we hold at the Village, my sweaters and booties are always in high in demand.

In 1993 we celebrated my 90th birthday. That was something! I used to think sixty was old. Here I was ninety! Thirty years had gone by since my 60th birthday in Japan. On that occasion I had been alone with Papa. For my ninetieth birthday the children asked me what I would like to have. I had only

Mama at her 90th birthday celebration, still "directing."

one wish. In all the years since we left Turlock the family had never been all together. For reasons beyond their control there had always been one or two children absent. Now Papa was gone. I told the children my wish. That they should all gather for the celebration. And they did! Each of them came, and all the grandchildren came. And even my first great-grandchild was there. We had a beautiful reception at the Village and several hundred people attended that afternoon. When I counted up all the cards that came for this occasion, there were more than 500 from around the world. The children and grandchildren sang, recited verses, and John gave a moving tribute to my life. Fred read a long poem he had written in my honor. And all participated in some way. It was such a pleasure to be with them. How proud I was of each one. They had all become useful and productive members of their communities. Mark, our cook at the Village, made the most beautiful canapés and provided a lovely table of food for the guests. There were endless bouquets of flowers and I don't know how many gifts. Telegrams came from Japan and Germany. What excitement! But the best part was seeing my family together and spending time with each of them. It was like the epiphany of my life.

After my 90th birthday my strength steadily declined. I found it increasingly difficult to get around. Somehow my feet just wouldn't carry me as far any more. So I gave up my ministry. Now I have to learn what one of my German friends called the greatest art in life. How to get old with a joyful heart, to rest when one wants to work, to be quiet when one wants to talk, and to carry one's cross quietly till God takes us home. I don't think any of these were ever my style. Yet I have learned to live from day to day, to enjoy and appreciate the small things—a beautiful morning, a newly opened rose in my garden, a telephone call from one of my children, a letter from a friend. Being has replaced doing. How interesting this process really is. I've always listened, but usually so that I knew what to do. Now I have learned to listen in a new way. It is a deeper source within me. A much quieter music plays there. But God still speaks to me. I may not be able to go out as much, and I spend more of my time in my apartment. But I still write to many people around the world. Every day I pray for my family and a long list of those who have special needs. Sometimes I still argue with God, but not as often nor as strongly. I have come to accept myself and the world as it is. I thank God that I still have a clear mind. One of the pleasures of old age is to reflect on the past. As I think about my life I feel richly blessed. It has been such an interesting journey!

This morning I sit looking out my window. It is a lovely spring day. Already it is becoming warm again. I think I will take my book outside and sit on the bench in the sun. Putting down my pen, I notice a card on my desk. It summarizes my feelings today, "Praise the Lord Oh my soul and forget not His goodness."

Epilogue

On April 7, 1998, six months after the manuscript of this this book was completed, Mama died of a series of quick heart attacks at the age of ninety-four. All her children were at her bedside, and for her death was a distinct going home.

As was noted in the preface, the idea for this book began with the celebration of her 90th birthday in 1993 and it came full circle with her death four-and-a-half years later. Mama enjoyed poetry and verse. It may be appropriate, therefore, to complete her book with the verse I composed for her 90th birthday which sums up so much of her remarkable life.

To Mama at Ninety

Who would have thought this day would come,
That one and all we would assemble here,
with cheer, to celebrate the life of one,
Whose ninety years still seem so young
To those of us who know her well,
and of whose tales we love to tell.

Who is this woman here before us?
Many ask, and some implore us,
Is she not that single lady,
Sunday School Teacher, Nurse and Preacher,
China bound by her intention,
Still to learn that intervention,
Whether divine, or humanly inspired,
could be quite specific,
and turn her much beloved China,
into the Pacific.

The South Pacific, to be exact,
a tract of water blue and wide,
dotted by isles,
whose names still bring us smiles,

EPILOGUE

Oneop and Truk, Mortlock and Lukunor,
Oh, what masks and shark's teeth, stuffed turtles,
and strange tools, these sites revealed to us children.
Pools of imagination, wrapped in brown paper,
and later, tucked away in the endless barrels of
missionary moves.

But Oh, what stories too!
Who can forget that outrigger canoe,
With Max at the prow,
Ordering, "Lord Send Us Wind Now!"
And the awful consequences,
As our Sunday School Teacher, Nurse, and Preacher
adrift, amidst the swift waves of a Pacific Squall,
canoe capsized, in jeopardy all,
with goods and chattels drifting away—
Held us entranced with heightened suspense,
hardly daring to say,
wide eyed and grim,
"But Mama you couldn't swim!"

Oh, for that raincoat that kept her afloat,
How many of us, hearing she had nearly drowned
in the Village Pool,
took up that auditory tool, the phone,
to remind her of that boat,
and of the need for that raincoat.
Without which all aquatic excursions
should be curtailed for new diversions.

Still we inquire, who was this Sunday School Teacher,
Nurse and Preacher?
This single lady, who left her village,
The "town of bears," all green with tillage,
for distant shores, and open spaces,
far from the Swabian rural places, of home and hearth.
To human fields in the Pacific,
Eastern Asia, and a terrific challenge in Japan,
to carry out God's plan,
for her, and for the men and women of this distant land.

How Grand!, we often think, from the bland natures
    of our home existence,
    when we contemplate at distance, the lives of others
    Missionary lives, for one,
    seem so romantic,
    from our own pedantic,
    preoccupation with mundane matters.
    Little do we know the tensions,
    no one mentions,
    of the struggle against self and loneliness.
    Amidst those Pacific Isles, palm trees, reefs,
    and native smiles,
    how could one pretend, not to be content.
    Indeed, so thought our single lady, Teacher, Nurse,
    and Preacher.

But as we know, God's own menu
    soon required a change of venue.

For there was Karl,
    A Municher from Liebenzell, who we must tell,
    had fallen for our single lady, Teacher, Nurse, and
    Preacher,
    Whom he had come to know in Tokyo,
    Where she had suddenly appeared,
    by way of Moscow, Harbin, and some other far-out places,
    Waiting for papers and passenger spaces,
    to go, to the Nanyō.

With her had come two brides to be,
    Karl's friends, it seems, were luckier than he,
    And there was Rose, still fully bent,
    on blessed singlehood, no matrimonial event, would
    seize her on her way to Micronesia.
    Or so she thought.

Karl had his own ideas it seems,
    Or maybe heaven had its schemes, to bring
    these two together, despite the weather, sickness,
    and a dirty little ship,
    that made its trip, six month apart,
    spoiling the art of written communication,

of love, and patience.
Messages of no and yes, and yes and no, seemed to go,
across each other's bow, and how, was each to know,
the vow, that both had made to their Lord, and to each other.
Finally a new invention, telegraphed Karl's intention,
across those boundless waves,
and brought the long delayed reply,
the telegram that stated why,
she said, "I'll come."

Oh, for our single-lady, Teacher, Nurse, and Preacher,
These were hard words of personal commitment,
promises to keep, and to cement,
with prayer and hope for the event,
that was to steer her to a new career.
With fear, and hope,
and with the harried words of her director,
who appalled at his defector,
told the world in words that carried,
"Like all girls" you simply, "Wish to be Married!"
What a put down!

But off she went to Japan.
And there was Karl,
Well not right away, he had missed the pier,
and that was scary, but nary a moment had passed,
until at last, he appeared, roses and carnations in hand,
and soon a golden band was on her finger.
That was 1933 and she was thirty.

Now a new world opened before her.
Much to explore,
to learn, to understand, on this new shore,
of Rising Sun Land.
The difficult language, so few ever mastered,
twisting the tongue, and the mind as well—
Pray tell,
how do you use your *kuchi* in Horinouchi?

Horinouchi is where they lived,
Here Papa started a new Church,
She a new family,

First there was John, then Anne, and Bill,
Endless household chores to fill,
and to see,
to the smooth functioning of her family.
Still, our (now) *Hausfrau* Teacher and Preacher,
never forgot her mission to be,
of service to her community.
To family, church, and women around her,
she gave of love, and life, and a profounder sense
of faith and place,
than simple sermons in church could trace.

Clouds now gathered on the horizon.
Angry words, and deeds,
national greeds, and hatreds, came to the fore,
and tore, at the very core of the lands to which she swore
her allegiance. And once more,
the message that she bore
of "Peace on Earth Good Will to Men" could not dispel,
what soon became a human hell.

All this, she and Karl could see
from their new home in Todoroki,
a place that means "thunder," and under whose gable,
she added to her table, now growing,
Fred, Rosalie, and Peter, not knowing how the food
could be got, to feed her little brood.
War was upon her, and Karl, and the mood was grim.

But as we have seen she had learned to swim,
if not physically then by faith,
and the Lord provided, and guided, and showed the way,
from day to day.
Hidden away in Karuizawa, flanked by towering Mt. Asama,
Mama learned, what we still treasure,
Human pluck, and God's own measure, will suffice.
And how much of that human pluck,
was taught her by a faithful duck.
How nice.

Like a bad dream, long suspended,
war cries finally were ended,

and the clouds of Mt. Asama,
gave way to another drama, and also to a new life.

This time it was America, to which she traveled,
children to educate, health to regain,
multiple cultures to explain, and experience.
New Jersey farm life, with too much live-stock,
soon gave way to the world of Turlock,
in California's San Joaquin valley,
a pleasant place in which to rally,
new friends and firm supporters to be,
for the Lord's work, which she, and Karl hoped to
continue in Japan.

Oh, how few of life's many places,
serve as genuine oasis, for the spirit and the soul,
for Mama and Papa Turlock provided these all,
with a generosity of spirit and human good will,
that still, resound with the profound good sense
of the American heart. An art form not found in many
another part of the world.

From Turlock it was back to Japan,
to God's plan,
for her and for those whom she served.
Family now split between three nations,
Oh, what a task at communications. To pray for her
children that each might be,
faithful to what she had taught,
and to themselves.

Now the years lengthened out.
More churches were built with increasing clout,
The children were largely children no more,
most had settled on the other shore,
to take up their own vocations,
in separate and distant locations.
Finally too, the time had come,
to say good-bye to the Rising Sun–
to so many years of hard work and tears–
and to a job well done!

Who would have thought that our lady Teacher, Nurse
    and Preacher would once again rally,
    to the challenges of a church in Scott's Valley,
    where she and Karl worked in retirement,
    to help others transform the local environment.
    How much she enjoyed her mountain cabin,
    and the green locality, with all the hospitality
    that she and others provided.

What golden years, indeed, these were,
    rays of sunshine through the clouds of passing time,
    And suddenly the sun was gone one day,
    and so was Karl.

She mourned, as we did all, and said good-bye,
    closing a chapter of her life,
    no easy task,
    and ask,
    where do I go from here,
    listening for that still small voice to appear,
    and give the answer.

And once again it came, God's menu,
    calling for a change of venue.

So here is our lady Teacher, Preacher, Nurse and Mother,
    still in place,
    running her race,
    not as fast as once she ran,
    but ever committed to God's plan,
    and still convinced that with a raincoat of faith,
    and a little vim,
    all of us can learn to swim.

Now let us raise our glasses high,
    and join in celebration,
    a life to cheer for ninety years,
    of love and dedication.

And with our friends across the sea, I cry,
    Banzai!

F. G. NOTEHELFER

Made in the USA
Columbia, SC
19 August 2017